THE TASTE OF WAR

Margaret Bourke-White, the celebrated American photographer and writer, died in 1971. This book is an anthology of her war memoirs edited by Jonathan Silverman, and drawn from her books: *Shooting The Russian War* (1942), *Purple Heart Valley* (1944) and *Dear Fatherland Rest Quietly* (1946). It includes sixteen of her original photographs and the result is a personal chronicle of World War II by a reporter whose nerve and keen vision have made her a world-famous legend.

Margaret Bourke-White's aim in creating photo-stories was to record the Big Thing of the Age, and in the early 1940s this was the war in Europe of which her written coverage is vivid and graphic. Whether on the spot in 1941, when the Nazis invaded Russia and subjected Moscow to air attack; under fire on the Italian front in 1943 or in Germany in 1945 to observe the effects of the Nazi defeat, Margaret Bourke-White always met head-on the risks inherent in recording history in the making. This professional relish ensures that these memoirs are dramatic throughout, and written with the freshness of contemporary observation, rather than the reflection of subsequent hindsight. As such, they are unique.

Jonathan Silverman is the director of foreign rights at Scott Meredith Literary Agency Inc., in New York City, and the author of *For The World To See: The Life of Margaret Bourke-White* (1983).

Also available in the Century Travellers series:

THE
TASTE OF WAR

MARGARET BOURKE-WHITE

Edited and Introduced by
Jonathan Silverman

CENTURY PUBLISHING

LONDON

Introduction

DANGEROUS AND daring assignments were always more attractive than others for Margaret Bourke-White. She liked pursuing pictures that no other photographer had attempted before; and if she had to travel long distances or endure hazardous situations in order to obtain the exposures she wanted, she welcomed the prospect with relish.

The thrill of taking risks was only a part of what made photography so inviting to her, however. From her earliest days as a professional photographer, Bourke-White's aim had been to record the *Big Thing* of the Age: the burning issues and central drama of the times in which she lived. Taking risks was warranted, she felt, for the sake of preserving history-in-the-making.

In the late 1920s, when she opened her first studio in Cleveland, Ohio, the Big Thing of the Age was Industry. The booming factories and construction projects, spawned by a decade of prosperity in America, stirred Bourke-White more deeply than any other subject, and the images she produced of the cranes, railroad yards, and other mammoths of modern design that had sprung up around Cleveland are among the most stunning industrial photographs ever made. In particular, her 1928 photographs of the making of steel, the first ever to convey the awesome visual power of the world inside a steel mill, had a very significant impact. Upon seeing those steel-making photographs, Henry Luce hired Bourke-White as *Fortune* magazine's first and only photographer in the spring of 1929.

Luce, who had begun publishing *Time* magazine in 1925, detected in Bourke-White's pictures the style that conveyed most succinctly "the dignity and the beauty, the smartness and excitement of modern industry", which was to be *Fortune*'s central focus.

When Luce hired Bourke-White again, in 1936, as one of the first on *Life* magazine's original team of four photographers, Industry had long since receded from its place as the Big Thing of the Age. The cold realities of economic depression had awakened America's artists and writers to the country's social ills and Bourke-White eagerly joined their ranks. She had her hands full flying around America for *Life* magazine photostories for most of 1936. But, true to her convictions, she also completed a project, in collaboration with Erskine Caldwell, that was designed to document the harsh and unjust conditions of sharecropper life in the deep South, which Caldwell had fictionalized in his bestselling novel and Broadway play *Tobacco Road*.

The book Caldwell and Bourke-White created, a unique marriage of photographs and text, entitled *You Have Seen Their Faces*, was immediately recognized as one of the most important social documentaries of the 1930s. But by the early 1940s, the importance of the sharecropper issue had paled. The Big Thing of the Age, was unquestionably the war in Europe.

Bourke-White had been an eyewitness to the early advances of Nazi terror while on assignment for *Life* in Czechoslovakia in the spring of 1938. She also had a burning desire to cover the war itself, when it fully erupted in Europe, and as fate would have it, in the spring of 1941, when the Nazis invaded Russia, Bourke-White was already on the spot.

The Hitler–Stalin non-aggression pact was in effect when Bourke-White and Erskine Caldwell (whom she had married in 1939) reached Moscow in May, 1941. Within a few weeks, however, the non-aggression pact had been scrapped. The Nazi army was storming Russia's borders, and Bourke-White was the only American photographer present to record the fighting. Her dramatic photo-reports on the bombing of Moscow, the bloody Yelnya battlefront, and other important aspects of the early clashes of the war in Russia, which appeared in *Life* magazine week after week between August and December 1941, awakened the millions of Americans who read *Life* to the unrelenting brutality of the Nazi forces and surely helped sway public sentiment towards accepting the military responsibilities America was soon to take on.

Bourke-White was indebted to *Life*, of course, for sponsoring her expedition to Russia and for bringing her photographs to the largest imaginable audience, but magazine work alone never fully satisfied her. Although she had provided the magazine with outstanding news material on the Russian war, Bourke-White had a great deal more to say about what was going on behind the surface of the news, and for six months in 1942 she worked on putting her personal insights and experiences into *Shooting The Russian War*.

Shooting The Russian War was, in fact, her second book on Russia. Her first, entitled *Eyes On Russia*, was published in 1931, following her historic journey as the first foreign photographer permitted to take pictures of Soviet Industry under Stalin's ambitious Five Year Plan. She travelled to Russia as a guest of the Soviet Government for three summers in a row between 1930 and 1932, making hundreds of exposures in every region of the country and on every aspect of life there.

Of course, the Soviet Union to which Bourke-White returned in 1941 had changed considerably from the country she had visited as an industrial photographer in the early 1930s. The towering figure of Stalin had replaced Industry as the country's singular obsession, an ideological chill had settled in, and Bourke-White keenly felt the difference in spirit.

Above all, however, Bourke-White saw that the Russians were unified in their determination to defend their land against the Nazi invaders, and that whatever political differences America might have with Russia, they were minuscule compared to the objective of defeating Hitler at all costs to which both countries were firmly committed by the end of 1941.

Bourke-White saw a very different picture, indeed, when she travelled to the Italian front in the summer of 1943. The United States Army and the German Army were pitted against each other on opposite hills overlooking Cassino Valley, where some of the hottest battles in the War were fought. The Nazis had the superior position, based as they were on the heights of Monte Cassino, and American casualties were so heavy that the battle zone was nicknamed Purple Heart Valley (after the medal awarded to U.S. servicemen who are wounded or killed in action).

Bourke-White had been under fire before, of course. Not only in Moscow, but also in North Africa where, in January 1943, she had become the first woman permitted to accompany an Air Force crew in action on a bombing raid. She had learned to endure enemy bombings and machine gun fire. In Italy, however, she was working under greater risk than ever from the constant threat of unpredictable artillery attacks, which she found much harder to accept with equanimity.

Bourke-White's assignment to Italy had come from the U.S. Army Service Forces, commanded by Gen. Brehon Somervell, who wanted Bourke-White to tell the story of "logistics", or how the soldiers in the field were supplied with everything they needed to survive: from food and ammunition to medical and even religious services. *Life* magazine used Bourke-White's photographs to show Americans how big an undertaking the war was, and how efficiently the military was handling the whole operation.

There was another aspect of the war in which Bourke-White herself was keenly interested, but which the U.S. military, and *Life* magazine more or less took for granted, and therefore ignored. Namely, the restoration of a democratic way of life in Europe. It chagrined Bourke-White to see how few constructive efforts were being focussed on eradicating the social damage fascism had caused.

"In Italy it seemed to me we were neglecting a magnificent opportunity. It was not enough to conquer this territory if we did not educate it in such a way that we could live at peace with it in the future. What is the use of all this bloodshed unless we insure the future for civilization and for peace? What is the use of leaving all these American boys on the battlefields, if we leave occupied countries unchanged when we move on? . . . There is no use fighting a war unless we leave behind us a better world, and to do that we must get the youth of Europe on our side."

In Italy, Bourke-White also developed a stronger sense of herself as a writer than she had had before. As she explains in her autobiography, *Portrait of Myself*:

"The very intimacy of the Italian conflict sharpened my awareness of human beings around me, and I began to listen to what people said. I mean really listen. Someone drops a phrase and you say to yourself, 'No one else could have said just that thing in that way. It is like a portrait of the man.' Until then, I had considered myself eye-minded and let it go at that, but much as I love cameras, they can't do everything. The American soldier with his bitter humor and his peculiar gallantry had opened my ears."

When Bourke-White returned to America in the fall of 1943, she assembled the copious notes she had taken in Italy, many of which had originally served as captions for her photographs in *Life* magazine, into her second book on World War II. Entitled *Purple Heart Valley*, the book is a remarkably vivid and comprehensive portrait of the conduct of the war in Italy. The bizarre disorder and violence she describes in *Purple Heart Valley*, however, are practically benign compared to the devastating chaos she later saw in Germany.

In *Dear Fatherland Rest Quietly*, Bourke-White's extraordinary account of the ending of the war, she wrote:

"I know of no way to convey the feeling of rising violence that we witnessed as we drove deeper into Germany: the waves of suicides, the women throwing themselves after their loved dead into newly dug graves, the passionate denunciations of friends and neighbors, the general lawlessness. Each street corner had its open tragedy; every life seemed shot through with its own individual terror. And over all hung the numbing realization that this newly conquered world was facing a sterile future."

Life magazine used Bourke-White's photographs of Germany in the spring of 1945, to tell the story of "Faceless Fritz", a report designed to give Americans greater insight into the character of the nation that had triggered the war, and kept it going with mindless intensity for so many years. Showing the faces of the German people, however, hardly explained the mentality behind the inhuman horrors that had been carried out.

Bourke-White therefore stayed in Germany through October 1945, long after her work for *Life* was completed, in order to determine for herself what made the Nazi mind tick. Her interviews with Germans at high, low, and in-between levels on the Nazi ladder make up a good part of the text of *Dear Fatherland Rest Quietly*, and shed considerable light on the "logic" of the Nazi phenomenon.

It troubled Bourke-White deeply that the patterns of thought responsible for starting the war were still not being confronted in earnest by the occupation forces. She felt that the evil persisted in Germany, and it frightened her.

"We turned our backs on our greatest opportunity to do something constructive with the youth of Germany. We had no plan, no desire, no willingness, it seemed, to teach a democratic way of life. We poured out lives and boundless treasure to win a mechanical victory and now we had no patience for the things of the spirit which alone can save us from another far greater catastrophe. It was time to go home."

Nonetheless, Bourke-White believed it was possible to make up for past neglect.

"Unless we do this war will be without meaning for us, and some of the hope for a good world will die down in the hearts of men everywhere."

After the war, Bourke-White continued travelling around the world for *Life* magazine. She covered the last two years of Gandhi's struggle for independence from Great Britain, and was the last reporter to interview Gandhi only hours before his assassination. Bourke-White also covered the Korean War for *Life* in 1952. But although she had become one of the eminent personalities on the American scene, was awarded honorary degrees, and made frequent appearances on radio and television, the final twenty years of her life were bitter ones, for the most part. In 1953, Bourke-White contracted Parkinson's Disease, which slowly crippled her, and forced her to stop all work with photography after 1957. She retired officially from *Life* magazine in 1969, and died at her home in Darien, Connecticut in August 1971.

The three books from which this volume has been compiled represent a reporter's personal chronicle of World War II. Although too personal, perhaps, to be considered works of serious history, the three books are also in a different class than most war memoirs, chiefly because Bourke-White herself was in a different class than most other reporters. Her implacable nerve, her keen sense of justice, and her humanitarian vision stand out prominently, and constitute Bourke-White's unique voice in these writings. She was a person who lived, above all, to record history, and in documenting the remarkable drama of this century, as she did, secured herself a remarkable place in history as well.

Jonathan Silverman

SHOOTING
THE RUSSIAN WAR

CHAPTER I

Halfway Around the World

I SUPPOSE it was those Irish ancestors of mine, deep-sea sailors all of them, whose sons in each succeeding generation ran away to sea when anyone tried to dry-dock them at home, who were responsible for my passionate love of seeing the world. If they were in a position to make observations, they would surely feel that it was a mistake to pass on their wanderlust to a female descendant, for in their day, as far as I have heard, the distaff side never ran off to sea. They might even think that I have an unfair advantage if they could know how quickly our flying boats take us from one part of the world to another.

In view of this ancestral roaming tendency, it was a lucky thing, I think, to marry a man who knows how to read maps. Before making this happy arrangement, I had managed to find my way with a camera through a little more than two dozen countries located on five continents, sometimes for *Fortune* magazine, sometimes for *Life*, and sometimes to satisfy my own curiosity. The only time I ever got seriously lost was in northern Canada, flying over the Arctic near the North Magnetic Pole, where compasses don't work anyway; but direction finding in the Far North was something my Canadian pilot excelled in, and he managed to find his way at last to a tiny Eskimo settlement.

However, when I come back from trips to Siberia or the Sahara Desert, my friends often marvel at how easily I can lose my way between Grand Central and Fifty-first Street while walking to the dentist. Just recently, driving home from New York to Connecticut, I managed to lose my sense of direction so completely within an eighth of a mile of our house that I had to ask the neighbors the way home. This astonished my neighbors, but it didn't puzzle me at all, for I am no good on the short hops.

But now that I am married, all is changed. My husband reads maps the way I read detective stories. The only difference is that he follows the clues of latitude, longitude, air and ocean currents, and topography, and emerges with the correct deduction, while I, even though attempting to follow that simplest of all clues—the person least suspected—rarely guess the murderer, for I am seldom able to deduce successfully who is the least suspicious.

Erskine Caldwell's map reading is much more than a simple matter of finding his way from one place to another. It is a whole study in agriculture, economics, and sociology. It is as though, through the surface of the map, he had felt the rainfall, the winds, the altitude, and the fertility of the earth. When he folds up his map, he reminds me of one of his own fictional characters, Jeeter Lester, who in the end of *Tobacco Road* lets a handful of soil sift through his fingers. Erskine has been feeling the land and he knows in advance what it can be expected to produce in the way of crops and men.

When two persons who have deep professional interests marry, there are two ways of pursuing those interests: together or separately. Russia was one of the countries which we selected to do together, and we had a joint and urgent conviction that we should get there soon, to record in words and pictures what we expected to be the coming tide of the war. We kept our plans somewhat secret, for we do not like to talk about things until we are sure we are going to accomplish them. The State Department granted us validations, although they accompanied our passports with a dutiful and somewhat ominous letter warning us that due to distressed world conditions, we could have no assurance of being able to get back to our native land again. The Soviet Ambassador in Washington promised us visas, which would be waiting for us in Chungking, but he warned me that photographs by visitors in the U.S.S.R. had been forbidden for some years, and I could have no certainty in advance that the camera ban would be lifted for me.

I was willing to take a chance on this, however. When I first went to Russia, in 1930, few photographs had come out of the country, and those few had been taken by Soviet photographers; foreigners had not been allowed to take pictures at all. This had sharpened my ambition to bring the first photographs, taken by a non-Russian, out of the Soviet Union. I had been successful in accomplishing this not because of any special pull, for I had none at all, but because when I arrived in Moscow and showed the Soviets the many industrial photographs which I had been taking in America, they decided that it might be a good thing after all to let an American industrial photographer record their Five-Year Plan. I was ready to take the gamble again.

I spent the entire month before departure planning my equipment and taking lessons in elementary mechanics so as to be able to repair cameras when I was beyond hope of assistance. Some of my most bulky photographic materials went ahead by ship to Hong Kong, where we would connect up with them at the end of our Pacific clipper flight. My quota of supplies included three thousand flash bulbs, peanut variety, a large quantity of film packs, five cameras, twenty-two lenses, four portable developing tanks, bottles of Dk21 fine-grain developer, several papers of dressmaker pins, duplicates of every screw found in all the minute parts of my lens mounts and synchronizing magnets, a synchroscope, and a jeweler's screw driver and pliers. In addition, I carried twenty-eight paper-bound detective stories.

My husband packed one small suitcase with his old corduroy jacket and a few shoes and shirts and got an extra ribbon for his portable typewriter. His professional equipment weighed seventeen pounds. My equipment weighed six hundred pounds.

At last all the preparations were completed, and in late March we took off from the West Coast. There is something about each new trip that fills me with a proud, secret excitement. Even if it is just getting on a train to go from New York to Indianapolis, I feel as if I were travelling toward an adventure. This was to be my first trip completely around the world, and I was walking on wings.

Hong Kong had the unreality of stereopticon slides. Its streets showed three dimensions, but even as we were rolled through them at breakneck speed in rickshas they still retained that insubstantial quality of one picture succeeding another.

The hillsides were piled high with crowded houses. Decorative Chinese-lettered signs were strung across the alleys, and fabulously plentiful flowers were sold under all the archways. The stores were spilling out into the streets with their stocks of Swiss watches, English woolens, carved ivories, and embroideries at fantastically low prices. Everything was cheap, because Hong Kong was a free port for foreign articles, and coolie labor made native products cost next to nothing.

We were astonished when a tailor arrived unsolicited with our breakfast tray. He quickly talked my husband into ordering a suit, which he copied from one of Erskine's old ones—for the Chinese can copy anything—and it was delivered with our morning paper the next day, perfectly tailored and finished down to the last hand-stitched lapel.

We were startled but delighted when, the following morning, the instant we woke up, a shoemaker was at my husband's bedside with a pencil to draw the outline on a piece of paper when his foot first hit the floor. A pair of Erskine's old shoes served as a model, and by noon my husband had a beautifully finished pair of new shoes.

I gave the shoemaker some jobs, too. I ordered cases of chamois leather, closing with zippers, for each of my five cameras, for each flash gun and chromium reflector, and for all of my filters. When they were finished they fitted each piece of equipment like a glove and acted as perfect dust protectors. When it came to final packing of supplies, I tore off and discarded all the cardboard protectors of my three thousand peanut bulbs. The bulbs themselves I packed into two large wicker baskets such as Chinese peasants carry. Merely removing the wrappers saved one third of their weight. I knew that it risked a great deal of breakage, but space would be at a premium as we flew across China. During my work later in Moscow, in that vast quantity of flash bulbs I found only six that were even cracked.

The luxurious Chinese world which Hong Kong presented began swinging toward the opposite extreme when we started our flight to the war capital of Chungking. We were taken to the airport at midnight to wait for an unannounced departure time. Since three hours of the flight were made over Japanese-held territory, the take-offs were planned when two layers of cloud would offer the best possible chance for the Douglas to pick its course between them, unseen from the ground, and with the hope of being undetected by enemy planes that might be scouting above. Since there was always the chance that we might have to make a forced landing back in the wilderness, in case an air raid over Chungking should make it impossible for us to land there, we were told to carry a couple of sandwiches.

We were flown by an American pilot and co-pilot, volunteers flying for the Chinese National Airways, who have since become famous in the group of American "Flying Tigers" who attacked the Japanese during the invasion of Malaya.

We flew in a plane laden with bales of money freshly printed to pay the Chinese soldiers, and every kilo of extra luggage brought for us, every camera and every film pack, displaced its weight in money. We sat on stacks of Chinese dollars, we tucked our legs around them, and I believe that if we had actually had to land in the wilderness we would have warmed our hands in front of fires built of money.

But the Japanese stayed out of our way that night, and after circling over intricately sculptured mountains, carved into whorls and arabesques by the agriculture of thousands of years, we darted down between two towering peaks and stepped out on a narrow landing field at the bank of the Yangtze.

At first I could hardly believe I was in Chungking; in the early-morning light it was difficult to see a human habitation anywhere. Then we began climbing the stone steps on the north bank—446 steep, by actual count—toward the capital on the mountaintop. Halfway up we began to see people, hundreds and thousands of people. They were carrying little baskets of cracked rock out of the newly blasted dugouts; they were squatting in the road, dipping chopsticks into bowls of rice; some of the luckier ones were riding in sedan chairs carried up the breathlessly steep streets by two human beings. The roads were lined with dugouts carved out of solid rock, dugouts not only for humans, but also for automobiles and trucks. Everywhere there was the never-ending activity of building.

The Kialing House, our hotel, in addition to being filled with its usual foreign population, was overflowing with a fashionable Chinese wedding, proceeding in the midst of much starched pink tarlatan and massed artificial flowers. The many cell-like bedrooms were being utilized by the gentlemen guests, who were changing to swallow-tails and tuxedos, the last costume that we expected to see in war-torn China. However, a corner cot was found for us, and depositing our luggage on it we made off to the Soviet Embassy.

Our journey up the precipitous path was one of extreme anxiety, not only because it seemed that our swaying sedan chairs might be pitched off our coolies' shoulders at any instant into the gorge below, but also because of acute worry as to whether our visas would really be there. People were delayed weeks, sometimes months, for Soviet visas—often to find that they were not getting them after all.

We saw the Soviet Ambassador after a wait of only five minutes and received our Russian visas after only fifteen. While our credentials were being stamped in our passports, we talked with him over glasses of Russian tea and munched little chocolate candies in wrappers stamped "Red October Candy Factory, Moskva."

Over our tea, we commented on what a target the Soviet Embassy must make, situated as it is on the highest point in Chungking. We knew that most of the diplomatic staffs of other countries had moved to the South Bank, which is much less frequently attacked than the main part of the city.

"We stay here," said the Soviet Ambassador, "because we think that if the Chinese people can stand the bombing we can share it with them."

This expression of solidarity with the Chinese people was demonstrated again a little later, when the Ambassador's secretary led us down to our waiting coolies. As we were hoisted in our sedan chairs to the shoulders of these human beasts of burden, the Russian said, "None of us in the Soviet diplomatic service ever use sedan chairs, because we do not feel that it is right to exploit the back muscles of other men."

It was not a pair of exploited backs, but a body by Buick that called to take us to the residence of the Generalissimo and Madame Chiang Kai-shek.

Their house might have been built for a well-to-do resident of Kansas City, Missouri. It had a square frame, regularly spaced windows, and mission furniture. The living-room suite, complete with sofa, was the same overstuffed style that has been multiplied time without number throughout the United States. There was nothing either beautiful or exotic about the house or its furnishings. The only Oriental touches lay in a few Chinese scrolls hanging on the walls.

But when Madame Chiang Kai-shek entered, it was immediately evident that there was nothing ordinary about her. I doubt if one would find that complex assortment of characteristics anywhere else. She has a combination of purpose and of glitter, of capacity for intensive hard work with a dash of the theater thrown in.

She spoke in a voice so soft-timbred and low that one had to listen carefully to hear her. Her spare but graceful gestures seemed studied, her beauty was of a restrained sort held back under an enameled exterior and glowing out of a pair of hot eyes. She was dressed in that severely cut tube dress which is so becoming to the slenderness of Chinese women; hers had tiny flower patterns woven in the black fabric, picking up the color notes of the emerald, sapphire, and diamond clips that gleamed in fashionable smartness on her tiny ears.

After a few minutes of conversation with her, the overwhelming impression of theatrical perfection was forgotten in the feeling that here was a person with a will like a stretched steel band.

While tea was being served, Madame Chiang and Erskine entered into such an absorbed conversation that I set down my half-empty tea-cup and got my camera into operation as quickly as possible. It is always a help to me when my subjects are interested in conversation while I work, because it gives me a chance to record a varied succession of facial expressions while they forget the camera. Madame's beautiful face was very expressive as she talked.

Erskine was telling her that she should visit the United States as soon as possible, in order to convince the American people that it was to America's interest to send more military supplies to China.

"But I have written a book for publication in the United States," said Madame Chiang. "That will do more good than anything else."

"A book will help some," Erskine said, "but your personal appearance would help China more than a dozen books at this time."

Madame Chiang was silent for several moments.

"I suppose that's true," she said, "but I can't leave China now. There is so much to do here that I wouldn't feel right if I didn't stay here every minute."

"Just the same," Erskine told her, "I wish you would go for a quick visit. Americans haven't been able to keep up with the world. They don't know what it's all about any more—and they probably won't find out until it's too late—or almost too late."

"But Americans should know that by helping China they are contributing to the defeat of our enemy, and theirs—Japan."

"The average American thinks this war is taking place on another planet," Erskine said.

At which point the photographs, which were progressing with the conversation, were interrupted by the entrance of the Generalissimo, who came in to have a cup of tea.

Generalissimo Chiang Kai-shek is a masterpiece of monotone. His hair and mustache are the texture of straw, his skin is the color of dried grass. He is as immobile as a wheat stack, and his general impassiveness contrasts with the striking personality of his dynamic wife. But here, also, one has that feeling of hard, strong purpose, and one hears constantly that the men fighting under him are ready to die for him.

I asked the Generalissimo's permission to take his portrait and went on working again: it seemed odd to photograph a general holding a tea-cup and sitting on a sofa with a lace antimacassar behind his head, but when you are a photographer you learn to take what you can get. While Chiang did not speak English, he gave the impression of not missing a single thing when English was spoken. At rare intervals he smiled, and I was able to catch a startling mouthful of false teeth, gleaming in his otherwise impassive countenance. When he talked with Erskine, Madame Chiang interpreted.

My husband asked Chiang if China was getting sufficient military supplies from the United States and England.

Chiang was quick to say that he was satisfied with American

help to the extent that it had been promised, but that very little had been promised at that time.

"What about England's help?" Erskine asked him. "Is it enough?"

"No! no! no!" Chiang said. "England has done very little. England does not understand. England is afraid of offending Japan. The British should realize that Japan will eventually attack them."

Erskine told Chiang of the crated warplanes he had seen on the docks in Los Angeles Harbor, waiting shipment to China.

"Did you see many of them?"

"Very many," Erskine said.

"Good! good!" Chiang said. "Were there any big bombers?"

"I am quite sure there were," Erskine told him. "We saw several shiploads of all types of bombers and fighters."

"Good! good! good!" Chiang said. "It is heartening to hear of planes on their way from America. That is what we have always needed. We can defeat Japan only with planes. Japan cannot be defeated without planes."

Every facility was to be provided for Erskine and me if we could take time to fly to the front, but since our destination was Russia we decided to take the first plane available to the U.S.S.R.

CHAPTER 2

The Last Days of Peace

IN THE middle of the Red Square, on the first day of June, hailstones pelted down on me while I attempted to take pictures. All through the month of May it had been snowing fitfully. Never in the memory of the oldest peasant, everybody was saying, had there been such a spring in Moscow. I was shivering and coughing in the heaviest coat I had, which I wore with equal impartiality at chilly breakfasts in our room or outside in the Red Square. It was the same red coat which had been frowned on during air raids over China, but here, at least, it was the right color.

We had been in Moscow for a month. On our arrival we had been greeted cordially by the Union of Soviet Writers, some of whose members had helped select and translate Caldwell stories for the U.S.S.R. and were eager to welcome the author in person. VOKS, the Society for Cultural Relations with Foreign Countries, which knew my Russian photographs from my three earlier visits, had obtained permission for me to take pictures again. There were many restrictions, but still I was happy that I could work.

The occasional limitations on subjects that I wished to photograph troubled me much less than the weather. It was the kind of weather that drives photographers alternately to ecstasy and madness. Piles of dazzling clouds let through the sunlight in short quick stabs, and before one could so much as whip out a yellow filter the skies became overcast and gray.

Not only did the weather delay my photographs; it retarded the crops as well. This did not worry the Russians as much as might have been supposed. War fears were growing. There was an ominous feeling that harvesttime might bring fighting with it; and when the unnaturally cold weather delayed the harvest of spring wheat for several weeks, everyone began repeating the favorite Soviet quip—that the Bolsheviks had learned to control even the weather.

While it was evident that uneasiness was growing, no one was discussing openly from which direction the war clouds were expected to gather. The nonaggression pact between Germany and the Soviet Union was in effect; Germans were to be seen in all the leading hotels; the Soviet press, which is government controlled, contained not an anti-German word.

Still, I was interested to observe that if the man in the street opened his morning *Pravda* or *Izvestia* and read that a British ship had been sunk, he felt very bad about it, almost as though one of his own ships had been sunk. And if, on another day, he read that British pilots had downed an unusually large number of German planes, he was apt to tap his neighbor on the arm and show him the good news.

It made me feel that the Russian people recognized the pact as a marriage of convenience, designed to give their new industries more time to turn out needed munitions while their country remained at peace. In recent history, as short a time ago as 1918, the Germans had invaded the Ukraine, only to be driven out by the Russians, and the people had not forgotten. In the thirteenth century, the Huns had invaded the Ukraine and were driven out by angry peasant hordes led by the great Russian hero, Alexander Nevsky. And the people of Moscow had this invasion clearly in mind, too, because a vivid moving picture about it had been released in 1939. It had played to packed audiences throughout the city until the very day when the German–Soviet pact was signed, at which time it was withdrawn so suddenly that some of the movie audiences were left in darkened suspense as the Huns and the Ukrainians, clashing at saber points, faded from the screen. They were not even given the "Continued Next Week" slide, which American movie theaters run as the thriller breaks off at its most exciting point. If some omniscient theater manager could have run such a sign, it would have read, "To Be Continued After Two Years." Its director, Sergei Eisenstein, however, had a bit of that kind of foresight. When we arrived in Moscow, he got the reels out of a safe where they were stowed away and gave Erskine and me a private showing. "We think," he commented sagely, "that it will not be much longer before *Alexander Nevsky* will be shown in public cinema theaters again."

Although technically, in early June, 1941, Germany was the friend of Soviet Russia, there were other rumblings. The most significant, to us, was a report that came to our ears about an address that Stalin had made to the graduating class of the Military Academy. Stalin's speech had already been printed in the Soviet papers, but we learned through one of the underground routes by which news sometimes reaches journalists that the printed version was merely the preamble to his fateful address. The main theme of his talk to the Red Army graduates had been: "Germany is our real enemy."

This was so sensational that some of the foreign correspondents who heard it tried to cable it out; but such a statement, not even published within the borders of the Soviet Union, could not be expected to pass the censors. One foreign correspondent who smuggled the story abroad was deported within a week.

The American Ambassador, Laurence A. Steinhardt, had been preparing for weeks for the emergency he thought was impending. A second embassy was being established in the country about thirty miles north of Moscow in a *dacha*, or country house. He was importing tents from the United States and preparing to set them up under the birch trees to house needy Americans who might be blasted out of their hotels if action started.

He did not know until it was too late to change that the spot selected for this safe retreat was close to a group of munitions factories. More dogfights were to be held over those tents than if they had been pitched in the middle of the Red Square.

Mrs. Steinhardt was very busy making the *dacha* homey and comfortable. She was choosing harmonizing wall colors and fabrics and was hanging curtains in attractive color tones and heavy enough to be drawn for blackout purposes. A perfectionist down to the last pleated valance, she had curtains matched for fringes and chenille edgings by the courier who carried the pouch to Stockholm each week, as the Swedish capital afforded a wider selection of drapery trimmings than could be found in Moscow.

Ambassadors' wives were faced with extraordinarily complex problems in the social field during those last confusing weeks that the German–Soviet pact was in force. Protocol was assuming such proportions that it could be tackled only by supertechnicians. Within diplomatic circles each dinner called for divisions for which Solomon would have needed an advisory committee. How many Axis or Allied plenipotentiaries could be mixed, if any, and in proportion to how many neutrals?

Many embassy hostesses expanded their operating budgets by giving all entertainments in twos. But even when this was done, which of the neutrals could be trusted to speak to which of the belligerents? Some brave ambassadresses flung everyone together and continued to smile glassily while the room coagulated into sections, with floating icebergs, unseen but plainly felt, bobbing in between. One of the Scandinavian ministers evolved a superb handling of the situation. He gave a reception in which two great rooms judiciously divided up the Axis and Allied guests. These salons were not adjoining, but were connected by a short hall through which the waiters and the more fancy-free of the neutrals circulated impartially.

Lady Cripps flew into Moscow from Stockholm in the same plane which carried the wife of the French Minister, who had been her intimate friend for many years.

"It was too dreadful," she told me. "We were the only two women on the plane and we felt so silly, not even being able to look toward each other. When the plane stopped at Riga, I found I didn't have enough Russian currency in my purse to phone my husband. There was no way to change it at the airport, and when I saw my dear friend go to the telephone and ring her consulate in Moscow, it would have been so convenient if I could have asked her simply to tell them to call up the British Embassy and let Sir Stafford know when I was coming."

The diplomatic colony was buzzing with a story which had recently leaked out, concerning the departure of Molotov earlier in the year for his visit to Berlin. The pro-Ally members of the diplomatic colony had been lucky in getting a long laugh at the German Ambassador, and long after the event the laugh was still good.

The station authorities had been notified, when it was time for Mr. Molotov to leave on a special train with the German

Ambassador, that no one without the proper credentials would be allowed to pass the train gates. This was a routine rule in such a case. The Soviet Commissar for Foreign Affairs had already gone on board when the German Ambassador reached the train gate, closely followed by an attendant carrying his bags. There were, of course, credentials for His Excellency Count Friedrich von der Schulenburg, but no one had thought to make out a pass for the attendant.

The fidelity with which Soviet citizens obey orders is one of their most admirable and, sometimes, most exasperating characteristics. His Excellency, of course, wanted his bags. Courteous regrets were expressed, but certainly the station guards could not be expected to break a ruling, particularly when such important personages were involved!

Hastily, because the train was due to pull out any moment, the German Ambassador decided to make the best of it and carry his bags himself. But how could this be permitted? No papers had been issued authorizing these articles to be carried within the gates.

Zero hour arrived, and Count von der Schulenburg, complaining in two expressive languages that he would not even have a clean shirt in which to disembark at Friedrichstrasse Bahnhof, sprinted for the train and jumped on it as it moved out.

Hurrying through the moving train, he at last found Molotov in an observation car, beginning to worry about the nonappearance of the Ambassador. As soon as the Commissar understood the difficulty he issued an order. Immediately, not only the diplomatic train, but all trains coming in or out of the station on near-by tracks were stopped, and in twelve minutes a trouble engine had brought up the German Ambassador's luggage.

During these last weeks of Russo-German peace, Erskine and I were living in a plain but comfortable room on the top floor of the old National Hotel. It was much like any European hotel room, but the service was greatly improved over Moscow hotel service as I remembered it nine and ten years ago. The bathroom plumbing worked, which it had not always done during the Five-Year Plan, and I was pleased to see small cakes of soap supplied daily with the fresh linen, for soap had been an almost unobtainable luxury in earlier years. At that time such efforts were being made to bring machinery from abroad that consumers' goods were forced to sink to a low ebb.

Our windows looked over Gorky Street, which is the Fifth Avenue of Moscow. It was a very different-looking Gorky Street from the narrow alley which I remembered from ten years ago. Whole rows of buildings had been pushed back on rollers to make an extremely wide thoroughfare, and modern office buildings and new shop fronts gave the effect of a complete face-lifting program.

From our windows we could see the names of a block of shops; there was a Cheese Shop, a Champagne Store, a Children's Store, with toys and frocks and suits designed for little boys and girls. Next to it was a new shop of which Muscovites were very proud. It was the Ice-Cream Parlor. We found that Eskimo Pies, which the Russians liked particularly because they considered them a symbol of Western culture, could be purchased there. But the store to which we paid the most frequent visits was the Dietetics Shop. Just inside the entrance was a door leading to the office of a doctor, who could be consulted free of charge by ailing customers who wished advice on diet. In the intervening years between the comparative famine of my last visits and the comparative plenty of this one, the Russians had discovered the vitamin and pursued it with unbridled enthusiasm.

While we were happily free from those ailments which made shopping at the Dietetics Shop necessary, it was interesting to see the array on sale. There were partially cooked meats and specially blended salads, prepared for people with specific diseases. There were thirty-two kinds of breads with various ingredients omitted or included for sufferers from ulcers, diabetes, and other illnesses. Then, there was one invalid product which we used to buy. We had discovered that an ordinary chocolate bar, at our disadvantageous rate of exchange, cost us the equivalent of $2.50; but in the Dietetics Shop, where prices were kept low for the benefit of invalids, their specially prepared excellent chocolate cost only thirty-five cents. So we became steady purchasers of diabetics' chocolate.

During our early weeks in Moscow we had many visitors and we made many Russian friends. We were singularly fortunate in the kinds of contacts we had with the Russian people because it is not easy, as a rule, for foreigners to mix with Russians. The changes in ideology—for example, like that which was then going on in regard to the Germans—were too unpredictable to the average Russian for him to want to take a chance on being seen too much in the company of foreigners. But our work, my photographs and my husband's writing, gave us a kind of immunity which was one of our greatest assets in learning to know the country.

The people we saw most often were members of the Writers' Union. The assistant to the editor of the foreign-literature department, young Elisaveta, who spoke almost perfect English, became one of the best friends I have had in any country. She was small and fragile-looking, with blue eyes and a cloud of black hair which she held back from her pale, sensitive face by a narrow ribbon tied Alice-in-Wonderland style. She had a warm curiosity about everything American and an almost fanatic patriotism about everything Russian. She went with me frequently while I took photographs, to act as interpreter. Each photographic expedition became at the same time a Russian lesson, for I was trying hard to increase my Russian vocabulary. I could understand short phrases, but I wanted to learn to follow longer conversations.

Interest in American magazines, whenever the Russians could get their hands on them, was tremendous. One day when I was unpacking some delicate pieces of camera equipment, Elisaveta came in and carefully smoothed out the sheets of old magazines that I had wrapped them in. When she saw that they were pages I had torn from *Vogue* and *Harper's Bazaar*, she exclaimed: "We must carry these to the House of Fashion Models."

She took me to visit the House of Fashion Models, on Gorky Street, and we found a fashion show in process of preparation. The chief designer received my old magazine pages eagerly. "We are improving on the American models to suit the needs of Soviet women," she explained. They were also adapting native peasant dress for city wardrobes. This latter effort I found the more commendable of the two, for with the coming of modern clothes, peasant handiwork is too easily lost.

During those prewar weeks, whether we were attending a writers' banquet with Petrov, or whether I was photographing schools and factories with members of the staff of VOKS, or whether I was just walking along the streets or sitting in a little restaurant with Elisaveta, I noticed that the jokes people told were beginning to take on a political significance. I have often thought that one can tell more about what the people are thinking by the anecdotes that they tell than any other way. Many of these stories were aimed at Hitler.

In one of their favorite anecdotes, Hitler goes to the edge of the English Channel and stands there looking longingly across the water. He decides that the problem is too much for him and summons the oldest rabbi in the countryside, who, he believes, can give him expert advice.

Hitler explains his problem, and the rabbi says, "Oh, that's not so difficult. Moses had the same problem three thousand years ago."

"What did Moses do?" asks the Führer.

"Oh, he solved it very simply," answers the rabbi. "All he did was to pick up a certain stick, strike the waters, and everything was handled."

"That's just what I wanted to know," exclaims Hitler. "Where is that stick?"

And the rabbi replies, "It's in the British Museum."

Another indication of the drift of international relations was a new rule that was passed, forbidding foreigners, even diplomats, from traveling outside Moscow without a government permit. This meant that even members of the diplomatic corps could not travel down to the Black Sea for a vacation without a special permit, which was not often granted. This annoyed the diplomatic colony at first, but soon they guessed that it was a measure aimed at the Germans, to keep them from seeing too much.

However, it was essential for us to break through this regulation if we were going to do our work properly, and with the help of the Writers' Union and VOKS, which felt it was all to the good to permit us to do a thorough reporting job of their country, in words and pictures, we were given permission to travel. Early in June we left for an extended trip through the wheat fields of the Ukraine, factories in Kharkov, Rostov, the Donbas Coal Region, the Caucasus, and the Black Sea.

CHAPTER 3

Way Down South in Georgia

AN UNNAMED Mason and Dixon's line separates Georgia, in the south, from Great Russia. Georgia was the last of the major republics to come into the Union of Soviet Socialist Republics, and its people are independent and proud. They have the same superiority in their attitude toward Russian northerners that our old Southern families have toward Yankees. The large-eyed, handsome Georgian people show the touch of their sunny climate: they sing more and joke oftener than their countrymen to the north, and their southern hospitality is fabulous.

In 1932 I had ridden on horseback through the Caucasus, accompanied by a group of Georgian soldiers and commissars. As we rode, they taught me a song which the Georgians have been singing for many years; the words of the chorus are, "Mamma, I want to go to America, to bring back an American girl who will come and sit beside you." It was unprecedented for them to have an American girl to sing it to; therefore, this fact warranted celebration. Every time we came to a new village, we dismounted and sang the song over the local wine. Each district in Georgia makes its own wine, of which it is justly proud, and which is drunk not from glasses, but from wine horns that are drained at one gulp. Whenever a toast is proposed, the toastmaster and the person to whom the toast is addressed must drain their wine horns, letting the last drop drip out on the thumbnail to show that the horn has been emptied. After the song to the American girl had been sung, with many improvised verses, and in the elaborate barbershop harmony of which the Georgians are masters, the toasting over wine horns began. Since I was their guest, toasts were addressed, not only to me, but to my father and my mother, my aunts, my uncles, my grandparents, and to my husband-of-the-future. Politeness demanded that I down a horn after each toast. This quantity of wine horns was only possible because it was spread out, usually, over the greater part of the day and accompanied by huge wooden platters of *shashlik* (lamb cut up and roasted on a skewer) served with rice and pomegranate seeds. Usually it was sundown by the time my hosts reached the final toast: to the husband they hoped I would have.

And now, after nine years, I had returned with that husband. The fact that he was also a Georgian was a never-ending source of inspiration to the makers of toasts. Parallels between the Georgia of Russia and the Georgia of America were recited in improvised verse, were sung in barbershop harmony, were celebrated in liquids both golden and red, dry and sweet, still and sparkling. As our excursion was conducted by the local Writers' Union, our escorts included the leading poets of Georgia, who turned their considerable talents toward rhyming every comparative feature between that "Paradise" of America and that "Garden Spot" of the Soviet Union. Both Georgias grew cotton. Both were famous for corn and oranges. Both had golden sunshine. Both produced beautiful women. But, best of all, both Georgias were noted as the birthplaces of the greatest writers in the land.

I whispered that *Tobacco Road* had never seen anything like this, but Erskine whispered back that they were just a lot of Georgia crackers here, same as back home.

The next morning, we boarded a plane at Tbilisi, and the group of poets and authors of the Writers' Union of Georgia, who had been our guides, saw us off. We flew over spectacularly beautiful mountain ranges until we came down in the midst of tropical vegetation by the Black Sea. It was, had we known it, the last civilian flight to be made in the Soviet Union. The next day all civil planes were withdrawn from service. Upon landing at the resort town of Sukhumi, we went swimming, coeducationally and in "bathing costumes," along the black gravel shores of the surprisingly salty Black Sea.

The next day was the twenty-second of June, and it brought an event of such magnitude that the whole course of our work was changed.

It was Sunday, and there was a peculiar tension in the atmosphere. Crowds of peasants gathered in knots around the loudspeaker in the public square. An important announcement from the government was expected, no one knew just when. (All over the Soviet Union, dance music, news, and government proclamations come over the government-controlled radio through a loudspeaker which blares out constantly in the center of each small town.)

We drove from one village to another, through the tropical vegetation that bordered the Black Sea, and in each public square stood knots of people, restlessly grouped about the loudspeakers, waiting uneasily for they knew not what.

We went back to our hotel and had tea, and at four o'clock Petrov went out to the square again to see if the news had come through. When he came back, Elisaveta ran down to meet him. For a long time we could see them from our balcony, walking back and forth in the garden below.

"I think the war has caught up with us," remarked Erskine.

"If it really has, I wish they'd come up and tell us something," I said.

"It's their war," said Erskine. "Let them talk it over first."

When they came into our room they were smiling, not with joy but with relief.

Molotov had spoken from the Kremlin. Before daybreak, German planes had flown over the Soviet border and dropped bombs on Kharkov, Kiev, and other Soviet cities. Troops were being rushed to the border, and the indications were that the most intense warfare in history had begun.

We drove from one collective farm to another that afternoon, and everywhere there were scenes of the most enthusiastic patriotism. Collective farmers were pledging their support, their work, their lives, to victory of their country. But everywhere there was one question on everyone's lips: where did Great Britain stand?

How could they, as Soviet citizens, guess what would be the policy of capitalistic nations? Could all this be a frame-up between England and Germany? Financial interests are powerful, the collective farmers kept reminding one another, and might swing the tide against the will of the people. The Russian people admired the brave citizens of England, who had showed so much courage during the bombings, and if they were to be together in the struggle it could mean much.

It was almost dusk when we reached a large citrus-fruit collective farm on a hill overlooking the Black Sea. The collective farmers had gathered in a clearing in an orange grove, where a loudspeaker had been mounted. Just as we arrived, the amplifier blared out a second announcement from the government: Churchill had made a speech, and the translation was being read from the Kremlin. Churchill had stated that Great Britain would stand with the Soviet Union to meet their common enemy.

I saw tears of joy stream down the cheeks of those farmers. "With Great Britain and the Soviet Union together against the invader," they began to shout, "the bloody Fascists will be crushed."

We packed our bags and drove from Sukhumi to Sochi, where we hoped to get a train back to Moscow. We were fortunate that the head of the district Party Committee had been able to lend us a car. All along the way, whenever we paused for petrol or water, dozens of people pressed up to us, wishing to engage our car if we could spare it. They were all trying to find transportation from their vacation spots so they could get back to enlist.

In the jewel-like resort of Sochi, steeply banked above the sea, the rest homes were emptying rapidly. Its principal street, twisting through flowering groves and over cliffs, was lined with resthouses: the sanatoria of the Arctic workers, of the Donbas coal miners, of the *Pravda* newspaper staff; the Red Army House, and the rest home for locomotive workers. This last, where we stayed, was a Pompeian, pillared structure, run according to the plan we had found in Mineralnye Vody —giving reduced rates or free vacations to *otlichniki*, the most efficient workers. But the *otlichnik* locomotive workers were leaving as fast as they could get room on the trains.

The Red Army House had been emptied before we arrived. It is a colossal glass and concrete structure, startlingly modern, and with a private funicular to shuttle vacationing soldiers down the dizzy grade to the beach. Now its pair of little cars stood idle on their sloping tracks.

Reaching the station, we found a crowd that pressed about it for blocks. Petrov forced his way into the throng, and the fact that he was able to return with tickets was evidence of the influential place which writers are accorded in the Soviet Union.

Our two-day train trip back to Moscow was an hour-by-hour struggle to get news. During each stop, we tried to listen to the station radio, but troop trains roaring in the opposite direction drowned out the loud-speakers. In the larger stations, Petrov would be out on the platform before the train stopped, trying to get a newspaper. But the papers vanished, the instant they appeared, into hundreds of outstretched hands.

The dining cars had been taken off all trains, and at each stop we bought whatever food we could find, usually black bread and cucumbers. While we shopped, during what minutes were available, Elisaveta tried to collect news by word of mouth. She would approach groups of soldiers first and then civilians and then run back into the train to give us what scraps she had found out. The Germans were bombing points in Bessarabia, attempting to break through to Odessa. At the next station, she would hear that they had been repulsed but were reported bombing fortresses near Leningrad.

At Rostov, a long stop, she walked up and down the platform with an old man in a Santa Claus beard, until the train started; whereupon she ran around to everybody in our car to tell them that during the first three days of the war the Soviets had brought down three hundred enemy planes.

Trainloads of naval guns and sailors passed us, headed south toward the Sea of Azov. Freight cars packed with motorbusses rolled by, directed west, to expedite the movement of troops on the front. A long line of cars carrying tractors—of the charcoal-burning type, to save gasoline—were being unloaded to hasten the harvest in the Kuban region, where the rye was growing as tall as a man's head.

At many stations along the way, we picked up copies of Churchill's speech, translated into Russian, Georgian, and Ukrainian and evidently printed by the hundreds of thousands. And at last, when we were within a few hours of Moscow, we saw our first newspaper. We still had not been able to buy one, but soldiers in a troop train moving in the opposite direction on the next track passed their paper through the window of our train. The newspaper traveled through our entire train, where it was read aloud in every car. Some dispatches were read more than once. These favorite items were cables of sympathy from various organizations in America, expressing friendship for the Soviet people and admiration for the way they had met the Fascist attack. As each of these cables was reread, the whole carful of Russians would burst into cheers. "With the friendship of the great United States," they cried, "and the solidarity of Britain, we will drown the Fascist head-hunters in their own blood."

We reached Moscow in a pouring rain the evening of June 27—the old chilly weather back again. Petrov asked us to forgive him for leaving us to rush out to the country. He had left his wife and two children at his *dacha* while we took our trip and he wanted to be sure that they were safe. Elisaveta hurried off to her apartment to find her mother.

At the National Hotel we were reinstalled, not in our old room, but in the vast corner suite that had been occupied, during the time of the nonaggression pact, by the leading German trade representative in Moscow. The hotel had previously been full of Germans, who had been seen at their best gloating over meat soups and saucers of sour cream and of butter in the hotel dining room.

The suite we inherited from the Nazis possessed a czarist magnificence that dazzled us. Cupids swung from the chandeliers. Cherubs winged their way across the murals on the ceiling. The rooms were so filled with tables covered with vases, lamps with china bases, inkstands of Ural Mountain stone, and ash trays mounted on the backs of lions that I wondered how our Teutonic predecessor in all his plumpness had made his way about without knocking off an art treasure at every step. In the adjoining bedroom the immense bed was piled high with quilts of yellow satin. The bathroom was a vast tiled cave. The drawing room was equipped with grand piano and great white bear rug, and its finest feature was a gold-fluted pillar bearing on its summit a blue cloisonné vase with the picture of Napoleon.

It was a month later when we discovered that we could swing Napoleon around on a socket joint and reveal the Empress Josephine on the other side. Erskine adjusted the vase after each military communiqué. When the invaders were doing well, he allowed Napoleon to face the world. When the

Russians seemed to be beating the enemy back, he turned Bonaparte's face to the wall.

All this splendor cost us no more than we had been paying for the narrow room we had occupied before we left. Ninety-six rubles—eighteen dollars at the current rate of exchange—had seemed exorbitant when we didn't have a grand piano and Napoleon thrown in. But when I walked through the double doors and stepped out on the balcony, I called back to Erskine, "This balcony alone is going to earn that eighteen dollars a day when I get a camera out on it."

Opposite us was the Kremlin, Lenin's Tomb, and the Red Square—a magnificent Moscow panorama. If the *Luftwaffe* did any work on the Kremlin, I knew we would have the best viewpoint in the city to photograph it. Against the lemon-yellow night sky stood the onion-shaped domes of St. Basil's and the five-pointed stars which topped the Kremlin towers. These stars were of ruby glass holding lighted lamps in peace-time, but now the city lay in complete blackout. Above this silhouette of domes and towers the sky gleamed unnaturally bright. It was the time of the "white nights."

I went back into the room. "Do you realize this hotel is so old it trembles every time a streetcar goes past?" said Erskine. "What's it going to be like when they start pounding the Kremlin?"

"Perhaps its very flexibility will help," I ventured optimistically.

The head chambermaid came in to show us how to adjust our black-out curtains, and as she chatted we learned that our hotel suite possessed certain elements of history. Trotsky had stood on our balcony, addressing the unheeding Trade-Unions at the time of his fall from power. Lindbergh had stayed in our suite during his visit to Moscow. (Later, after we moved out of it, Lord Beaverbrook moved in, while attending sessions of the American-British Economic Conference.) But its most recent occupant had been the chief delegate of the "Fascist bandits," the chambermaid stated specifically.

"When did the Germans leave?" I asked.

"It was an odd thing," she said. "They had been checking out of the hotel all week, and Saturday night they were all gone but two, that thin Gestapo one and the fat one who had these rooms. At seven in the morning they went running out of the hotel without their suitcases and even without their breakfast. We wondered where they were going so fast, and later, when we heard Comrade Molotov over the radio, we knew that we would never see them again.''

"Did they pay their bills?" I inquired.

"No," she replied. "Not a ruble from those Fascist reptiles."

CHAPTER 4

The First Days of War

I WOKE up the next morning to find that the military authorities had issued a ukase proclaiming that anyone seen with a camera should be shot on sight. Here was I, facing the biggest scoop of my life, an opportunity so great that a photographer would conceive it only in an opium dream: the biggest country enters the biggest war in the world, and I was the only photographer, on the spot, representing any publication and coming from any foreign country.

The anticamera law was decidedly inconvenient. But I had only to reflect on the supreme convenience of being within the country's borders at all, at a time when all sorts of other news photographers were hammering vainly on the gates, to be willing to face almost any difficulty, even that of shotguns. I did think, however, that to have to face German bombing planes and Russian firing squads on the same side of the same war was rather a lot for even a photographer to do.

But a greater inconvenience even than the military law was the fact that we were supposed to be evacuated. When a war breaks out, an ambassador always has to evacuate somebody, and there was hardly anybody left but us. All the embassy wives and half the embassy staff had been sent out even before the invasion took place. Mrs. Steinhardt had boarded the last crowded plane to Stockholm, with only that percentage of her wardrobe which she was able to wear directly on her own little figure, and her worried husband was still hoping that some miraculous way might open up to get her suitcases to her.

The telegrams of distress that began coming in from *Life* magazine in New York made me guess that our evacuation had already been reported in the American papers. And yet, surely, I thought, anybody would know that I would start throwing my lenses like hand grenades at anyone who tried to carry me away from such a scoop as this.

When Mr. Steinhardt called us to the embassy, Erskine counseled me, "Don't talk too much. Let the Ambassador feel that he's doing his duty. The less we argue, the better chance we have."

The Ambassador warned us that it was his duty to protect the lives of American citizens. "No one knows how soon Moscow will be bombed," he said. "And when it begins, the loss of life and the destruction are bound to be terrible. There are still two seats left on the train to Vladivostok. It might be your last chance. Later, after bombing starts, there may be no means of getting you out. You may be trapped. Yes, I really have to point out that to stay will be to risk the greatest danger."

"Don't forget we came here to work, Mr. Ambassador," we reminded him.

"However," he continued after a meaningful pause, "if after thinking over the perils to which you are exposing yourselves, and if after seriously weighing the dangers involved, it is your considered decision to stay, our embassy will help you in every . . ."

He had no chance to finish, for within the next instant the United States Envoy and Plenipotentiary Extraordinary found himself being kissed by a photographer.

We tripped out of the embassy and walked back to our hotel, and as we passed through Arbat Square the marquee of a cinema theater caught our eye. When we had left on our trip for Georgia, the theater had been playing *The Great Waltz* to capacity audiences which had thronged in for the rare chance to see an American moving picture. Today a long queue waited for seats, and the title on the marquee was *Alexander Nevsky*. Eisenstein's anti-Nazi picture had been brought out of its two-year retirement.

As we entered the hotel, we found Elisaveta waiting for us. She had come to tell us there were meetings being held all over the city. From the lobby we could hear a roar of voices sounding down the stairwell, and we hurried up to the second floor, where, in the large dining room, a clamorous meeting of chambermaids, chefs, and waiters was in progress. The speakers were jumping up on the tables, and the long room rang with oratory.

The hall maid for our floor was shouting: "When we heard the words of Comrade Molotov about the barbarous attack on our country, we remembered the saying: 'They that take the sword shall perish by the sword.'"

The cheering of the hotel workers drowned out her voice now, and the second-floor supervisor leaped to a table, snatching a feather duster from the nearest chambermaid and waving it over her head until she could be heard. "We will wipe Hitler's fiends off the earth," she called, waving her feather duster as though to show how it was to be done. "The hangman hordes shall perish!"

A resolution was passed providing that the women workers of the hotel would take over the tasks of the men in addition to their own, whereupon the hall porter jumped to a table and called for volunteers to the Red Army down to the last waiter and dishwasher, at which the male personnel broke into cries that resolved into a chant: "We shall meet the Fascist bandits with a wall of fire."

"Let's get out and see things," I said, and we went out into the streets. We were swept along with the throng until we reached the October Railroad Station. The freight yard was jammed with locomotive engineers and mechanics, rallying for active and reserve service in the army. A red-draped tribune had been hastily set up at the end of the yard, and a brakeman was calling through a megaphone, "We volunteer to fight not only for the life of our fatherland but for the whole of progressive humanity."

In the Red Night Rubber Factory we found the women volunteering to take over the work so that the men could go to the front. At the Stalin Auto Works the pressure of volunteers was so great that a restraining speech was being made, explaining the necessity of keeping key men at their jobs until women could fully take over the production. The head of the pattern shop, who had been requested to stay at his post, jumped to the platform and shouted, "The motors we turn out shall be better than those of our enemy, for ours are made by free men and theirs by slaves."

During those first dramatic weeks of the war, you could go

into any factory, and side by side with almost every man there was a woman standing. Sometimes it was his wife, sometimes it was his sweetheart; or it might be a woman brought from a less important industry; but the man was teaching that woman his job. Realizing that it is not an easy thing to take over a skilled job, the women were going to night school to increase their factory technique. They took great pride in keeping production up to the level that had been maintained by their husbands and brothers.

And the women, who wanted so much to go to the front, too, dramatized their jobs as only Russians would think of doing, by referring to their tools and industrial processes with military names. Even in the meat-packing plant, the girls were happier if they could refer to a "spearhead attack" on their masses of beef and if they could speak of the cutting operations along the conveyor belt as a "bayonet advance."

Soviet citizens, who have always taken the principle of work earnestly, undertook the work of defense with the utmost seriousness. Everyone began studying to do something new or something better. Salesgirls were learning to be truck drivers, schoolteachers were studying shooting. I talked with a group of algebra teachers who were learning to operate and to clean machine guns. Factory workers of all kinds were studying in their spare time to be nurses. I visited a cinema theater which had been turned into a school for delegations from apartment houses, who were organizing classes in their homes for instruction in various defense tactics. In the first-aid section an anatomy class was studying a very animated-looking skeleton. At a signal from the director they began bandaging up each other's heads with an amount of energy that would have bound up a whole wounded army. Near by, a group of high-school girls were studying the internal construction of a fire extinguisher, in a room lined with ladders, fire hose, buckets, and fire helmets.

Children patrolled the streets at twilight to warn householders who allowed threads of light to leak through their blackout curtains. It was the special function of children to keep sandbags and water pails constantly filled in case of incendiary raids. The Young Pioneers volunteered to do the marketing and help with the housework for the many women who had gone into the factories to replace the men who had left for the front.

Petrov and Elisaveta dropped in every day to tell us what was going on. Petrov had desired keenly to go to the front, but he had been requested to stay at his desk and take over the editorship of a second publication. His office was in the *Pravda* organization, and in addition to the magazine *Ogonyok*, of which he was editor, he now had charge of *Crocodile*, a humorous weekly. He always had anecdotes and bits of news to tell us before they were published, valuable material for Erskine's writing; often he brought in colleagues from the Russian newspapers, newly returned from trips to the front, whom Erskine could interview. Petrov had been promised that he could go to the front later.

Elisaveta had a similar ambition. "I just hate medicine," she told me. "I loathe the sight of a bandage. But I'm taking night courses in first aid because I know that's the only way I'll ever get to the front, and I simply have to go."

She took me to visit the medical-training centers which had sprouted up at every street intersection, like the corner drugstore. Schoolgirls, housewives, and working women were going to night classes, and the applications for front duty as "medical sisters" were stacking up like mounds of snow. I was glancing through them one night, with Elisaveta looking over my shoulder.

"Why, that's Lenin's adopted daughter," she exclaimed as we came to the name Barbara Alexandrovna Armand.

"I can no longer stay out of the struggle," the letter ran. "I have had a good education and can do either nursing or cultural work at the front. I beg you not to refuse me."

Her wish to serve was granted, I found later, but not to nurse the wounded. She was sent into the country to take care of children who had been evacuated.

Evacuation of children was never announced as a fact, even with the growing tension of German front lines moving steadily closer to Minsk, steadily closer to Smolensk. It was announced that twenty thousand school children were being moved during their summer vacations "for scientific research in the Arctic regions," that fifty thousand youngsters were going on an expedition to central Asia "to make geological surveys."

As the Germans drew closer to Moscow, the streets around the railroad stations were narrowed into lanes by the overflow of thousands of mothers with their children, camped on their sacks of belongings and living within sight of the station gates until space could be found for them on the trains.

When I went into the hotel barbershop for a shampoo and a manicure, I was met with the announcement, "There are no more manicurists left in the city of Moscow."

"Why not?" I asked.

"They have all been sent to the country to take care of the children."

There was no more nail polish either. I brought down my own little bottle of lacquer, which, after its long voyage from America, retained only a small sticky residue in the bottom, and the cashier obligingly helped me to apply it. This became a weekly practice, with mutual benefits, for when she had given me my coat of polish she would dab the brush back into the few drops that remained and apply a coat to her own fingers. In Russia the use of lipstick and nail polish is considered "cultured," but the red capital has only introduced the most flaming shades. The softer tone of "Cyclamen" was quite a novelty for her.

Day after day, underneath our balcony, passed those husbands whose wives had taken over their machines. We used to see them marching to the railway stations en route to the front. Often their womenfolk walked quietly at their sides. The process of volunteering had been stopped for the more efficient procedure of mobilization. Theatrical performers and opera singers who wanted to enlist were not accepted as soldiers but were sent instead to the mobilization offices, where enrollment went on to the tune of arias. As the mobilized groups were moved outward, the concert and theatrical troops followed and continued their entertainment tours right up to the front lines.

No one knew where these front lines were. According to the Soviets they were far to the westward, with small forward thrusts being permitted the Germans only for the purpose of allowing the Soviets to capture the enemy in the pockets thus formed. According to the German radio, to which we foreigners but not Soviet citizens had access, the Nazis were on the outskirts of Smolensk.

"When Smolensk is taken," said Mr. Steinhardt, "the bombing of Moscow will begin, because the Smolensk airport will make a convenient hopping-off point only an hour away." (It turned out later that he was right.)

The war was not quite two weeks old when we went to a garden party at the Spazzo House, the Ambassador's residence. We were attending what was probably the most exclusive reception to be given by any embassy, any time, anywhere. It was exclusive because there were so few Americans in Moscow left to go to it. The kindly Ambassador, worrying over the safety of his small flock of Americans and overworked with detail because of his greatly reduced staff, had still not forgotten that it was the Fourth of July.

During this time we had succeeded in obtaining the unprecedented permission to broadcast "live"—that is, directly into the microphone to America, without making a previous recording to be broadcast from a phonograph. In the month of July I broadcast irregularly, and Erskine went on the air regularly every other night and every afternoon.

Just before dawn one morning I happened to be leaving the studio after speaking to America for an evening broadcast, which, with a difference of eight hours, meant early morning in Moscow. I was just putting on my hat and coat when I was told that an important speech was coming through in a few minutes from the Kremlin. I walked home sleepily, in the conviction that nothing of real importance could be broadcast at such an hour, and had just stepped through the door of our hotel room when I heard the loudspeaker over the square blaring out. I hurried onto the balcony. From the amplifier mounted on the roof over my head a strong voice spoke out: "Comrades, citizens, brothers and sisters! Men of our army and navy! I am addressing you, my friends!"

Wondering what leading official could be speaking at six in the morning, I ran for the hall porter and brought him out on the balcony.

"Who is that speaking?" I asked.

"The enemy is cruel and implacable," continued the voice. "He is out to seize our lands watered with our sweat, to seize our grain and soil secured by our labor."

The porter was listening like one transfixed. "He has a Georgian accent. Yes, I am sure of it! That is Stalin's voice."

Stalin had not spoken to the people since 1938. "Imagine

President Roosevelt giving an unannounced fireside chat before breakfast!" I thought.

I hurried into the bedroom and woke up my husband. The coming night would be his turn on the radio, and I knew he would want to report on the reaction of the people at first hand. When I was finally able to convince him that it really was Joseph Stalin who was making a dawn speech, he leaped into his clothes and we hurried into the Red Square.

Small knots of people had stopped near the amplifiers and were listening in dead silence. "A grave danger hangs over our country," Stalin was saying, as though preparing the people for news of losses. "In case of forced retreat of Red Army units, not a single engine must be left to the enemy, not a single railway car, not a single pound of grain or gallon of fuel." Larger and ever-larger crowds gathered around the loudspeakers as the voice continued. My Russian was not good enough to get all that he said, but Stalin spoke slowly and I could catch the drift of the "scorched-earth" tactics which were later to become famous. "Diversionist groups must be organized to blow up bridges, roads, telephone lines, and set fire to forests and stores." As I looked at the determined faces around me I could tell that here were people willing to burn their homes, destroy their crops, give their own lives, before one iota of comfort or help should fall to the enemy. "Our cause is just," concluded the voice. "The enemy must be crushed. We must win."

When he had finished, an old woman standing near us spoke her thoughts aloud, and what she said so manifestly expressed the sentiments of the crowd that it sent Erskine back to the typewriter to use her words as a lead for his evening dispatch. "He works so hard!" the old woman said. "When does he sleep? I worry about his health!"

When Stalin spoke at dawn it may not have been timed to be heard by the greatest number, but it was certainly planned to be read. *Pravda* and *Izvestia* devoted their entire front pages to the speech. Queues a block long moved steadily toward the newspaper kiosks as people waited in line to buy copies. By midafternoon, reprints of the speech were pasted up on walls and billboards throughout the entire city. There they hung, through sun and rain, faded but still readable, throughout the difficult months that were to follow.

CHAPTER 5

The Half-Ton Bomb

IT WAS a thrilling day for Erskine and me when the American Ambassador came to visit us for tea. This was not only because we liked Mr. Steinhardt very much, but also because we were always enthralled by his escort of secret police.

The ambassador of a major power is allotted six members of the NKVD, as the former OGPU is now called, who act as bodyguard. Lesser diplomats receive an escort in diminishing size, depending on their importance. The stated purpose of the guard is protection, but the prevailing opinion is that though fifty per cent of the reason for their assignment may be protection, the other fifty per cent is the fact that whatever a foreign diplomat does is bound to be interesting.

Mr. Steinhardt seldom had any conversation with his guards, but he told us that he had become so accustomed to them in the two years he had been Ambassador to Moscow that he had grown to like the boys and would miss them if they weren't around. They were referred to by Americans as the Four-Letter Boys or, more often, the YMCA.

They went with the Ambassador to the theater and to the opera. Once he took us to a restaurant which happened to be the best dining place in Moscow. Since it happened to be the most expensive as well, I was interested to observe that the diners at the table next to ours, without a question or a protest, got up immediately, leaving their meal half finished. The partly eaten dishes were carried away, and the bodyguard ordered a new and lavish dinner. Who paid for the unfinished meal and who paid for the new one, I was never able to discover.

On the Saturday of July 19, when Mr. Steinhardt visited us (it was after the Germans had been hammering their way into the Ukraine for four weeks), the NKVD followed their customary procedure. Two of them stayed in the street to watch the

Ambassador's car and one guarded the door of the hotel. Three came up to our floor, and of these, one watched at the head of the stairs and two stationed themselves outside the door of our suite. They fared less well with us than they had at the restaurant, for they received no tea.

As the Ambassador and Erskine and I sat sipping our glasses of tea we discussed the question which was on everybody's lips: "When would the first bomb fall on Moscow?"

A ukase had appeared, compelling everyone not on active watch duty to go into a shelter when the siren sounded. Blackout was enforced so strictly that anyone allowing even a crack of light to show from his windows at night was subject to fines and imprisonment. During the preceding ten days there had been several alarms. We had gone into shelters, and after a few minutes the all-clear had sounded, and we had been told that it was just a practice alarm.

As we sat drinking our tea we heard the loudspeaker in the square outside our window blare an announcement. We opened the window to hear more clearly, and suddenly the voice of the announcer was swallowed up in the rising wail of the siren. We looked at each other and said: "This time it's the real thing."

We hurried out of our room, down the steps, and out of the hotel. As we crossed the street to the subway I looked over my shoulder and observed that precisely two paces behind us the secret-service men were following us, with military exactness.

Thousands of people were pouring into the great entrance of the Metro. In orderly fashion they were guided to the escalators, on which they descended to the safe depths a hundred feet below. It was interesting for us to watch this human stream, and here our secret-service squadron proved of aid. The YMCA boys cleared a vantage point for us beside a soda-pop stand at the head of the escalator and formed a cordon to keep the crowds from our corner, so we could watch everything that took place.

After forty minutes, the all-clear sounded, and we came out to the streets, where we were told that this was another rehearsal.

"Perhaps," said Mr. Steinhardt, "it's not just we who are rehearsing. Perhaps the Germans are rehearsing."

On the following Tuesday night, July 22, at exactly ten o'clock, the alarm sounded, and Erskine and I went across the street into the subway, hoping that we would not have to stay in the shelter very long, as we each had a great deal of work to do. I was mixing chemicals preparatory to starting a quantity of films through the developer, and Erskine was polishing off a radio script.

The Moscow subway is something very special, war or peace, as visitors to the New York World's Fair in 1939 will recall. The platforms in the stations have multicolored marble pillars, the ceilings are decorated in gold and blue mosaic, and some of the stations are finished with archways bound in stainless steel. Eisenstein, the Soviet moving-picture director, remarked to me, "The Metro is exactly what Metro-Goldwyn-Mayer would think an air-raid shelter should look like."

Going into the subway was in itself an adventure, for a triple set of escalators raced downward at a speed three times as fast as that to which New York's underground system has accustomed a Manhattanite. As we coasted down the escalator to the lower platform, we discovered that the trains had been stopped and the power turned off from the tracks. People had been conducted to the tracks, where they sat, uncrowded, several thousand strong. Sitting on the tracks in the Moscow Metro is something you can do in your best clothes, for Muscovites are so proud of their subway that it is kept as clean as a whistle.

Erskine stayed on the platform, where he could try to talk his way out if the all-clear did not sound before his broadcast time, and I went back into the tunnel with the crowd. I sat on the tracks and counted the hours. It hardly seemed that a practice alarm would keep us there so long. Down the tracks, a man wearing overalls and an embroidered Kazak cap read an illustrated edition of the poems of Pushkin. I pulled out of my pocket the Russian textbook I always carried, and that night I added to my vocabulary a number of words which I might never have acquired if the alarm had been shorter. I glanced at my neighbor and noted that she was a schoolgirl doing cross-word puzzles. "When I can do a crossword puzzle in the Russian alphabet," I thought, "I'll feel that these hours spent in shelters are worth while."

Finally, after five and one half hours, the all-clear sounded, and the downward movement of the three escalators was reversed, shooting the thousands of us quickly up into the street. The early dawn light hung green in the sky. People were running toward the Kremlin, and I ran with them. There, beside the Kremlin wall, and within only a stone's throw from our hotel window, was a huge bomb crater. The first bombs had fallen on Moscow.

Hundreds of people crowded up to look. Immediately trucks carrying repair squads arrived and dozens of men set to work to fill up the hole. "They can't hit our Kremlin," a familiar voice beside me exclaimed. It was the reception clerk from our hotel. She grabbed me by the hand and led me running toward the Red Square. "They can't hit our Red Square either, and they can't get Lenin's Tomb."

The Germans had undoubtedly tried very hard to hit the Kremlin that night, and while they did not succeed they did do a thorough job of smashing up both the Italian and the Japanese embassies.

The next night, knowing we would be forced into air-raid shelters by zealous citizen guards whose job it was to see that everybody made for cover, Erskine and I went to the Spazzo House. This was the Ambassador's residence, now being used as an embassy, and here we knew no one would prevent us from having an unimpeded view of the spectacle in the heavens. On arriving we found that the Ambassador had left early with his entire staff for the *dacha*, his country house. It was very plain that the Germans had designs on the munitions factories along the Moscow–Leningrad road that led to the *dacha*, and he wanted to get his people home before raiding started.

My husband and I felt a little thrilled at taking charge of the American Embassy for a night. The two or three Russian servants who had been stationed there to put out fire bombs, if necessary (three had fallen on the embassy grounds the night before), made us comfortable and brought us tea in the garden.

"I'll make a bet with you," said Erskine. "I bet that they come again at ten o'clock, just as they did last night."

He sat with his watch in his hand, and it was exactly five seconds before ten o'clock when a hum in the sky from the north told us that German planes were on their way.

We went up to a convenient stretch of roof just outside the

Ambassador's office windows and began our watch through what will always be one of the outstanding nights of my life. I have seen bombings before in other cities, but I have never before seen the entire heavens filled with shooting stars, with hanging parachute flares, with dot-dashes of tracer-gun fire, with red, white, and blue Roman candles, and streamers like the tails of red comets shooting out into space. Around the complete circumference of the horizon the beams of searchlights swung restlessly, as though a horde of insects turned over on their backs were waving their luminous legs in the air. Once while we watched, these shafts of light came together in a knot and caught in their focus a plane which glowed like a silver moth against the sky. For minutes the knot of light kept the moth imprisoned as it dipped and turned, trying to escape, until suddenly it twisted violently and fell; we had seen our first German plane shot down.

At a quarter after one my husband had to leave to go to the radio station. I found out later that the car from the studio, the only one at that time with authority to be on the streets during a raid, had been hit by a bomb. So Erskine had to make a dash for it in our car, racing not only through falling bombs, bricks, and shrapnel, but rushing past militiamen who might have machine-gunned him had they discovered that the car did not have air-raid credentials.

Left alone on my roof, I began putting my camera to work. Incendiary bombs had begun falling now, so the horizon was bright enough to aid in focusing. Spasmodically, flames began shooting up in scattered spots where fire bombs had found enough timber to work on. The drone of planes sounded more frequently directly overhead, and the beams of searchlights swung upward, crossing and recrossing until the whole heavens were covered with a luminous plaid design. I had not realized that there is so much music with an air raid. The most beautiful sound is the echo of the guns, which returns on a deeper note, like the bass of a Beethoven chord. The total effect is as though two types of music were being played together—formal chords with overtones of jazz thrown in. The peculiar whistle, which one soon learns to recognize, of bombs falling in the neighborhood is like a dash of Gershwin against a classic symphonic background.

I cannot tell what it was that made me know the bomb of the evening was on its way. It was not sound, and it was not light, but a kind of contraction in the atmosphere which made me realize I must move quickly. It seemed minutes, but it must have been split seconds, in which I had time to pick up my camera, to climb through the Ambassador's window, to lay my camera down carefully on the far side of the rug, and to lie down beside it myself. And then it came. All the windows in the house fell in, and the Ambassador's office windows rained down on me. Then something else came down on me, which I did not recognize at the time to be a Japanese screen. Fortunately, a heavy ventilator blown out of the window had missed me by a comfortable margin. I did not know until much later that my finger tips were cut with glass splinters. I only knew that the basement would be a very pleasant place in which to be.

Getting there was the longest journey of my life. My cameras went too, of course, and with my arms full I started toward the stairway but lost my way so completely that I elbowed around the Ambassador's bathroom three times before I reached the stair. Here I had the hardest job, for each landing was ankle-deep in glass, and with the house spasmodically trembling I had to try to choose moments for each crossing when I would be less apt to slip on the glass. When I finally achieved my three-flight descent I found the basement not only a pleasant but a sociable place. The A.P. and U.P. correspondents had arrived to sleep in the comparative safety of the cellar shelter, and at dawn my husband got back from the radio studio.

The all-clear sounded, and we were about to start home when it suddenly occurred to me that I was leaving a lot of good news pictures behind. It was too dark then to photograph the wreckage, so I made my way about the house and on each of the biggest piles of glass I left a note: PLEASE DON'T SWEEP UP GLASS TILL I COME BACK WITH CAMERA.

Home we went, and I fell into such a sound sleep that it was only with difficulty that I aroused myself sufficiently to answer the loud jangling of the telephone. It was Mr. Steinhardt's secretary saying, "You'd better come over here at once if you want to take pictures of this glass, because Mr. Ambassador wants to get the house cleaned up." For which I could hardly blame him; and I hurried over without my breakfast and began to photograph the wreckage.

The bomb, a thousand-pound one, had fallen on the Vachtangov Theater fifty yards away, completely demolishing the building. Muscovites grieved because its beloved director, Kuza, had chosen that night to do his patrol duty on the roof and had been lost, along with a popular actor, Christiakov. Of its two underground shelters, filled partly with theater workers and partly with passers-by who had taken refuge from the street, one was completely destroyed and many in it killed. In the second the occupants escaped without a scratch.

When I returned to the hotel with my films I began immediately to develop them in the bathtub; but no sooner were the cherished results of my work immersed in the developer than another air raid started. The only chance of saving my films was to stay with them, something not so easy to do in a hotel where a dutiful patrol shepherds all tenants into the shelter. As a knocking sounded on the door I found that the space under the bed fitted my measurements very exactly. I could hear the guards enter and go through our rooms until they had satisfied themselves that everyone was absent. And as their steps echoed down the corridor, and the symphony again sounded over Moscow, I completed the developing, hypoing, and rinsing process well known to all photographers.

CHAPTER 6

Moscow Air Raid

THE OPENING air raids over Moscow possessed a magnificence that I have never seen matched in any other man-made spectacle. It was as though the German pilots and the Russian anti-aircraft gunners had been handed enormous brushes dipped in radium paint and were executing abstract designs with the sky as their vast canvas.

This spectacular quality was due to the intensity of the ground barrage. London, for all the severity of its blitz, had more scattered ground defenses: inevitable because of the large size of the city. But Moscow is smaller, and its defense rings were concentrated. Also, the Russians were so eager to keep the Germans back that they flung an enormous amount of ammunition into the air, at what must have been prodigious cost. During that last week in July and through the first half of August, the prodigality of the barrage continued. Later, even on nights when bombing might be heavier, there was usually less to see. There were fewer searchlights used, and the Russian ground crews had learned to employ their defenses more economically.

Sometimes, with that thoroughness which is a characteristic of the Russian race, the patrol would come back and send us scampering to our respective hideaways again; but finally the hall would quiet down and we could come out and watch the raid.

My own position was made more complicated by the fact that the alarm usually caught me with three or four film packs in the tub, in the process of developing, and while the search went on I would lie under the big bed, counting the seconds and minutes and hoping I could get back to the tub and throw the films into the hypo before they were too badly overdeveloped.

The nights took on a curious routine. First, while the action was still confined to the outer defense rings in the distance, I had a multitude of preparations. All the art objects had to be moved against the far wall and under the piano. After my experience with miscellaneous articles shooting inward at the embassy, I did not wish to be knocked out with a china lamp or agate inkstand. Profiting by the knowledge that eight embassy typewriters had been put out of commission by being dashed onto the floor, I would set both our typewriters under the desk. I never received much encouragement from Erskine during these operations, which he considered old-womanish. Sometimes, the concussion works in reverse, he would tell me, and things blow out. But I would explain that when a ventilator has missed your head by inches, you take an entirely different attitude toward movable objects.

In a future world, if wars continue, I believe modern architecture will develop a severity that will surpass anything yet attained. I used to think about modern architecture, as I crawled around under the piano in the darkness, stacking those statuettes and vases. I used to picture rooms with built-in wall seats and sunken lighting fixtures, with recessed cabinets and all surfaces that one might bump into, rounded and smooth, with nothing loose around the place and not a single object in the middle of the floor. If I ever get out of this, I would say to myself, I'll go back and tell those modern architects that they're on the right track but they should carry modernism even farther.

It is strange how in a bombing everything in the room seems to rise up against you and become your enemy. The Napoleon pillar was too heavy to move, and in the darkness and the vibration I feared Napoleon more than Hitler.

But once the bric-a-brac was stowed away, the place was my workshop, and my whole attitude changed. It has always been my experience that a camera in my hands produces a subconscious transformation. A few years ago, for example, I did a considerable amount of photography on some skyscrapers under construction. If the photographic needs of the job required walking over a scaffold eight hundred feet above the street, it seemed as routine as if the sidewalk were only eight feet below. But I felt this ease only when working, when it seemed of some purpose.

Photographing the bombings was much the same. Once I began viewing the skyline through the ground glass of a camera, my world became one of composing streaks and dashes of light, of judging the length of exposures, of trying to make each sheet of film bring out the most intense portions of the unearthly beauty unfolding before the lens.

I had begun making time exposures (varying from a few seconds to eight or twelve minutes each) with one camera in operation. As the raids increased in intensity I worked with four. The size of the raid was measured by whether it was a two-camera, three-camera, or four-camera night. But I never operated all five at once.

My fifth camera, along with a couple of lenses and half my store of films, flash bulbs, and synchronizing equipment, I had transferred to the basement at Spazzo. I was always afraid that the tools I was working with might get smashed up during a raid. The possibility of being left without a single camera grew to be an obsession, so I always took care to divide the risk.

As time went on, our routine was perfected to the point of seeing that our room was stocked with beer and sandwiches well before the alarm sounded; and later, as other journalists moved into our hotel, we used to keep open house during a raid. One after another, when the patrol had completed its round, silent pajama-clad figures would steal into our room. I believe that most of the Moscow raids described in the American press were viewed from our splendid balcony. But during those early weeks we held vigil alone.

People in London and Barcelona used to say that they minded a raid much less if they were in a crowd. I never noticed this, perhaps because my cameras were such absorbing company; but there was one night, early in August, when this objective point of view deserted me.

Usually a raid approaches gradually, and by the time the action has reached the center of the city one becomes adjusted to it, in a way, and the whine of bombs and deafening banging from guns on near-by roof-tops come as less of a surprise. But this night, before I got the first carved-lion ash tray on the floor, the bombs started whining. We had no time to put away typewriters and china lamps, although I did manage to get the four cameras going, two on the broad marble window sill overlooking the Kremlin and two pointing in opposite directions through the grille of the balcony.

Then all time was thrown out of joint. As each finely machined specimen of high-grade steel, streamlined like a bird's wing, was dropped out four miles over our heads, we could hear it screaming its way closer and closer to earth. It seemed as if it would never reach the ground. Erskine would grab me in those strong arms of his and carry me to a little vestibule between two sets of doors, which divided our bedroom from the parlor. We would wait and finally, when the crash came, we could hear that sickening sound of bricks giving way: like toast being crumbled inside your ear. Then we would think: at least that one missed us. Next I would run out and change the films, knowing that such a jar had blurred the exposures then in process. Then another and another would send us back between the doors. But each time, no matter how close the shriek came, I always felt safe when my husband carried me back in his arms.

Even during a raid we could always tell the time, for the Kremlin clock, its gold hands and figures concealed under gray paint, still chimed out each quarter hour. It was Erskine's night to broadcast, and at one-thirty he had to leave for Radio Center. We had been wearing our Russian military helmets whenever we approached the window sills or the balcony, but now he changed his for an enormous helmet which the Mayor of Moscow had provided especially for going to broadcasts. It had a steel visor that projected over his face, and a metal apron that swept around the sides and back, and it might have been designed for a Martian invasion.

"If they set fire to the hotel, you go right down to a shelter," he directed. "And don't waste any time. The Huns are expert at bombing burning buildings."

"I'd hate to get shown up now after all these days of making believe that I'm not here," I said.

"Never mind that. If it gets any worse you get into a basement. Do you hear?"—with which he was gone.

Only a few minutes after he left, the loudest scream of all sounded through the air. I ran back between the double doors, feeling very lonely, while the bomb executed its interminable descent, and when it finally landed I could hear the skeleton of a building across the street give way. I hurried out to the balcony. Just behind the Kremlin wall an enormous plume was rising into the air. It seemed to hang there, frozen against the moonlit sky. Then planks and bricks began dropping out of it. I could hear the shouts of soldiers and patrolmen running toward it across the square.

The damage was concealed behind the wall and it was a week before I was able to find out that a whole Kremlin palace had been blown to bits. It was not the building used by Stalin for offices, but a palace used as a barracks by the Kremlin guard. Not this, however, nor any other hits made on the Kremlin were ever permitted by the censors to be released in news dispatches.

The raid began dying now. The Germans were going away, and the ground fire was drawing into the distance. I rested on the broad window sill.

Air raids affect people in various ways. Some people grow very hungry afterward, others become sleepy. Most of my Russian friends developed an appetite and had to eat as soon as the raid was over, but I was one of the sleeping kind. When the guns grew quieter I would drop off at once, often right on the window sill beside the cameras. Sometimes a wave of planes would come back, and the blasting of guns on rooftops near by would jar me awake. I should start up to see the square below dancing with fireflies as the shrapnel tinkled down on the pavement. But as soon as the sound started to grow softer I would be back in slumber on the marble ledge, my cameras, set for time exposures, still recording any streaks of light that might flash through the sky.

When my husband came back we would get into the wide bed that had held the Lindberghs, and the German trade commissioner, and perhaps Trotsky too, for all I know, and very comfortable under the yellow, satin quilt we would doze off, and wake up again if the shooting picked up, watching it through our big windows.

Finally at dawn we would hear the loudspeaker on the roof above us call out, "The enemy has been beaten back, comrades. Go home to your rest." As confused voices rose from thousands of people leaving the subway, we would fall into a deep sleep.

The war, it seemed to me, had brought about unprecedented unity among the Soviet people. Outsiders who thought the stress of conflict would cause the Communist system to crumble were wrong. The Russians gave the impression of being strongly united behind their political system. By now a whole generation has grown up under it. Soviet citizens have seen their standard of living steadily improve, they have had a certain amount of government representation under their constitution, and apparently they have no wish to change. The overwhelming majority of Americans, brought up in a democratic society, would find it difficult to accept the absence of freedom of speech which Soviet citizens take as a matter of course. The Communist system, which apparently works very well for the Russians, would have little appeal to Americans who are accustomed to arguing loudly and vehemently over anything with which they disagree.

Soviet citizens can disagree with safety about certain things —how a factory is run, for example, whether the operation of a store is efficient, whether the collective farm of which they are members is operated to the best interests of everyone concerned; but in matters of major policy they would consider it unwise to lift a dissenting voice.

The unity of the Soviet people has been assured because whatever dissension existed during the last few years was wiped out. Thus no organized opposition is left. These drastic measures offer another explanation of why there is no fifth-column movement in the country—one secret of the Soviet Union's strength. But the all-sweeping corrective measures which were taken did leave a wake of fear. Even among the patriotic and loyal, this fear was noticeable.

It was quite evident, for example, when we arrived before the outbreak of war. Ten years before, during my previous visits, the spirit of experimentation was everywhere. It was noticeable in all walks of life, but especially in creative fields, such as the theater. Many of the creative efforts were clumsy and crude, but they were always interesting because the germ of trial and discovery was there.

When I returned in the spring of 1941 I found that a crystallization had taken place. There was less of that refreshing experimentation with new things, and more conformity. No one could afford to make a mistake in ideology.

But in regard to this fear, the war was the great healer. With each month of the conflict, unity became more pronounced and dread lessened. Citizens had so many new tasks to do, tasks which demonstrated their loyalty, that they no longer had to fear whether their patriotism might be open to question.

And, despite the lessening of experimentation, the theater, ballet, and opera were still excellent and the acting, dancing, and music always superb. The theaters remained open even through the bombings, although matinee performances became the custom. There was always a performance of Shakespeare running somewhere in the city. In the Moscow Art Theater Sheridan's *School for Scandal* was playing to packed audiences, and the great favorite was, and has been for years, *Anna Karenina*, in which jewel-like sequences and flawless acting build up a perfection seldom matched on any stage.

The Moscow Opera was so crowded that tickets had to be bought far in advance. Whenever Barsova, the leading coloratura soprano of the Soviet Union, or Lemeshev, the handsome young tenor, sang, the workers and collective farmers in the audience stood in the aisles and cheered at the end of each aria. Lemeshev, in particular, had such a following among the younger generation that girls of high-school age cheered and screamed when he appeared. In the middle of the last act of *Eugen Onegin*, where Lemeshev in his character of the young poet, Lensky, is killed in a duel, these throngs of girls would pelt the stage with bouquets of flowers and rush out of the theater in a body so as to be able to catch one more glimpse of Comrade Lemeshev as he left by the stage door.

Toward the latter part of the summer, as more members of the British Military Mission continued to arrive in Moscow, the occasional sprinkling of British military uniforms through the opera audiences attracted as much favorable attention as the stars on the stage. During intermissions, when the spectators flocked into the lobby to get tea and big rolls stuffed with cheese and chopped meat, many smiles and friendly glances followed the trim uniforms. Whenever the Britishers appeared, a murmur would run through the crowd: "The British army and the Red Army are now fighting together against Hitler. It is good!"

This approval of the members of the British Military Mission was enthusiastically shared by the Caldwells. We had a standing invitation from big, bluff General Mason MacFarlane, the head of the mission, to drop in for air raids. This was valuable to me, for having used our splendid balcony to the utmost I needed new viewpoints for night pictures. The British Embassy faced the opposite side of the Kremlin from our hotel and was situated at the edge of a mass of roof which became alive with activity when bombing started. Many times when the alarm began sounding we would jump into our car and make a dash for the British Embassy. We had this procedure so perfectly timed that we could reach the embassy, some eight blocks away, before the siren stopped blowing. Erskine would watch the raid from the embassy until it was time for him to go to the broadcasting station, while I remained to take my pictures.

On one night when we arrived—it was during the third week in August—so much began to happen all at once in the sky that the embassy staff was running back and forth through the darkened house, watching through the windows. It takes a spectacular raid to get Britishers out of bed, they have witnessed so many of them; but on that night even Sir Stafford Cripps was hurrying about in pajamas and fuzzy bathrobe, running to the windows first on one side, and then the other, watching the raid.

It was plain that for me it was going to be a "four-camera night." The General led me up to the attic and held a guarded flashlight while I picked out the lenses and film-pack holders I expected to need. We buckled on our helmets. Mine was the regulation Russian-army type, shaped like a mushroom and so heavy that I had to develop a whole new set of neck muscles before I learned to keep it on for more than a quarter of an hour at a time. We filled our pockets with camera equipment and climbed up a little ladder through a trapdoor in the roof.

There is something unearthly about being on an open roof in a raid. The sky seems so startlingly big, with its probing spears of searchlights and flaming onions hurtling their way through space, that a human being appears too small to count at all. But as this raid got under way I had so much to do that I could not think of anything outside the four cameras I was trying to operate at once. There are no rules for exposure on a subject like this—at least, none that I know of. The most I could do was to guess, by the mounting action, which points of the horizon would be the most interesting to photograph, and then, after the spurts of firing had taken place, try to estimate whether the illumination had been correct for the exposure of each of the four negatives in process.

Once I became so engrossed in calculations, as I focused on a group of cathedral towers with anti-aircraft guns sending up decorative spurts behind their onion-shaped domes, that the General reproved me. "You can't hesitate over your decisions in war, you know."

"But I'm not a general, only a photographer," I said, so apologetically that when I completed my focusing arrangements he added kindly, "Are you sure you are quite happy about that camera now?"

As we started on all fours down the slope of the roof he suddenly called out, "Get behind that chimney. Those things will be hot when they come down." I did not realize what "those things" were, as I heard a swish like satin through the air, and then within less than a minute a rain of fire bombs had fallen within eye range all over the city. From a hundred rooftops I could see spurts of flame. Some of them caught and spread into a steady red glow, but most of them vanished almost at once. I knew that all over the city, on each rooftop, were stationed groups of citizen fireguards who had been training for weeks for just such a night as this; but this was the first chance I had had to see the results of their work on such a broad scale.

A garage building somewhere off to the side caught into a blaze, and a fire truck rushed up and pulled into the drive. By now the grounds were illuminated with red light and I could plainly distinguish the fire engine's crew. It consisted not of men, but of girls wearing firemen's helmets and asbestos suits and mitts.

"May we take a short cut through your driveway?" asked a pleasant woman's voice. "We have come to liquidate the fire."

The blaze was still confined to the corner of the garage, and the liquidation was rapidly effected, where upon the firewomen took off toward the Lenin Library, near which another spurt of flames was mounting toward the sky.

By this time another phase of the raid had begun. A second wave of the *Luftwaffe* was returning with demolition bombs, hoping, I suppose, to take advantage of the light from the fires that had been set. I wondered how the city looked to them up there and whether the considerable amount of "liquidation" accomplished between waves of planes would annoy them. The peculiar whooshlike whistle of bombs began, caused when a quarter of a ton of steel rushes down through the resisting atmosphere, and at regular intervals we could hear shrapnel tinkle on the roofs and streets about us. The General said, "It's getting too thick to stay out here. Come inside for a while," and we climbed through the attic window.

Periodically I would have to go out to change the films in my four cameras, and as the General helped me out the trapdoor he would say, "Do it as quickly as possible, and if you hear something little coming, stand up, because you're less of a target; but if you hear something coming that sounds big, lie down." I was never able to analyze whether the various descending articles were big or little, so I just buckled my wobbly helmet on tighter, made the rounds, changed films and checked the focus, and then returned for a short breather on the ladder.

We had been joined at the trapdoor by Rear Admiral Miles, a slender, hawk-faced man with the clear eyes typical of all seafarers. He had taken part in many battles at sea but, until he came to Moscow, had never witnessed an attack on land.

Then something began floating down that was so spectacular we all crawled out on the roof and crouched along a railing by a drainpipe to watch it. A flare had been dropped directly overhead and was drifting down toward the Kremlin, close enough for us to count the ribs in the enormous parachute that held it. Suspended from the giant umbrella was a ball of blazing magnesium, so bright that it hurt our eyes to look at it.

"They're certainly looking for something very specific in the neighborhood when they burn up as much magnesium as that," said the General. "That stuff costs plenty."

"It's not just the cost," said the Rear Admiral. "There's only so much of that stuff in the world."

It took half an hour for the mammoth parasol to drift to earth, and it was a fruitful working time for me. Photographers have for years taken pictures by the light of magnesium, but I certainly never expected to have the assistance of a fleet of German pilots dropping flares from the sky to light up my night pictures of the Kremlin.

It was one of those seemingly endless nights, when all the ammunition that the world has ever made seems to come pouring out of the sky and streaming up from the earth. Just as the sound of guns began dying away we heard a new wave of Nazi planes approaching, and the shooting started up again. The General had taught me how to distinguish between the sound of the Soviet and the German planes. The Russian planes have a kind of steady hum, and the Germans have a peculiar throbbing beat. I set my cameras again, focusing them toward different parts of the horizon and opening the shutters in readiness, and it was then that I heard what I had been too busy to listen to before.

On a cluster of rooftops at the back of the embassy, the fire watchers were calling out to each other. Some of the voices had a surprisingly youthful quality, and I guessed that this must be one of the children's squads which had recently been organized into fire-fighting brigades. While my Russian is not good enough to understand long conversations I can usually catch short phrases, and as the next spattering of fire bombs was dropped I heard boyish voices call out: "Let me have the next one." "The next one's mine!" The General, whose Russian is a bit better than mine, began translating to me, and I to him, as we each caught a phrase, and finally we realized that these schoolboys were arguing with each other for the privilege of putting out the next fire bomb because each child wanted to make a record.

At last the satin-swishing of the fire bombs died down, the throbbing of the Nazi planes fell away into the distance, and the humming Soviet planes took possession of the air over the city, blinking their green and red lights to show the gunner's crews below where they were. I folded up my cameras, and from the square near us we could hear the loudspeaker blaring out: "Comrades, the raid is over. Go to your rest."

The General, the Admiral, and I climbed through the trap-door, and there, hanging on the ladder like a little furry bat, was Sir Stafford Cripps in his woolly bathrobe, where he had been watching the end of the raid. We all went downstairs and had a whisky and soda, and as the Ambassador settled himself comfortably in a big armchair, his dog Joe pattered in and sat down at his slippered feet.

CHAPTER 7

We Go to the Front

THE RUSSIANS are a secretive people, and while this may have
its military uses it is a distinct barrier to correspondents who
wish to gain a firsthand view of what is going on. Perhaps all the
restrictions in wartime are a good thing.

However, regardless of wartime restrictions, Erskine and I
felt that it was of supreme importance for us to get to the front
and see at first hand the operations of the Red Army. Ever since
the beginning of the war we had been begging the authorities to
let us go, and the middle of September had arrived with still no
result.

Finally, the matter was argued out over a pair of butter
horses. The horses, sculptured beautifully in butter, were table
decorations at a remarkable dinner given by Narkomindel to
the press. First, enormous bowls of caviar were served (with the
perpetual cucumbers), then little quail with frills around their
matchstick legs, swimming in luscious sour-cream sauce, followed by a dessert of frozen fruit. One hundred members of the
Soviet and foreign press were present, including the inevitable
Mr. Hatenaka, the Japanese correspondent of *Nichi-Nichi*, and
many distinguished Soviet writers, such as Ilya Ehrenburg,
author of *Out of Chaos*, Mikhail Sholokhov, author of *And Quiet
Flows the Don*, our friend Eugene Petrov, and his novelist
brother, Valentine Kataev.*

The last toast was drunk and the party filed into the salon for
coffee and apricot brandy, but Mr. Lozovsky and I still sat

---

* "Kataev" is the family name of the brothers, and Valentine Petrovich
Kataev is the author of *The Embezzlers* and other novels which have been
translated into English. Eugene Petrovich Kataev took his father's name of
Petrov as his pen name, in order not to be confused with his distinguished
brother.

behind the banks of flowers and the butter horses while the waiters began carrying away the scraps of the feast.

"I can't go back to America without photographing the front," I said. "I simply can't. What will I say when my fellow countrymen discover that I have not seen with my own eyes the heroism of the glorious Red Army? They will exclaim, 'Why were you not allowed to witness those noble deeds about which we hear so much? Perhaps, then, they do not really exist!' "

It sounded a bit oratorical, but continued association with Russians makes such speech seem natural.

"It is very dangerous at the front," said Mr. Lozovsky. "Aren't you afraid?"

I get rather tired of being asked if I am afraid when I believe that the mention of danger may be merely a convenient form of refusal.

"There's only one thing I'm afraid of. That's of going home without having finished my job."

This seemed to sink in, so I added, "I came here to photograph your country. If I had wanted to be safe I would have stayed at home. If the Red Army soldiers can face the danger, why shouldn't I?"

"Fighting is their work," said Mr. Lozovsky.

"And photography is my work."

The waiters were clearing off the champagne ice buckets now and were removing the screen of flowers. The butter steeds were still rearing their satiny legs and waving their golden manes as though they were charging toward victory.

"Hmm," said Mr. Lozovsky, enigmatically, through his mahogany beard. "You are a very determined young lady."

Two days later we were called late in the evening to Narko-mindel and told to come back the next morning prepared to take a trip. We were instructed to wear plenty of warm clothing, in preparation for rough places and cold weather. But beyond that we were given no inkling of where we would be taken.

There is such a thing as being too happy for speech. What little communication was necessary, the rest of that night, we carried on in whispers: not only Erskine and I, but Tatiana and the day chauffeur, who helped us get ready. They felt that it was their victory too, because even though they were not going they had known all along how much it would mean to us.

Tatiana lent me her heavy yellow sweater; the night chauffeur lent me a woolen scarf. I had no extra socks, because earlier
in the summer I had sold them to Alexander, the day chauffeur,
who had admired the bright colors I wear with slack suits. Now
I bought some of my old socks back from him. I wore the only
heavy slacks I owned, a gray tweed pair. But when it came to a
warm coat I had nothing but the bright-red one which even the
Chinese had realized was not the proper thing to wear at a war.
There was nothing to do but wear it, and be glad that it had a
black-satin lining. All during the trip to the front, I was
whipping it off and turning it inside out whenever we came
within the range of guns.

It was cold and dark when we left the hotel to go to the
entrance of Narkomindel. In the half darkness around the
bathtub, which was still filled for fire-bomb duty, a small group
of newspapermen had gathered. They must have been the
result of the most painstaking selection according to Foreign
Office protocol. It was evident that great care had been given to
selecting British and American representatives. There were five
Britishers and six Americans. I was pleased to find that Mr.
Hatenaka, the Japanese correspondent, and his Leica were not
among us. The youngest of the three censors came along.

The most weirdly dressed of the correspondents was Cy
Sulzberger of *The New York Times*, who wore his Greek battle
dress, a kind of white shiny tunic of the Isadora Duncan school.
The most de luxe was Alex Werth of Reuter's, who wore a
dazzling short coat of white dog fur. And the most natty was
Philip Jordan of the *London News Chronicle*, in his khaki military
outfit worn by British war correspondents in Africa. The other
men wore just clothes, and as each muddy day passed by they
were reduced more and more to something that resembled a
uniform, so covered did we all become with the earth and mud
of the Russian steppes.

We were distributed in a fleet of five cars, with an armed
chauffeur and a military officer-guide packed into each.
Around our feet were disposed various bundles carrying food,
and one of them contained objects of a familiar shape. It seemed
incredible to me that we should be carrying champagne to the
front; but that proved later to be the case. The chauffeurs were
supplied with their own hand grenades, which they kept in the

front pockets along with cranks and tire-mending tools. As Erskine and I pulled out of the Narkomindel courtyard, past the bathtub, our secretary and day chauffeur stood on the sidewalk, waving us off as proudly as though we were their children just leaving for boarding school.

All that day we could feel a good hard roadbed under our wheels, but that was the last day that we were fated to have anything under us more firm than mashed potatoes.

The autumn rains had begun and were drilling their wet needles into the roads and fields. At intervals we drove off the highway into the woods and gobbled down some of the slices of peppery sausage and fistfuls of black bread which we carried with us, eating them between bites of the inevitable raw cucumbers which Russians include in the simplest or most elaborate meal. Cholerton, the British correspondent of *The Daily Telegraph*, who has lived in Russia for almost twenty years—so long that he has grown a long black beard like a Russian—ankled through the wet ferns and picked little white mushrooms which he brought back to the car with him and nibbled contentedly, as we drove on through the rain.

I had known big, bearlike Cholerton on my visits to Moscow in previous years. Most of the other correspondents on this trip were new to the Soviet Union, although I had met some of them on other fronts—in wartime one encounters the same journalists in many parts of the world. For example, I had met blond, slight, whimsical Philip Jordan, of the *London News Chronicle*, on a Cairo balcony overhanging the Nile, at the beginning of the African campaign. In Chungking, Erskine and I had known and liked the *Chicago Daily News* correspondent, Arch Steele: gaunt, sparing of words, Lincolnesque in appearance. Arch Steele was justly respected by his fellow correspondents for his astuteness. We all called him the Admiral.

I had met Cy Sulzberger during the first year of the war, in Bucharest, when we were covering the Balkans, he for *The New York Times* and I for *Life*. Cy, with his prominent light-blue eyes and still more prominent chin, always reminded me of a tightly wound watch spring. His manner was so quick and positive that everything was usually being done his way before the rest of the crowd woke up to what was happening. He rushed about during our trip along the front as though he expected the

Russians to dry up their roads and mop up the mud so that he, Cyrus, could move faster. Whenever his car became hopelessly stuck in the mud, as all our cars did at intervals, he began reminiscing about his fiancée, a beautiful Greek girl, and wondering how soon he would be able to join her in Turkey, where she was waiting for him. (Four months later, the Greek refugee became Mrs. Cyrus Sulzberger in Beirut.) Vernon Bartlett, a roly-poly, elderly British M.P. who was representing the British Broadcasting Corporation, was even more impatient with the discomforts of the roads than Cy.

Alexander Werth, tall, dark, with a rather gloomy face, was a useful addition to our party, for he was half Russian and made a perfect translator of speeches and toasts at banquets. He was a living example of a popular Soviet quip about Leningrad, for he had been born in St. Petersburg, educated in Petrograd, and did not leave for England to complete his schooling until after the city had become Leningrad.

The quietest members of our party were the Associated Press and United Press correspondents. Diminutive Henry Cassidy had been the A.P. correspondent in Moscow for several years, and star-reporter Wallace Carroll had just arrived from other war fronts.

Our party pushed its way on toward the front over a succession of rivers of mud which had once been called roads. Sometimes the rivers widened into lakes, where the boundaries of the road had blended with the meadows and all were mashed to a uniform consistency by the treads of tanks and heavy artillery which had poured in steady streams to meet the enemy. We might have been traveling over Camembert cheese.

Once when we became mired to the hubcaps and our party had to rebuild stretches with stones and logs in front of each helpless wheel—a backbreaking job which took two and a half hours before all cars were extricated—I remarked that at last I had met the famous General Mud face to face.

"Oh, no," said our chauffeur, "in modern warfare he has been reduced to the rank of colonel."

But it was my private opinion that the Red Army had succeeded in promoting him to the post of generalissimo.

Sometimes while we were negotiating these almost liquid highways, small units of the *Luftwaffe* would appear and put in their own bit of work on the roads. The first time this happened we dashed out of our cars and slithered across the slippery surface to the edge of a meadow, where we threw ourselves down in the low shrubbery.

It is odd what images become engraved on your mind. I remember noticing that we were lying in the largest patch of fringed gentians that I have ever seen. The gentians were at a level with my eyes, and over this blue border I watched three great curtains of mud rise into the air and hang there shimmering, as though suspended on invisible curtain poles in the sky. When these heavenly draperies descended to earth again, there were three large sludgy pits, perfectly round in shape, in the road behind us, and our cars were undamaged, though glistening with a coat of mud laid on thick, like maple icing on a cake.

I began gathering fringed gentians, but the soldiers who were driving our cars had something much more practical to gather. They began pulling boughs off the shrubs and trees and tucking them around the fenders and tying them on the tops of the cars. When we moved on again we looked like a nursery on wheels.

At twilight we reached a schoolhouse within six miles of the German lines. The benches where children had sat during the years, studying their arithmetic lessons with beads on an abacus and writing compositions on the life of Lenin and the philosophy of Karl Marx, had been piled against the wall. Their places had been taken by cots packed tightly down the long schoolroom. So thoughtful of our comfort was the Foreign Office which had planned this trip that a barber was even waiting to give the correspondents a shave.

CHAPTER 8

Death and Life on the Battlefields

THE DAYS alternated between trips through the eternal mud and banquets within the sound of enemy guns. The nights were spent in a bewildering succession of field headquarters, sometimes under canvas and sometimes under thatched roofs. Once we slept on the floor of a little resort cottage above the swollen Dnieper, near the fire-gutted town of Dorogobuzh. We slept all together in a room so small that we lay elbow to elbow, our feet against the heads of the row of men in front of us. Erskine rolled me in my blanket over against the far wall and took his place beside me to give me a maximum of privacy. Occasionally I woke up and saw the sentry, bayonet in hand, guarding us, while a single candle flickered on his immobile face.

Often at dawn I would slip out ahead of the others so as to use the valuable early hours before we started on the move. There were always interesting types among the soldiers: Mongols, Ukrainians, Siberians, Uzbeks, Kazaks, and Turkmenians, their faces wet under their dripping raincapes. And it always was raining.

I used flash bulbs to augment the weak light. One by one, my shutters began sticking in that helpless, half-open way which is the worst sight that ever confronts a photographer. And as each lens in its crippled shutter went out of commission, I drew reluctantly on the dry ones which I was saving in my camera case.

These morning hours were often the only times that we were stationary during daylight long enough for me to make character studies and photograph soldiers doing their daily camp tasks. I usually worked until one of the correspondents would stick his head out between the flaps of the mess tent, coffee cup in hand, and call, "Come on, Peggy. Everybody's starting now. Don't hold us up the way you did yesterday," and I would hurry my equipment into the car and we would be off.

Once we were under way Erskine would slip his hand into his overcoat pocket and bring out something salvaged from breakfast. The morning he handed me the long, strong drumstick of a goose I was pleased indeed.

Sometimes the feast time, later in the day, gave me a little more time, and I developed a certain banquet technique. As soon as the toasts had begun I would steal away with a piece of black bread in my hand, loaded with salt herring or a slab of cheese, and scout around for photographic subjects.

Once, when I came back at the end of a luncheon, there had been such enthusiastic toasting of Anglo-American-Soviet friendship that it was small wonder one of the correspondents had slipped unobtrusively under the table. We were being piled into cars and were about to be taken to a group of field batteries directly on the first firing line when my husband missed him.

"Don't leave him behind," said Erskine; "he'll never get over it when he finds out what he's missed." So my husband raised the unconscious correspondent in his arms and placed him in the back of one of the cars, where he was brought along, quite unaware that he was being carried to the very brink of no man's land.

The completeness of his coma lasted until far into the night, which we were spending, packed tight as crackers in a box, on the floor of a tent. Suddenly we were startled awake, for our reviving companion, still under his spell, was chuckling and laughing to himself.

"Shut up and let us go to sleep," somebody called. "There's only one of you and there's a dozen of us."

"If there's a dozen of you I'll take you all to the baker," he announced, after which there was complete silence until dawn. At breakfast our correspondent could hardly believe he had been taken almost within a vodka breath of the German lines. He wrote up his story from the notes the other correspondents lent him.

Finally, a difficulty developed that worried me more than the weather. Some of the correspondents decided they had had enough of the rain and the mud and the disproportionate amount of time it took to go from one place to the next. They wanted to return to Moscow. It took so long to travel along the front, they argued, that they might as well start back and write up the things they had seen. The things they had not seen they could imagine. The simple solution of dividing forces and letting those who wished to see more of the front do so, and those who so elected go back home, was immediately rejected: that might give a scoop to those who remained.

The front faction and the home faction were about evenly divided. Erskine and two or three of the other Americans, especially Carroll and Steele, were steadfast supporters of the front group; but otherwise the membership fluctuated so frequently that when matters grew crucial I stuck around because my vote might be needed. Whenever I set forth my side of the case, that we had been promised we would be shown many more interesting subjects, and that surely if we kept on I would get my break of sunlight sooner or later, I was reminded that the needs of photographers are different from the needs of journalists. Well, they *are* different. No doubt about it. Quite different. And there was only one of me and ten of them.

The homing instinct reached its peak over one of the raw-fish breakfasts. The discussion grew so lively that the Russian officers accompanying us had retired, along with the censor, to the next room, to allow us to decide the matter for ourselves. (I often wondered what those army officers thought of our discussions. They had been so hospitable.)

And then it was one of the medical sisters who really swayed the vote. We looked up from our plates of raw fish to see her coming into the room with a steaming mound of mashed potatoes. Golden pools of butter were nestling in the hollows. Everyone's spirits rose, and the vote was cast to continue on through the mud and rain and see whatever the Russians were willing to show us.

I was overjoyed, because I had a deep feeling that I was going to get my break at last.

I always had interesting little adventures on the evenings that I slipped away from the banquet table. Once the soldiers showed me a big cache of captured German mechanized equipment hidden under the fir trees: some Skoda reconnaissance cars, a huge troop carrier with its caterpillar treads blown partially off, a Mercedes gun hauler, field guns, machine guns, and disabled tanks with swastikas painted on their sides.

Once a tankist returning from a battle where several enemy tanks had been surrounded and captured told me how the enemy tank drivers had filled every available bit of space around their feet, inside the tanks, with women's clothing which they had rifled from Russian villages. One tank, he said, was filled with women's underwear and another was crammed full of peasant embroideries, taken, I suppose, as souvenirs for German soldiers' wives. I was glad they had recaptured that tankload of embroidered scarves and blouses, for Russian peasant handiwork has a richness that is hard to match in any part of the world today. I would not have liked to see it go to the enemy.

Frequently, groups of pilots would return from the fight and show me their captured trophies, for a pilot always saves his enemy's medals if he is able to get them. Each of these pilots had his captured Iron Cross, and one of them had seven of them. "All the Fascist pilots want to get Iron Crosses," he said to me, "but we give them crosses of wood."

I was interested to learn that the Soviet fliers frequently recognized captured German pilots who had parachuted to safety when their planes were shot down. The *Luftwaffe* evidently made full use of the men who had flown passenger planes over the commercial line operating between Berlin and Moscow in peacetime—men who were thoroughly familiar with the route. Sometimes the Russians knew these captives well enough to call them by their first names. The Germans, however, never showed a sign of recognition.

Sometimes I talked with scouts who had penetrated far enough back of the enemy lines to make contact with the guerrillas, for the Red Army maintains connections with partisan troops wherever it can. Wherever possible, the regular army smuggles guns to the partisans. One returned scout told me about a group of villagers who were successful in halting an oncoming munitions train by tossing burning trees across the railroad tracks. When the German soldiers ran up to try to clear the tracks, the villagers shot at them from an embankment with the only two rifles they had, and when those gave out they threw rocks at the Germans. In the end more of the partisans than the German soldiers were killed, but the enemy had been delayed.

Another scout came from a region beyond Smolensk, where a detachment of partisans had hidden in the tall grass along the highway, waited until a group of tanks came opposite, and tossed bottles of flaming gasoline* at them, disabling three tanks. As this scout worked his way back, he passed through a town where a group of partisans had actually fallen on two invading tanks with hammers and axes. Machine-gun fire from the tanks killed several of these villagers, but finally, led by the village blacksmith, they managed to bend the machine guns out of commission and then, beating on the armored walls, they created so much din and dust that the tank crews had to surrender.

One of the scouts had come from a tiny village, nine miles behind the lines, with a report of how when the Germans moved in, the men went back into the woods, believing the Nazis would be less suspicious of the women. The German officers took up their quarters in a log schoolhouse, and at midnight the peasant women set fire to it with gasoline-soaked hay. Then, when the officers rushed half dressed out of the burning building, the women set on them with pitchforks.

In the Soviet Union when territory is captured one does not see the swarms of refugees which have clogged the roads of other invaded countries. The government has previously instructed civilians to stay and become partisans. They have been given directions in the art of sniping and in guerrilla warfare, and if their village is captured they know just what they are expected to do. Guerrillas cannot win a war, but they can do a great deal to make the enemy uncomfortable.

The person whom I remember the most vividly among the Russians I came to know at the front was Tanya. Tanya was a nurse, with widely spaced blue eyes, honey-colored curls that spilled down shoulder length, and a strong, chunky little body. We were in the Yartsevo sector when I met her, not far from Smolensk, and Tanya had been born here. She knew every footpath, and at night, as soon as it grew completely dark, she would buckle on her sidearms and go crawling on her hands and knees through the long grass and low shrubbery, across to

* This is the Molotov Cocktail, used so successfully by guerrillas in the Spanish Civil War.

the German lines. There, behind the lines, she would learn what she could about the movements of the enemy and the location of German guns, and creep back just before daybreak to report on what she had seen. Then she would sleep a few hours, go to the hospital tent to help tend the wounded, and at night if she was needed she would be off again.

The area she was working in had changed hands many times between the Germans and the Russians, so she was much needed. It is a sector that is still changing hands, and as I write this today I believe it is being regained by the Russians. So the experience of scouts like Tanya has great value.

Later, the night that I met her, we were allowed to visit an action point. We were led to the edge of our little wood and told that we could run across an open meadow to another grove of trees about a quarter of a mile away. We were instructed to run single file and keep three meters apart. As we reached the middle of the meadow the whole horizon was ringed with light and there was the sound of thunder above us. It was the Soviet battery firing over our heads, and the Germans began answering toward us with machine-gun fire. We quickened our pace, and as we approached the grove for which we were headed the Germans began sending up star shells, to light the front lines so as to be able to see scouts who might be slipping across. Even as I ran I could not help but notice what a brilliant glow the star shells threw on the ghost-white birch trunks. I hoped that Tanya, wherever she might be at that moment, was sufficiently hidden. And then, in an instant, we were inside the grove.

The action point was less than a quarter of a mile from the Germans. We had to walk on tiptoe and talk in whispers. Here, of course, I was not able to take pictures, because flash bulbs would have revealed our position. Under cover of the darkness, the battery crew moved like clockwork, loading and operating their big guns.

When we returned and started on to another section of the front, it was a little past midnight, much too early for me to find out if Tanya had made the journey safely. I shall always wonder about her.

The next day, we had left the woods and groves behind. We were approaching the great battlefields of Yelnya, where war had lashed back and forth in all its fury, the land sometimes in enemy hands, sometimes in Russian hands, until at the end of six weeks of some of the most savage fighting that the world has perhaps ever seen, the Russians had reclaimed it again. This was sacred soil, for this was the first land to be won back for the Soviet flag, and we arrived directly on the heels of this victory. Here there were no picnic groves, no little woods of fir and birch. We were entering a man-made desert.

The fields were chewed up with the treads of tanks, and we were passing "scorched-earth" villages, with only patches of ashes darkening the ground to show where homes had stood. On the side of a hill, above a small stream and facing the road, was something that looked like a Zuñi village. Just as our American Indians built their holelike houses, tier above tier, up the sides of the mesa, so as to be able to see and face the enemy as he approached, so the Germans had dug themselves into the hillside of Ustinovo. And they had dug in with them several tanks which they could use as pill boxes. Communication trenches had been dug, joining links with forward positions and command posts. Each little cell-like dugout was banked with sandbags and braced with timber, and inside were metal cartons and wicker baskets which still contained hand grenades and land mines bedded in straw. The Germans must have been driven from this hill suddenly, for large stores of ammunition had been left behind for the Russians.

I heard Erskine shouting to me from the top of the hill. He was waving a German helmet, so I picked up one of my own. There were plenty to choose from; hundreds of them, savagely gashed and broken or riddled with bullets, were lying around in heaps. The metal they were made of was thin, much lighter than the heavy mushroom-shaped casques that protected Russian heads. I selected one that was fairly intact. The owner's name, Herbst, was lettered in white inside, and a single bullet-hole over the left ear showed how Herr Herbst had met his end. I have the helmet at home now, in Connecticut.

We went on along the wind-swept road, between bursts of rain and hail, and late in the afternoon we came to Ushakovo, where the great battles of Yelnya had been fought.

There was none of the sylvan character we had seen in our earlier views of the front when we reached the battlefield of Yelnya. Here the Germans had poured across the fields, filling up this area like breath being blown into an expanding balloon. After six weeks of fighting, through August and September, the Russians had managed to snip off the balloon and deal with the captives within the Nazi bulge. And now the place looked like the end of the world.

Here were the ghosts of blasted trees, great trunks split and smashed as though a giant hand had picked them up in bundles and dropped them broken back to earth. As far as the eye could reach was wasteland, pitted with shell holes, channeled with trenches, littered with the remains of war which had swept in concentrated fury back and forth across it during those desperate weeks.

The Russian dead had been buried in a common grave, marked with newly planted firs and surrounded by a fence topped with red-painted tin stars. Field asters still showed touches of lavender and purple where they had been laid on the freshly piled mound of earth. The Germans had been hastily shoveled into their own trenches, unmarked—many thousands had been dug into the ten-mile-square battlefield where they had fallen. Like hundreds of empty turtleshells lay the German helmets, some decorated with little swastikas painted in white, many cracked viciously through the top where the metal had given way during battle.

Erskine called me and pointed to a zigzag trench. The bottom was sprinkled unaccountably with dead mice.

Everywhere was the paraphernalia of life—a torn sleeve, the piece of a boot, a tattered raincoat, fragments of rain-soaked German newspaper. Erskine stooped over and pulled out a handle projecting from the ground. It was an officer's broken sword.

We had to be careful where we walked because the ground was full of unexploded mines and shells. Once I stepped on something soft, and a green cloud rose into my face. It was a heap of moldy bread which still retained the shape of loaves, so recently had men been breathing and eating there. Near by was a chased-silver samovar, pierced with a bullethole, which raised an image of Russians drinking tea in what seemed like a bygone age.

When we reached the town of Yelnya, fighting was still going on near by. The front was only a few kilometers away, and the rattle of machine guns and the deep roar of artillery sounded restlessly to the west. Yelnya had had an estimated population of five thousand, and now it was a ghost town. When we drove into its ruined streets I knew that here at last I had the pictures I wanted, pictures that would look like war. It was almost twilight, but the clouds, as though they had heard my prayers at last, began lifting, and the rays of the setting sun poured down on the skeletons that had once been homes.

I jumped out of the car and hastily set up a camera. I had just begun work when one of the reporters, a member of the home faction, dashed past me, notebook in hand. "Hurry up, Peggy," he called. "We're clearing out of here in five minutes and we'll be halfway back to Moscow tonight."

It was too much—all the hopes and disappointments, all the fighting to salvage something through the mud and rain, all the arrivals at the most interesting places after dark, the tearing away in the mornings before I could complete my job. "I can't work this crazy way," I said aloud to the empty road. And I began to cry.

Crying doesn't do much good, because it interrupts focusing. I knew this, but I only stood there weeping, wasting my time. And then the censor came along and guessed what the trouble was, proving that there is some use for censors after all.

I shall never forget how he gathered a squad of soldiers to help me and instructed the officer in command of the town that I should be given all the help I needed. The plan was to have the correspondents go on to a banquet that was waiting for them sixty miles back on the road toward Moscow. Erskine would stay with me, of course. And the censor put a little pile of chocolates in the back seat of our car, cautioned me not to take too long, because the sound of the guns was rising, and the crowd was off.

Darkness was beginning to fall now, but the soldiers helped me string out my extension cords so we could light up portions of the road with flash bulbs. As it grew darker I brought all three of my flash guns into use, each with extension wires, and the soldiers strung out with them along the road, watching me for signals while I capped and uncapped the lens. It was too late to get instantaneous exposures, but it worked.

I was interested to see that the only building left even

partially intact was the cathedral with its coppery-green dome, now being used as a Red Army barracks. But for the most part the town had been reduced to a collection of skeleton fingers, pointed toward the sky. These were the central chimneys, some of them still smooth with the polished tiles that are characteristic of peasant dwellings. Still, wherever two walls came together, or wherever there was a scrap of roof, people were creeping back to their homes, so resilient is the human race. Sometimes they were welcomed back by their cats, which have a way of lingering around the house even after bombing, although dogs turn wild and run away.

It was getting late now, and the garrison commander thought we should be on our way. Erskine was talking with a group of soldiers by the church, and I took one last walk, down a side street, and watched some people cooking food, which the soldiers had given them, over what remained of their brick and plaster ovens. They were setting up housekeeping in the midst of the ruins, and I noticed that they were using strange cooking utensils. I examined these utensils more closely. They were not mere pots and pans bent out of shape from bombing. They were pieces of wrecked German planes, and portions of metal sheeting from captured enemy tanks. Bent into shallow shapes they serve well enough as baking tins or broiling pans.

The officer and my husband were both calling me now, and their voices were almost drowned out with the rising thunder of guns. The star shells that soared over the front lines to the west were gleaming in a cobalt-blue sky. It was time to go.

But as I walked back to the car I paused to look at a woman borrowing some hot charcoals from the fire of a neighbor. "What is she carrying them in?" I wondered, as I watched her heading homeward. The shape was familiar. She was bringing home hot coals in a Nazi helmet.

CHAPTER 9

White Nights in the Arctic

"WHICH DO you think will be quicker," puzzled Erskine, "to go home by way of Australia, or by way of the Arctic Ocean?" We were back in our Moscow hotel suite, and he was lying on the white bear rug, studying all his available maps. To get world coverage it was necessary to use some maps printed in Russian, some in English, and even the enormous one of Asia and the Pacific, which we had bought in Lanchow. The map of Asia covered the entire floor and was printed in Chinese characters.

It was October, just after our return from the front, and we both had lecture tours starting in less than a month, so we had to get home the fastest way possible. We did not know that Pearl Harbor was less than two months away, but we did want to come home. Even the most stimulating travel in foreign countries, I find, sharpens the desire to return to your native land, where, with an instinct deeper than reason, you feel that you really belong.

The Australia-versus-Arctic question was fantastically difficult to decide. It is impossible to get exact information about travel through warring areas, and even after accommodations have been made there is always the likelihood of being tossed out of your places whenever a couple of generals come along. We had already discarded a possible Africa-to-South America course, with the Cape of Good Hope coming in for serious consideration. The Australia route involved a choice between transit through Iran or Turkey, a flight by British-Oceanic Airways across India to New Zealand, and then return by air across the Pacific. The Arctic trip could only be by ship, and this was the most uncertain of all, for the movements of convoys are protected by the deepest secrecy.

It was Sir Stafford Cripps who finally decided us, by arranging with the British Admiralty for us to travel on the first convoy to leave Archangel Harbor. Furthermore, he obtained permission from the Admiralty for me to take photographs en route, and the handsome credentials that arrived from the embassy, beautifully embossed with the seals of the United Kingdom, were irresistible.

But we found that we could not take the trip without a special dispensation from our own State Department, because of an American law which forbids citizens to travel through belligerent waters on the vessels of a nation at war. An exchange of messages thereupon took place between Moscow and Washington, conducted all "in gray" (in code) so that information about the convoy could not be picked out of the air by the enemy. While these negotiations were being conducted, we thought we had missed our convoy.

However, it happened that some German scouting planes had been seen over the White Sea, and the departure of the convoy was delayed in the hope that it might be possible to shake them; and just as news of this delay came from Archangel, the American Ambassador called us over to Spazzo House to inform us that the State Department had granted us permission to take the convoy trip.

It seemed like extraordinary luck that word had come from Washington just in time. Mr. Steinhardt commented, "There is just one thing you have that I envy you, Margaret."

"What could that be?" I asked.

"That horseshoe that seems to hang always around your neck."

And was there anything else that we needed, he wanted to know.

"Oh, yes," I said, gratefully, "there is one thing I need very much. But you're going to be stuck here without supplies, and you must tell me honestly if you can't spare it."

"And what is it?"

"A new toothbrush."

So the American Embassy in Moscow did its last kind deed for its departing nationals. A splendid new toothbrush was requisitioned from the commissary for me, and another for my husband.

We had been instructed not to inform anyone, either at home or in Moscow, how we were going to travel. We had to get some

word to New York, so we cabled: WE WILL DISAPPEAR FOR ABOUT
THREE WEEKS DON'T WORRY.

While our visas, toothbrushes, and Admiralty decrees were
being obtained, the developing of the films from the front trip
proceeded in such numbers that it took both the day and the
night chauffeurs, working together, to hang them up as fast as I
got them out of the tub. The bathroom overflowed quickly into
the bedroom, and soon the edges of the bedspread and the
borders of the window curtains were pinned with wet negatives.
Then they began filtering into the sitting room; cords were
strung between the legs of the grand piano and back and forth
among the cupid chandeliers; and finally even Napoleon and
Josephine on their revolving pedestal supported their share of
dripping squares of celluloid.

When they were dry and sorted, Tatiana took them to
Glavalit, the same censors who had passed on our radio scripts.
They were all passed—not in a routine way, but in the midst of
many speeches to the deepening of Soviet–American friendship
and understanding—and were finally done up in neat packages
bound in lead seals.

Then there was that job which for a photographer is the
worst one of all: packing the endless paraphernalia so that it
will not jar, vibrate, or crush. Into the spaces in my cases left
vacant by used-up supplies I packed a collection of vividly
painted plaster dolls, brilliant in Russian costumes. They had
been made in peasant villages, and Elisaveta had helped me
shop for them in the Moscow handicraft stores.

Clothes were reduced to a minimum. I kept only the heaviest,
to get me through the Arctic. Tatiana received my raincoat, my
extra blouses, and all but my sturdiest pair of shoes, which I
would need for the homeward trip. My heavy slacks, still
showing trench mud, went with me for the convoy; my linen
pair I gave to Elisaveta, who had decided to try to make Soviet
women slacks conscious. Both girls received nylon stockings.
As silk stockings are rather scarce in Russia, and are not very
good, when word got around among my acquaintances that I
was packing, I had various feminine callers who hoped to make
purchases. The few pairs of stockings I still could spare I sold
for eight rubles each, the equivalent of the $1.60 which they had
cost me in America. (The Soviet department stores sell rather

ill-fitting silk hose for thirty-five rubles, or $7, a pair, and since mine were nylon, unheard of in the Soviet Union, I could easily have charged twice that sum if I had wished to profiteer.) My millinery collection, if my assortment of little bright-colored leather beanies could be called that, was divided equally between the two chauffeurs' wives.

Then there was the last great banquet at VOKS with all our friends invited: Eisenstein, Alexandrov, and Orlova from the movie colony; Eugene Petrov, Elisaveta, and many others from the Union of Soviet Writers; the Mayor of Moscow; the director of the Art Theater; and an assortment of opera singers. Erskine was presented with the most unique gift that it was in their power to give: a collection of captured German insignia which included iron crosses of the first and second class, medals for marksmanship, the insignia of the *Luftwaffe* and Panzer, and the aluminum skull which is the sign of the Death's-Head Division.

Early the next morning most of the party guests appeared on the station platform to wave us off. There were no "soft cars" on the train, so we were to travel "hard class," which means sleeping on a wooden shelf. Our car had these shelves in tiers of three. We had engaged two of the lower ones, and those over our heads were already filling up with soldiers. Our friends shoved great bunches of flowers into my arms, our long troop train moved slowly out of the station, and soon Moscow was left behind.

The woman conductor brought me fruit jars of water, and our bedshelf blazed with gladioli, zinnias, and roses. During the three days which it took us to reach Archangel, the heavy boots of soldiers who occupied the crowded shelves above hung down over my flowers. However, the soldiers seemed to enjoy the flowers as much as I.

We ate sausage, crackers, and salt caviar paste out of our wooden supply box. Once we had hot food, when the train stopped at the large station of Vologda long enough for me to run out and get steaming bowls of *kasha*, a rough cracked-grain cereal which peasants eat. Finally we reached the sprawling town of Archangel—clapboard shacks interspaced with a few modern stucco office buildings, lining a marshy harbor.

Our clothes had never been chosen for an Arctic climate, so

we found a furrier and bought splendid hats of stiff reindeer fur, which came down over the ears and tied under the chin. My flowers were still fresh, and I carried them onto the cutter, which we boarded in the darkness. After bobbing around in the dim, windy spaces of Archangel Harbor for an hour, searching for the convoy, we suddenly found the flagship. It loomed black above us, not a crack of light showing. We climbed a ladder up the side—cameras, flowers, and all—and we were on board. We were handed life belts immediately and told to wear them at all times, even when eating and sleeping.

The next morning our ships began slipping out, one by one, under cover of mist. It was such a good fog that the captain had decided to take advantage of it very early without waiting for the Russian tugs which ordinarily would have maneuvered the boats out to sea. This meant fast out and fast around the bends under our own steam, but we managed to negotiate the tortuous twists of the estuary successfully.

As the shores widened to form a bay, and the ships swung into their prearranged grouping, we found that we were in a convoy of twenty-two vessels: fifteen were British, one was Dutch, and six were Russian. All the ships except three of the Russian freighters were armed. Ours, an eleven-thousand-ton troop ship, which had been used for African cruises and was not insulated against Arctic temperatures, was well armed with machine guns on the upper deck, depth charges strapped to port and starboard sides, and four-inch guns mounted in the stern.

We were escorted by two destroyers, four trawlers, and a cruiser which was startlingly camouflaged with decorative scrolls in smoke and putty shades, interlaced with wavy lines of lime green.

When we reached the White Sea it was evident that those German planes were still on the trail. Most of the time we could not see them, because of the fog, but we could usually hear them. Occasionally we would catch a momentary glimpse of dark specks chasing through the clouds, and then the fog closed them away again. Sometimes they dropped things—we could not tell whether it was bombs or mines. Then we would shoot back at them. But the fog pressed so densely around us that they could not quite find us and we could not quite find them.

For two days this game of hide-and-seek went on. During that time I lived on the top deck, my helmet buckled on in case of shrapnel, and my camera ready, although I knew very well that if events took place which deserved photographic record-ing, the fog was so thick I wouldn't be able to get good pictures. The Commodore, however, was mightily pleased about the way the fog held, and by the beginning of the third day we had left the Germans behind.

"The Hun doesn't like to attack convoys," the Commodore remarked. "He thinks twice about it." Commodore Dowding, a compact, barrel-shaped Scotsman, was in a position to know a good deal about the habits of the Hun. He had been torpedoed in the Mediterranean in the last war, his destroyer sunk beneath him, and during the present war he had made it twice across the Channel at Dunkirk. "Once those Nazis do decide to attack," he went on, "they've got odd ideas. They shoot you in the water. Even in our most savage moments the British don't get to that. He's an odd chap, the Hun."

I discovered that even Commodore Dowding did not know where we were going. The movements of convoys are directed daily straight from the Admiralty in London, by wireless code. The codes are frequently changed to make translation by the enemy more difficult. The flagship receives the messages, but never replies. She travels "silent," for if she transmitted mes-sages her sending apparatus would act as a direction finder, and she uses it only if she must send "distresses."

So cautious is the Admiralty about the movements of its convoys that before the Commodore left England for Archangel he and the officers and crews of all the ships were told to bring light clothing for tropical weather. Just before setting sail they were informed that warm clothes would be needed, but it was only after they had been at sea for three days that they knew they were being sent to Russia.

A convoy traveling over open sea forms an active little community. There is always a picturesquely conducted con-versation going on between ships. They fairly chattered among themselves by means of flags and blinking searchlight signals, the lights for daytime use only. To make sure that the Russian skippers understood the signals, one of the destroyers cruised in broad circles, weaving its way through the convoy, while its junior officer shouted out the directions through a megaphone. Every so often the cruiser's plane was catapulted off the deck to scour the seascape, trying to spot submarines.

On the fifth day, to the astonishment of everyone, even the Commodore, our handsome cruiser ran up signal flags which said: "Good-by, have a good trip," and she was off, no one knew where. We felt rather lonely without her; but exactly one hour later, another cruiser had taken her place. Our new escort was less decorative, for instead of the whorls and curlicues of camouflage she was painted a uniform battleship gray; but she was bristling with fully as many guns.

We were in the Barents Sea by now, and still heading north. In order to skirt around areas which might be infested with submarines, we went so far north that we crossed the Arctic Circle and at one time were within less than nine degrees of the North Pole.

Here, again, we had the unearthly white nights. Through the long hours of darkness an uneasy splendor hung over the sea. Before turning in, Erskine and I would tie on our reindeer bonnets, wrap blankets around our shoulders, and walk around the deck. Between the translucent sky and icy water floated the barely distinguishable shapes of our fellow ships, not a glimmer of light showing as they traveled at their uniform speed of eight knots an hour.

Sometimes we would pass the Commodore, looking like a little rabbit in his cashmere cloak and hood. "It's strange, way up here," he would say. "It must be the reflection from the ice. But even in the dead of winter it never gets properly dark." And then he would continue on his rounds, straining his eyes through the ghost light, trying to assure himself that all his flock were still there.

Once, half an hour before midnight, we had unexpected visitors. An oil tanker, with a small convoy, appeared out of nowhere, refueled the destroyers, and disappeared into nothingness.

Early each morning my husband and I would hurry around the deck and count, to make sure that all our twenty-two ships were still there. One of the Russian freighters, a slow one, was slipping a little behind.

Then, as we worked back to lower latitudes, near Iceland,

there was an afternoon when from the point on the top deck where I was posted with a camera I could hear tense voices from the bridge, "Have they made contact? They're making contact!" Searchlight signals blinked rapidly, and the ships wheeled out into a scattered formation, leaving wide spaces of water in between. The whole sea seemed to shudder under us as the destroyers, several miles away from us now, dropped depth charges. Four hours later the Commodore passed me and stopped to tell me that they thought they had detected a submarine and hoped they had been able to shake it. The ships were being signaled back into their regular formation now, and by twilight all twenty-two were plowing through the water in their customary pattern.

The next morning, however, when Erskine and I made our count, there were only twenty-one of us. The slow Russian freighter was missing. We never knew what became of it. Possibly the Admiralty knows, but we were never told.

The following day we were passing through the Norwegian Sea, and the water was alive with an enormous school of porpoises. Countless thousands of glistening jet bodies cut through the water and skipped briefly through the air. They were racing the ships. For hours the sea was ink black, and boiling with leaping shapes as streamlined as shell casings.

One day more and we were in the North Sea, and again the water was filled with strange objects. This time it was floating mines. Fortunately, we reached their neighborhood by daylight, so that we could steer around them. Like great basketballs, with prongs like porcupines, they bobbed along within a stone's throw of the ships.

After fifteen days we had traveled through literally seven seas: the White Sea, Barents Sea, the Arctic Ocean, the Norwegian and North Seas, across a strip of the Atlantic, then through the Irish Sea; and finally we reached Scotland. Above Scapa Flow the sky was like a dotted-swiss textile, with cumulus cloud puffs and white barrage balloons. The ruins of Scottish castles on the cliffs were as gray as the shapes of battleships which lay everywhere about us. Like chains of beads, submarine traps were strung through the water.

At Scapa Flow an excessively courteous Admiralty official came on board to take up the films I had exposed on the sea voyage, for Admiralty censorship. Only half of them came back, but it was to be expected that many naval subjects would be censored out, and permission to take photographs had been given with that understanding.

One day more on through the Clyde, and we disembarked in Glasgow. Erskine had always wanted a glimpse of Scotland because his people came from there, and I had always desired a Scottish kilt. We went into a Glasgow tartan shop and inquired whether there was a Caldwell plaid.

"No," said the clerk, "Caldwell is a fine old Scottish name, but the clan has never had a tartan."

"Is there an Erskine tartan?" I asked.

"Why, certainly," she replied, "there is indeed an Erskine tartan. As a matter of fact, there are *two* Erskine tartans."

So I had a chance to choose between the black and white plaid, and the red and green. I selected the red and green and was measured for the voluminously pleated kilt, which was to be made, complete with huge safety pin, as the Highlanders wear it. We asked the cost.

"Eight pounds and eighteen coupons."

"What are coupons?" we demanded.

"How is it possible," exclaimed the clerk, "that you don't know what coupons are?"

"Well, we've just arrived. How should we know!"

"How can you eat? How do you exist, if you don't have coupons?"

We were to learn soon enough that on the British Isles everything is apportioned by means of coupons. The clothing ration was sixty-six coupons a year. So we regretfully relinquished the idea of the Erskine kilt.

A week later in London we were dining with an official from the Ministry of Information, and I happened to mention the Glasgow episode. "We have been asked for a lot of peculiar things," he said, "but no one ever before asked the Ministry of Information for a kilt."

The next day a deck of complimentary coupons were sent to our hotel, and we were able to order a kilt of the clan of Erskine.

England was restless. Groups of soldiers were being moved from one end of the islands to the other, and they were uneasy with their forced inactivity. Everyone was clamoring for firsthand news about Russia. They had just been promised, in a speech by Churchill, a more comfortable Christmas in 1941 than the last had been. The British people did not want more comforts. If their Russian allies were denying themselves in their efforts to annihilate the Germans, they wanted to help.

The unaccustomed luxury of the Savoy, of the Ritz Bar, seemed strange to us. Going to the movies was an unbelievably vivid pleasure. We walked over the acres of rubble around St. Paul's. British Broadcasting asked us to take part in a program to occupied Europe, so as to try to let the enslaved nations know what was going on in Russia. In the next booth, in the subcellar which B.B.C. is using since its building has been bombed, was General de Gaulle, also talking to occupied Europe.

We visited Lord Beaverbrook at Cherkley, his country home in Leatherhead, and ate apples with him which he had just brought back from Moscow. We found out that the handsomely camouflaged cruiser which had left us on our fifth day out had returned to Archangel for the express purpose of picking up his Lordship and Mr. W. Averell Harriman, who were returning from the Economic Conference. We also learned from the "Beaver" that he had quizzed "Brother Joe" on how he had liked being photographed by an American girl. Lord Beaverbrook had been in the Kremlin with the Economic Mission, shortly after I had made my portrait of Stalin.

Then to Bristol, a scarred patch of desolation, more completely wrecked, block for block, than London. As we entered the devastated town, air-raid sirens began wailing. Bristol, which had been quiet for months, was bombed as soon as we reached the city.

The next morning we took off for Portugal in a sealed plane, the windows blacked out to prevent passengers from watching possible naval operations underneath. On the way I read the last of my stock of detective stories, an Ellery Queen which had traveled with me on the whole trip. (All my heavy baggage, except one small suitcase, was being shipped to New York by Atlantic convoy.)

In Lisbon we stayed in a penthouse hotel suite where Magda Lupescu had stopped during her flight through Portugal. Its enormous violet bathroom, with a purple bathtub set at the top of a flight of gold mosaic stairs, and over it a mirrored ceiling, seemed more suited to the glamorous refugee than it did to a couple of reporters. A screened-in porch, high above the city, was bright with bougainvillaea vines during the day and commanded a brilliant spread of city lights at night. The effect of lights was startling, as it is to all travelers who return from the blacked-out areas of war.

It was in Lisbon that a new word entered my vocabulary. I had heard it before, but had never used it myself—until I came back to America, where I found everybody using it. That word was priorities.

After listening to alarming accounts of travelers through Lisbon, waiting sometimes for weeks to get Clipper accommodations, it was with some trepidation that we entered the office of Pan American Airways. My husband walked up to the counter and inquired about the reservations being held for Mr. and Mrs. Erskine Caldwell. The clerk looked us over indifferently and went back to his filing cabinet, where he shuffled through a bundle of cards. Finally he returned and, looking at me in a condescending way, said, "There is only one reservation being held. And I think, Mrs. Caldwell, that your husband has the priority."

We both had to get home. I had a lecture tour on the East Coast and Erskine had one in the West. If I hadn't been so conscious of that football physique of my husband, who is twice my size, I think there would have been a free-for-all in the Caldwell family right there, and I am not at all sure that the Atlantic seaboard would have won. But I begged the clerk, "Please look once more. There must be a reservation. Please do something to fix it up!"

He went back and looked through his cards once more, and when he returned he was shaking his head. "No," he said, eying me coldly, "there's only one more place being saved. And that's being held for a lady from Russia."

I thought, "Heavens, who's scooping me?" and I asked, "What's her name?"

He said, "Her name is Margaret Bourke-White," and so I was able to come home, too.

Erskine cabled our secretary from Lisbon, ARRANGE SUNDAY DINNER WITH BOTH STEAK AND FRIED CHICKEN ALSO ALL KNOWN FRUITS AND VEGETABLES BOTH IN AND OUT OF SEASON, and we flew to the Azores, on to Bermuda, on across the Atlantic, and arrived home in time for Sunday dinner. We had completed our trip around the world.

Within less than twenty-four hours I was facing my first lecture audience. As I began to speak about the things I had seen, it came to me in a rush what an eventful trip this had been. I had seen history in the making, had had my cameras in focus when nations were on the march. I had made new friends among a brave people and had watched them defending their country, courageously, with that fervor and self-forgetfulness which people show only when they believe in what they are working and fighting for. But I was happy to be home again, talking to Americans. These were my people, these listeners in the straight rows of seats in front of me. They were the kind of men and women with whom I had grown up, with whom I felt at home.

It was not till two days later, however, that something made me realize I was indeed in my own country again. I was at the University of Tennessee. The students had gathered for chapel, and just before I spoke they rose to sing.

I had heard the music many times before. I must have listened to the words, and sung them, hundreds of times; but this time they sank into my mind. "Long may our land be bright, With freedom's holy light." It seemed to me that never before had I actually heard the words of *America*, and suddenly I found I was standing on the platform before all those university students—crying.

PURPLE HEART
VALLEY

CHAPTER 1

Over the Lines

"THIS STRIP is really a nerve jerker," Lieutenant Mike Strok called to me over his shoulder.

We were circling above the tiniest airfield I had ever seen. The landing strip was so pocked with shell craters that I did not see how my Grasshopper pilot was going to slip in among them. It was nothing more than the beaten edge of a plowed field, but for the Air OP's, the "Eyes of the Artillery" as they are called in heavy-gun circles, this strip was their most forward operating base.

Lieutenant Strok had to divide his attention between the shell pits below and the sky above. This was because we were landing in the region airmen called Messerschmitt Alley. If an unarmed, unarmored observation plane such as our Cub is attacked, the pilot's means of escape is to outmaneuver the enemy.

"Good idea to make sure there's no Jerry fighter hanging about," said Lieutenant Strok. "If you can see him first, then he doesn't get the chance to blast the daylights out of you."

A final inspection confirmed that the sky was clear, and he brought our tiny Cub to a standstill on a piece of earth as big as a back yard in Brooklyn.

The commanding officer of the field and his ground crew of one ran up to greet us.

The ground crew spoke first. "If that ain't an American girl, then I'm seeing things!" he exclaimed.

The young officer laughed. "Sorry we're out of red carpet," he said. "We live like gypsies up here."

The CO of the Grasshoppers was twenty-six-year-old Captain Jack Marinelli of Ottumwa, Iowa. He was chief pilot and supervisor for a group of artillery liaison pilots who hedgehopped along the front lines in their Cubs, acting as flying observation posts to spot enemy targets and adjust fire for Fifth Army artillery. I had seldom seen a flier who bore less resemblance to Hollywood's idea of a pilot than Captain Marinelli. He looked more like the tractor and hay-machine demonstrator which I learned he had been back in Iowa before the war. He was plump, pleasant, and easygoing. This last characteristic, I was to find, faded as soon as the enemy was in sight. He had the reputation of being the coolest and most resourceful artillery pilot on the Fifth Army front.

Mike Strok explained that I wanted to take airplane pictures of the front, and Captain Marinelli said, "Well, I've just had a call to go out on a mission. There's a *Neberwerfer* holding up an infantry division and they asked me to go out and try to spot it. She can come along if she wants to."

"Jees, you don't want to take a girl on a mission," said the ground crew of one.

"She'll go if you'll take her," stated Lieutenant Strok.

"What's a *Nebelwerfer*?" I inquired.

"You've heard of a screaming meemie, haven't you? Wicked weapon! It's a multiple mortar: eight-barreled rocket gun."

By the time the screaming meemie was explained to me, I had been strapped into the observer's seat, and the ground crew was adjusting a parachute to my back and shoulders.

Knowing that one of the functions of observer is to watch all quadrants of the sky for enemy planes, I said to the Captain, "I'm not going to make a very good observer for you. Most of the time I'll have my face buried in my camera, and even when I haven't, I'm not sure I'll know the difference between an enemy fighter and one of ours."

"Don't worry about that," Captain Marinelli said. "If you see anything that looks like an airplane, you tell me and I'll decide whether it's a bandit or an angel."

I placed my airplane camera on my knees and arranged additional equipment and a couple of spare cameras, telephoto lenses, and some aerial filters on the low shelf behind my shoulders. The space was so cramped, and any extra movement so pinched, with the parachute crowded on my back, that I wanted to be sure I had everything near at hand where I could reach it in a hurry. There was no room in the Cub to wear helmets, as our heads touched the roof. Someone had lent me

one of the fur caps used by our Alaska troops, and I tucked my
hair back under it and tied it firmly around my chin. When you
lean out into the slipstream with an airplane camera, any
escaping strand of hair will lash into your eyes and sometimes
blind you during just that vital second when you are trying to
catch a picture. The Captain lowered the whole right side of the
airplane, folding it completely out of the way so I would have an
unobstructed area in which to lean out and work. Then he
spoke into his microphone. "Mike-Uncle-Charlie! This is
Mike-Uncle-Charlie five-zero. I'm taking off on a mission.
Stand by!"

"Who is Mike-Uncle-Charlie?" I asked.

"That's our brigade HQ's code word for today," replied the
Captain. "Just our phonetic alphabet for MUC—today's call
letters. When I find something that radio guy will be sitting up
there with his ear phones on, listening."

The ground crew spun the props. "We'll be back in time for
lunch," shouted Captain Marinelli to Lieutenant Strok as we
started to taxi between the shell craters. I glanced at my watch,
which registered quarter after eleven, and couldn't help
wondering if we really would be back for lunch. I was trying
hard not to wonder whether we would be back at all.

As we headed toward the front I was impressed with how
regular the pattern of war, seemingly so chaotic from the
ground, appears from the air. The tracks of pattern bombing on
an airfield were as regular as though drawn with ruler and
compass. In some olive groves the traffic patterns made by
trucks and jeeps which had parked there looked as if a school
child had drawn circles in a penmanship exercise, his pen filled
not with ink but with a silvery mud-and-water mixture which
held the light of the sun. Each bridge had been demolished with
a Teutonic precision. The delicate arches of the small bridges
were broken through the crest; larger bridges were buckled like
giant accordions. Paralleling these were bypasses and emergency bridges which our engineers had thrown up. Most regular of
all was German railroad demolition. Between the rails an
endless succession of V's marched into the distance, an effect
produced by the giant plow which the retreating Germans had
dragged from their last railroad train, cracking each tie in two
so neatly that it seemed as if someone had unrolled a narrow

length of English tweed, flinging this herringbone strip over the hills and valleys of Italy.

The irregularities were furnished by the smashed towns, so wrecked that seldom did two walls stand together, and never was a roof intact. Flying low, sometimes we could see Italian civilians picking through the sickening rubble that once had been their homes.

As we flew over the ghastly wreckage of Mignano and headed toward the still more thoroughly wrecked town of San Pietro, suddenly our plane was jarred so violently that it bounced over on its side, and we heard what sounded like a thunderclap just below.

"That's a shell leaving one of our big hows," Marinelli said as he righted the plane.

"Sounded close," I said.

"I'd hate to tell you how close," Captain Marinelli replied.

"How are you going to know when you get to the front?" I asked.

"Oh, that's easy," he explained. "When you stop seeing stars on things you know you've left your own side behind."

I looked down and saw our jeeps, trucks, and half-tracks crawling along Highway Six below us, each plainly marked with its white star.

"But the best way to tell is by the bridges," he continued. "As long as you see trestle bridges below you know we're over friendly territory, because those are bridges our engineers have built. When you begin spotting blown-out bridges you know we're approaching no man's land. The last thing the Germans do when they pull out is to blow up their bridges, and if they haven't been repaired it's because it's been too hot for our men to get in and mend them.

"When you see a stretch of road with no traffic at all, that's no man's land. And when you see the first bridge intact on the other side, you know you're crossing into Jerry territory."

We were flying over the crest of hills which surrounded Cassino valley like the rim of a cup. Highway Six wound between bald, rocky mountains here, and we almost scraped their razorback edges as we flew over. I could look down and see entrenchments and gun emplacements set in layers of rock.

Then the land dropped away sharply, and all at once we were high over Cassino corridor.

As I looked down, the earth seemed to be covered with glistening polka dots—almost as though someone had taken a bolt of gray coin-spotted satin and unrolled it over the landscape. I knew these were shell holes, thousands of them, and made by the guns of both sides, first when we shelled the Germans here, and now by their guns shelling us. As we rose higher I could look down and see hundreds of thousands of these holes filled with rain and glistening in the sun.

"It's been so rough down there," said Captain Marinelli, "that the boys are calling it Purple Heart Valley."

I could hardly believe that so many shells could have fallen in a single valley. It was cruelly contradictory that with all this evidence of bloodshed and destruction, the valley seemed to clothe itself in a sequin-dotted gown.

As we flew on, we glanced back toward our own territory and could see the muzzle flashes from our guns winking on and off as though people were lighting matches over the hillsides. Each gun flash left a smoke trail until our Allied-held hills appeared to be covered with the smoke of countless campfires.

"The worst of that smoke is from our howitzers," Marinelli said.

And then he added, "Usually we don't fly across the lines unless the mission absolutely requires it. But it looks to me as though we're going to have to today, to find that *Nebelwerfer*. O.K. with you?"

"I'm right with you, Captain."

We circled lower over a loop of Highway Six where wrecked tanks were tumbled around the curve of road. "First day they've brought tanks out into the open," said Marinelli. "I want to radio back a report." The tanks seemed to have been picked off one by one as they tried to round the bend, but I could see one tank charging bravely ahead. Then as we bobbed over it, I could see a giant retriever coming in with a derrick to evacuate one of the blasted tanks.

Just beyond we began seeing demolished bridges, and we circled above these also, because the Captain's secondary mission was to report on any bridges that had been blown up. He was just phoning back his observations, and I was taking pictures, when suddenly our plane was rocked sharply back and forth and we heard a sound like freight trains rumbling under us.

"Jerry shells," said Marinelli. "High explosives! You know, they've been missing that road junction by a hundred yards every day this week."

We were tossing around violently now, and dark whorls and spirals of greasy smoke were blanketing the ground beneath.

"We've got infantry troops down there," the Captain said. The realization was almost more than I could bear—that our own boys were trying to slog through that fatal square of earth being chewed up by high-explosive shells.

An instant later we were flying over a desolate stretch of road with no traffic at all. This, then, was no man's land. At the farther end we saw a beautifully arched ancient bridge, its masonry quite intact.

"Jerry territory," said the Captain, and took the plane sharply upward.

Over our own side the Cubs make a practice of flying low, because this makes an attack by enemy fighters more difficult, as they cannot come in under; but when the observation planes cross the lines, they must increase altitude, for without armor they are very vulnerable to small-arms fire.

In search of the German rocket gun, we flew four miles over enemy territory and Captain Marinelli began hunting for the *Nebelwerfer* in the region of San Angelo.

"That's the 'Gargling River,'" he pointed out. "GI for Garigliano. And there's the Rapido." The road to Rome stretched forward into the distance, with a railroad running parallel some distance to the left. A hairpin turn branched upward toward the Benedictine monastery, at that time still intact. The ruins of Cassino lay in white smudges at the foot of snowcapped Mt. Cairo.

Cassino corridor presented an extraordinary appearance, with white plumes rising up at intervals from the valley floor. These were phosphorus shells from our own Long Toms, falling on the enemy. Whenever one landed close below us we could see it opening out into a pointed splash of fire, which quickly became transformed into a rising chunk of smoke.

Suddenly I spotted a tiny silhouette in the sky, behind us. "There's a plane," I yelled.

"Just another Cub out on a mission," said Marinelli. "But you did the right thing. Tell me anything you see."

Just then he picked up the flash of the German *Nebelwerfer* —too quick for my untrained eye—and caught sight of the shrubbery blowing back on the ground from the gun blast.

"Mike-Uncle-Charlie," he spoke into his microphone. "This is Mike-Uncle-Charlie five-zero. Enemy gun battery located at co-ordinate 86-16-2. I can observe. Over."

Then to me, over his shoulder, "It's going to take them a little time now, because they've got to compute their data and consult their fire-direction chart to see which guns can reach the target. They'll let me know when they've assigned a battery. We'll be hanging right around here, so speak up if you want to be put into position for anything special."

There were many things that I wanted to be put into position for. Below us it looked as though someone were shaking an enormous popcorn shaker with white grains of popcorn bursting all over the valley floor. These were thickest in front of Cassino. The Captain maneuvered the plane so that I was practically lying on my side over the valley, and—strapped in safely—I could get an unobstructed view of the battleground below.

In a few minutes a message came through that Xray-King-Item would fire. While I took pictures of the popcorn-sprinkled valley, Marinelli carried on his radio conversation with Xray-King-Item, the battery assigned to knock out the *Nebelwerfer*.

I was overwhelmed to learn that it would be my pilot, up in our little Cub, who would actually give the command to fire. The next message he received was, "Mike-Uncle-Charlie five-zero, this is Xray-King-Item. Will fire on your command. Over."

"Fire," said Marinelli, and the reply came back, "Seventy-two seconds. On the way."

It seemed amazing that the shell travelling from the Long Tom battery several miles back of us would take almost a minute and a quarter to reach the enemy gun target below. The Captain was checking with his watch. "Don't want to sense the wrong round," he explained.

He had to make this precise time check because with other guns peppering the valley it was easy to make an error, and it would have caused great confusion had he started correcting the aim of some other gun.

On the seventy-second second, a white geyser began rising toward us from below, and we knew that this was Xray-King-Item's smoke shell. Marinelli spoke into his microphone: "Xray-King-Item; this is Mike-Uncle-Charlie five-zero; five hundred yards right, one hundred yards short. Over."

Then he explained, "We've got to give them a little time again to make their correction. They're laying number-one gun on it now. When they get it adjusted they'll tie in the whole battery."

Soon another message came from Xray-King-Item: seventy-two seconds on the way. Again at the end of seventy-two seconds a feather of smoke rose from below. The aim was closer now: "Five-zero right; seven-zero short," Captain Marinelli radioed.

I realized that the Captain was handling a great many tasks at once. Not only was he checking his watch during each seventy-two-second interval, radioing his sensings in terms of deflection and elevation data, but he was keeping an eye on the sky for enemy planes. And taking care of me, too! Every time I saw a fresh shell burst I would yell to be put in position, and he would maneuver the Cub so that I could photograph while he observed.

Suddenly he exclaimed, "We're being shot at." We could hear faint sounds as though twigs were snapping against the plane—a little like hot grease spitting in a frying pan just beyond us. "It's a Spandau," said Marinelli, and he knew exactly what to do. Since the Spandau, a German machine gun, has an effective range up to 2400 feet, he simply circled up to 3200 feet, where he went on making his observations and I went on taking photographs.

"Hands cold?" he called.

They were almost numb. At our higher altitude the air was colder and I had been leaning out into the windstream with the camera. The Captain, more protected by the nose of the Cub, stripped off his gloves and gave them to me.

The whole process of adjusting fire had gone on for about

fourteen minutes when Captain Marinelli finally radioed, "Deflection correct, range correct. Fire for effect."

"They're bringing in several batteries this time," said the Captain. "And this time it will be HE shells."

At the end of seventy-two seconds we could see that whole area being blanketed, not with white smoke bursts as before, but with the deadlier high-explosive shells. Curls and twists of black smoke spurted over the ground and billowed upward, and we knew that the *Nebelwerfer* was being chewed to bits.

"This is Mike-Uncle-Charlie five-zero," called Captain Marinelli. "Target area completely covered. Fire effective. Enemy battery neutralized."

Less than a minute later he exclaimed, "I see a fighter." Then, "I see two fighters."

Coming around Mt. Cevaro I could see them too: a black speck growing larger and behind it another smaller speck. In less time than it takes to tell, they had taken on the size and shape of airplanes.

We were in such a steep dive by that time that I was practically standing on my head, when I heard Marinelli say, "I see four fighters."

Sure enough, there were four shapes coming toward us, looking unmistakably like Focke-Wulf 190's.

This was the steepest dive I had ever been in in my life. I tried to take a picture, a plan I very quickly had to abandon because, with the whole side of the plane completely open, and the shelf behind me full of cameras and lenses, it was all I could do to hold back my equipment with my elbow and shoulders, to keep it from sailing into space.

I was bracing myself with the back of my neck when Captain Marinelli exclaimed, "I've lost my mike. Can you find my mike for me?" I knew he needed his microphone so he could report the fighters as a warning to all the other Cubs in the air. Groping with my left hand, and holding back my cameras with my right elbow, I retrieved his mike and handed it to him. We were still gliding down at a terrific angle when he reported, "Four enemy fighters sighted."

We were within fifteen feet of the ground when he pulled out of that dive. I have never seen such flying. He ducked into a gully and began snaking along a stream bed. Soon we were behind a small hill and over our own territory, where the fighters could not follow us in so low. In another instant we were behind a mountain and blocked from sight of the enemy planes.

We flew back to our field in time for mess, and when we rolled into the tiny landing strip, the ground crew came running up, bursting with news. To Captain Marinelli this news was much more exciting than being chased by four Focke-Wulfs: there was steak for lunch.

CHAPTER 2

Number-Three Priority

I HAD come to Italy by air, flying by Clipper to ETOUSA and by troop transport plane to NATOUSA. ("They sound like aunts of Hiawatha," one of my friends wrote.) In the abbreviated vocabulary used by the Army, these stand respectively for European and North African Theaters of Operations, United States Army. After completing my work in NATOUSA, I was sent from MBS to PBS: from the Mediterranean Base Section to the Peninsular Base Section.

As war correspondents, we go through the same formalities as Army personnel on transfers; although we may choose our spots, subject to Army approval, we obtain orders from the office of the commanding general. Our passage is free, but it must be authorized by the military authorities to whom we are responsible.

My travel orders—number-three priority—were headed cryptically in big red letters: U.S. CONFIDENTIAL EQUALS BRITISH SECRET. This sounded very hush-hush indeed. But it was less so than if they had been marked: U.S. SECRET EQUALS BRITISH MOST SECRET. Army legend has it that the ultimate in secret documents are classified: DESTROY WITHOUT READING.

My papers may not have been MOST SECRET, but they certainly were most impressive. They were supplied to me with six carbons, and they read:

SUBJECT: Travel orders
To: All concerned
1. Following will proceed by first available transportation from North Africa to Italy, to such places within the Theater as may be necessary for the accomplishment of her mission.
2. Travel by military aircraft is authorized. Rations in kind will be provided.
Margaret Bourke-White, Photographer
                    By command of General EISENHOWER.

Even traveling with all this CONFIDENTIAL EQUALS SECRET stuff, I still found myself resorting to what we correspondents call hitchhiking. You hang around an airport until something is going your way and there is room for you on it. In my case, in addition to finding space for myself, I had to find room for one Speed Graphic, two Rolleiflexes, three Linhofs, a Graflex fitted for telephoto, a battery of interchangeable lenses, various filters, film packs, flash guns, flash bulbs, a bedroll, and a typewriter.

Several months before, when a torpedoing during the North African invasion had made almost a clean sweep of my photographic equipment except for a few small odds and ends I had managed to take with me in the lifeboat, I had resolved, while still bobbing around on the high seas, that if I ever reached shore I would replace my cameras with smaller sizes. It took a torpedoing to make me really appreciate a Rolleiflex, that admirable, compact, featherweight camera. I had to comb the entire United States to replace the rest of the equipment, but I did it uniformly in $2\frac{1}{4} \times 3\frac{1}{4}$ size. I am a fanatic about interchangeability of parts. Especially in a war zone, where it is so easy to break things and so impossible to replace them, I carry duplicate cameras so I can pull out a new one when the one I am using gets out of order, and I have all my accessories and lens mounts machined so that any item will fit into any camera. Each of the three Linhofs was fitted with a range finder and infinity stops, so it could be used either on a tripod or hand-held like a Speed Graphic. All lenses, including those on the Rolleiflexes, were fitted with synchronizers for flash-bulb equipment. This arrangement proved invaluable in Italy, for it rained so much that I would have lost many daylight pictures had it not been for synchronized flashes.

The paring of my film size from the $3\frac{1}{4} \times 4\frac{1}{4}$ I had used on previous voyages to the $2\frac{1}{4} \times 3\frac{1}{4}$ size used on this trip shaved two hundred pounds off the weight of my raw film stock and supplies. All told, my seven cameras with their thirty-odd lenses, their infinite repair parts and accessories, along with sufficient quantity of film and peanut flash bulbs to last half a year, weighed 250 pounds. This was an improvement over the 450 pounds I had carried to the wars the year before, and a great reduction from the 800 pounds with which I had flown across China into Russia at the outbreak of the war with Germany. To compress my equipment and supplies into 250 pounds I had figured down to the last ounce.

My clothes fitted into the fifty-five pounds allotted airplane travelers in war zones. This poundage was not easy to achieve either, as it had to include both summer and winter uniforms, skirts for those occasions when even a war photographer has to wear a skirt, trousers to work in, heavy field clothes, boots, and woolen underwear.

What a war correspondent wears has been carefully laid down in the rule books by the War Department in Washington. A war correspondent wears officer's uniform but without officer's insignia. We have an insignia of our own which has made striking progress since the beginning of the war. First, it was a green armband (green signifies noncombatant) bearing the unfortunate letters WC. Many war correspondents were made happier when this was reduced simply to C for the reporters and P for the photographers. (Photographers in battle areas are classified as war correspondents.) Now we have replaced the wide green armbands, which were always clumsy and slipping out of place, with a neatly designed patch reading U.S. War Correspondent. In place of the usual shoulder bars worn by officers, we wear metal cutout insignia bearing the words War Correspondent, and on our caps and lapels we wear the army US. The purpose of our uniforms is not only to take on protective coloration among soldiers, but to save us from being shot as spies if we are captured. If we are taken prisoner we have another privilege in addition to staying alive. We receive pay, just as Army officers and soldiers do, under international law. Since we have no actual rank, we were given an arbitrary rank which at the beginning of the war was second lieutenant. Imagine my delight on my return to the battle zone last fall to find that we had been promoted. We are now theoretical captains. But we have to be captured before we start collecting that captain's pay, and we are always subject to certain Army regulations, and may be court-martialed.

Becoming a war correspondent is a matter of the most thorough investigation on the part of the War Department, as to background, patriotism, and reliability. By the time you are accredited you have no secrets from the War Department and neither do your ancestors; but it is right that this should be so because as a war correspondent you have access to many sources of vital military information. You are in a position of great trust.

I was a very proud girl indeed when I first received the Army credentials for which I had applied, as *Life* photographer, shortly after our country went into the war. The War Department had a new problem with me since I was a woman photographer. They had shown no discrimination, I am happy to say, because of my sex; the difficulty was in deciding what I should wear. They knew what the men should wear, because that had been laid down in the Army handbooks, but no one had ever had to dress a woman war correspondent accredited in America. I spent five days in Washington going over materials and details with the Army War College, and finally it was decided that I should wear just what the men war correspondents wear: the same type of blouse, coat, field cap, etc., as an officer wears, but with a skirt for "dress."

I had my uniform tailored to fit me, and I loved it. Then, during the torpedoing I have mentioned, all but the clothes on my back were sunk. The losses included some prized items: a fine pair of jodhpur boots which had been made for me in London, as only Bond Street can make them, and a neat little "battle jacket" such as pilots wear. These Air Force togs had been designed by General Eaker, and he had given the original jacket model to General Spaatz, who still wears it. Mine was made by London military tailors, during the time I was accredited to the Eighth Air Force, and it was the first that had ever been made for a woman.

I was almost as distressed by having these clothes sunk as by losing my cameras. When I finally arrived like a drowned rat in Algiers, I was taken for a drying out by my Air Force pals to the gingerbread villa then occupied by General Spaatz. Inside the door the first person I ran into was General Eaker, who had flown down for a conference with "Tooey" Spaatz.

"I lost that wonderful jacket you designed," I blurted out, "and my beautiful jodhpurs."

So General Eaker, on his return to London, called up the shops, found they had my measurements on file, and a new pair of jodhpurs and a new battle jacket arrived in time for the Italian campaign.

After a torpedoing everybody helps you. General Doolittle had greeted me with the words, "Margaret, what do you need most?"

"I'd love to have another shirt to change into," I said. And then I hesitated.

"What else?" he asked.

"Well, of course I lost all my pajamas."

"Now I know why I've been carrying my sister-in-law's pajamas all these years," said kind General Jimmy. "She gave me green silk ones. I've never used them because I always sleep raw, but if you want them, they're yours."

The pajamas were wonderful, and the shirt with which he presented me had a history. After the bombing of Tokyo, when Jimmy Doolittle landed by parachute with his men in China, and finally made his way to the outside world, he arrived in Cairo with as meager a wardrobe as the one in which I had survived the torpedoing. Since he was going to be given an official banquet that night, something had to be done. He found an Egyptian tailor who promised to make a uniform in a single day. By six in the evening a uniform of sorts was completed, but the blouse was so short, reported General Jimmy, that it reached up to his chest, and the shirt was so wide that it needed tucks. It was this shirt that he gave me, and I took it to an Arab tailor on the edge of the Sahara. The Arab spoke French, so to him the shirt was *la chemise du Général*. Cut down to fit me, the Doolittle shirt did splendid service, although to the pilots with whom I worked it was always known as the General's chemise.

So in the fall of 1943, when I packed for North Africa and Italy, into my fifty-five pounds went the Doolittle shirt, my new jodhpur boots, and the new battle jacket designed by General Eaker. And at the bottom of my flight bag went one unwarlike item—an evening dress designed for me by Adrian in Hollywood. "I want something to dance in with soldiers," I had told him; adding, "if I get the chance. And it must pack up so small that it would fit in the palm of your hand."

Adrian had created just the right dress. It had a transparent white shirtwaist top and a cleverly draped black filmy skirt. Off, it was one of those little numbers that look prim on the hanger; on, there was nothing schoolteacherish about it.

As on all trips, I carried cosmetics in a little pigskin-fitted case. I think I would have gone to the battlefield without rations before I would go without face cream. I remember once when this so fascinated a certain infantry major with whom I shared a dugout during a night at the front that he nicknamed me Crisco-puss. I also carried vitamins, but I might have spared those ounces of weight, for Army food is so well planned and substantial that never once did I feel the impulse to reach for a vitamin.

Each year, when I prepare for my trip to the war fronts, the selection of which spot I am to cover is the subject of much attempted crystal-gazing among the editors of *Life* and myself. We get together and discuss how we think the news may develop and what places I am most interested in covering. The final choice is a mutual one. I always want to get to the spot where we think there will be the biggest news, and this is just where they want me to be to take photographs.

So far our guesses have been good ones, although none of us profess to be prophets. Much credit for the selections goes to Mr. Wilson Hicks, *Life*'s executive editor, formerly of AP, who seems to have an almost instinctive sense for how the news will unfold.

In the spring of 1941, both my executive editor and I believed that Russia would soon be big news. Only a month after I arrived there Germany invaded the Soviet Union, and I was fortunately on the spot to photograph the Russian war. In the summer of 1942, before a single Flying Fortress had flown over enemy territory, Mr. Hicks foresaw that the growth of our Bomber Command would be one of the great stories of the war. This was a happy choice, for I love airplanes. I became accredited to the Air Force, working with our heavy bombers during those early history-making flights from England, and following through with the North African campaign.

So in the summer of 1943, my editor and I again brought out the crystal ball and did our guessing about how we thought events might develop.

"I'd like to see the war on the ground," I said. "I'd like to photograph artillery. And see what the Engineers are doing.

And there must be dozens of things that go on to make up a war that our American public doesn't know much about."

Just at this time an inquiry came for my services from the Army Service Forces in the War Department. Under General Brehon Somervell, the ASF was doing a gigantic job of supply about which our American people knew little. Sixty per cent of the war was a matter of supplying our troops with food, ammunition, medical and even spiritual services (the latter under chaplains). All this was the result of a chain-belt system which girdled the world—reached from our factories to the front lines, according to a process known to the Service Forces as "logistics." But to most American people "logistics," if they ever heard it, was just a word. That was where I came in. From their headquarters in the Pentagon Building, the ASF issued a request that I go overseas with our Army to show how supplies are brought to our troops: to tell in photographs the great story of "logistics."

This logistics business suited everybody. It pleased *Life*, because they could show in pictures that "it's a big war," which was the title they subsequently gave to one series of pictures I turned out during my mission. It delighted me, because it gave me a chance to follow up many of the subjects in which I was most interested. Having always liked industrial photography, I was eager to portray the Engineers. ASF in addition to Engineers and Quartermaster, includes Medical Corps, Transportation, Signal Corps, WAC's, Chaplains, and Ordnance. Through Ordnance I would reach Artillery. Through many of these diversified activities I would reach the soldier at the front and picture his activities from a new point of view. The focal point of all this gigantic system of service and supply was the front-line soldier, and that was the story that I wanted to tell in pictures.

I left by plane on Labor Day, 1943, and flew by way of England to North Africa. I carried in the pocket of my new summer uniform an informal note which brought me the world. It read:

WAR DEPARTMENT
Headquarters
Army Service Forces, Washington, D.C.

3 September 1943

Commanding General, NATOUSA
Army Service Forces

Dear Tom:

Margaret Bourke-White is coming to the North African theater to take pictures of Army Service Forces' operations; I have felt for a long time the need for such a service and was quite happy to accept her offer and that of her employer to do the job for us.

I am particularly anxious that Miss Bourke-White be given opportunity to photograph the complete supply and service story in the actual theater of war and will appreciate any assistance you and your staff can give to her.

Sincerely,

/s/ Bill
BREHON SOMERVELL
Lieutenant General
Commanding

That "in the actual theater of war" phrase was the most helpful one General Somervell could have written. It did much to overcome that natural reluctance in some quarters to allow a woman into the combat zone.

The "Tom" to whom it was written was a two-star general in NATOUSA who turned out to be someone with whom I had ridden horseback in Montana. It had been when *Life* magazine was still in the planning phase, before it had reached the newsstands, that I was sent out to cover some of our large government power projects. Major General Thomas B. Larkin, then a colonel, was in charge of construction of the Fort Peck Dam. He was helpful to me then in securing photographs which were used as the cover and lead feature for the first issue of *Life*, and he was equally helpful to me during my work in NATOUSA.

It was "Dear Tom" Two-Star who facilitated my quick passage to Italy when Naples fell. It was members of his equally helpful staff who brought Corporal Padgitt into my life.

Corporal Jess Padgitt from Des Moines was blond, neat, and twenty-one. He was a member of an infantry guard, and he was assigned to help me in my work. He looked like any nice kid from Iowa, and talked about as much as Harpo Marx. He was one of those rare souls who never had to be told anything twice. In fact, Padgitt seldom had to be told anything once. With no previous experience in photography, he noticed that I reached for articles in a certain order when taking pictures. On our second day out, he started handing me those items in that order. He observed that after each picture I wrote certain caption material. With no instructions from me, he produced a notebook and kept this data: name and home town of soldiers photographed; what jobs they held before entering the army; what jobs they wished to go into after the war.

It used to amuse me to see the way he had even adopted my wording: "Do you mind telling your age?" or "Are you married, engaged, or in love?" Possibly once a fortnight he would drop a voluntary comment. If he particularly liked a soldier whom I photographed, I might hear him murmur, "That was a good Joe," or conversely, "What a jerk!"

Otherwise, his reactions toward the world, and his ambitions, he kept to himself, with one exception. "Gives a guy a chance to learn something," he might say, after some new experience. Or, "Hope I can learn something in this man's army that will be useful after the war."

I love people who don't talk. Especially when taking photographs. Photography, unhappily, takes a lot of thinking about, and assistants like the Corporal, who don't interrupt you with chatter, are rare indeed. So we did our work in mutual near-silence for several weeks before I found out what he wanted to learn to "be useful after the war."

His sole aim in life, the lodestar toward which he pointed, was law. Somehow the Corporal had come into possession of a legal tome as heavy as man's head. It was the *Army Manual of Courts-Martial*, published for the Judge Advocate General's office, and contained documents, processes, and decisions of a legal nature. It was evidently love at first sight between the Corporal and the Judge Advocate General's manual. By the time I made Padgitt's acquaintance he had practically committed it to memory, and during our subsequent travels through wartorn Italy this volume never left him.

When he was assigned to be my man Friday, he was

voicelessly overjoyed to be rescued from what had been a rather monotonous job as guard before the front door of AFHQ. It gave him "a chance to learn something." And when my flying orders came through to go to Italy, he was in a silent agony of fear that he would be left behind. However, when my last lens and flash bulb were packed, the Army moved in its mysterious way. Between AFHQ and NATOUSA, and possibly "Dear Tom" Two-Star for all I know, Padgitt's U.S. CONFIDENTIAL EQUALS BRITISH SECRET orders suddenly came through.

The Corporal's orders were only slightly more detailed than mine. They began:

Following will proceed from this station to Italy on temporary duty in order to carry out the instructions of the Commander-in-Chief, and upon completion of mission return to proper station.

He also was to receive "rations in kind."

There were no details about the "instructions of the Commander-in-Chief." I, evidently was the lucky personification of his "temporary duty."

"This really is keen," was Padgitt's comment.

We were loading the equipment into the jeep for the airport when another powerful document came through from headquarters. This bore no CONFIDENTIAL or SECRET labels. With it was provided a handful of "certified true copies" which I was entitled to show to any interested party, in quarters where it might have beneficent results. It was from another Two-Star, the Deputy Theater Commander and commanding general of NATOUSA.

This glittering document read:

The bearer of this letter, Miss Margaret Bourke-White, has been specially assigned by the War Department for the particular purpose of preparing a photographic record of the activities of the supply and other services.

Miss Bourke-White's reputation as a photographer more than justifies a request on my part that she be given every facility and every opportunity for viewing and photographing activities relating to supply, maintenance, and hospitalization of the American Army.

Miss Bourke-White should be permitted to take pictures of any activities without regard to censorship, which will be exercised by proper authorities at the completion of her mission.

Please provide Miss Bourke-White with any necessary air or

ground transportation in order that her mission may be accomplished as promptly as practicable.

/s/ Major General, USA
Deputy Theater Commander

"What are we waiting for?" said Padgitt, and we jumped into the jeep and drove out to the airport.

At Maison La Blanche, the airdrome, we found there was room for only one in a bucket-seat job bound for Tunis. The El Ouina airfield at Tunis was a good bet for making connections to Sicily or Italy, and I flew on to try my luck there. Padgitt would follow as quickly as he could get the breaks.

When our plane circled over Tunis Bay and prepared to land at El Ouina, I could hardly believe that we wouldn't be shot at. During the North African campaign I had been permitted by General Doolittle to go along on a bombing mission and to photograph the raid from the lead plane of our formation of Flying Fortresses. The El Ouina airfield had been our target, and from a height of six miles our planes had dropped their loads, setting such huge fires among the enemy planes massed on the field below that columns of smoke had risen thousands of feet into the air. Enemy ack-ack batteries had opened up at us, and we had been chased homeward by Messerschmitts.

But today the lovely Tunis harbor and the fine El Ouina airfield were in Allied hands. When we came in for a landing, we rolled down a runway still bordered with the twisted wrecks of the planes I had photographed burning during our bomb run. Across the road was a German graveyard, dotted with the wooden swastikas which the Germans use instead of crosses. Ninety per cent of them bore the same date: January 22—the date of the raid I had photographed during the war for Tunisia.

While I waited for transportation in Tunis, I again stayed at the Villa Spaatz. This had even more gingerbread than the one requisitioned for him in Algiers. It was done completely in lattice-carved marble. The ground floor was bisected through its entire length by a sort of alabaster ditch, intended, I suppose, for goldfish, but useful only in tripping up all of us during blackout and getting everybody's feet wet.

"Tooey" Spaatz is the most modest and lovable of generals; he still looked unprepossessing even against this fabulous background. At the foot of a cliff below the villa lapped the sapphire Mediterranean. Someone had given General "Tooey" an amphibious jeep, from which we could all go swimming. It would be hard to decide whether General Spaatz looked more incongruous happily puttering around in the Mediterranean at the wheel of his amphibious jeep, while the various generals in his official family splashed in the water around him, or whether he made a more remarkable picture against the alabaster and gold-leaf background of his villa.

All business at Villa Spaatz, whether it had to do with housekeeping or the Air Force, passed through the able hands of pretty, black-haired Sally Bagby. Sally was a WAC and had one of the most interesting jobs in the Army. She had come into the General's service as a secretary and had shown such intelligence and reliability that he had made her his aide. During my brief stay, she was raised from lieutenant to captain, a promotion which made all of us very happy, for Sally was considered perfect by everyone. Sally did everything, from being hostess to the many transient house guests, of which I was one, to keeping the General's poker scores. In addition, she knew more about each forthcoming campaign than most of the generals knew. The one drawback to this unique job (Captain Bagby was the first woman to be made a general's aide) was that except when she traveled with the General, she was a virtual prisoner in the villa. The information she possessed was so vital that she was not allowed to leave the house, even to go swimming.

Several times each day I went to the airfield and scattered the carbon copies of my CONFIDENTIAL EQUALS SECRET travel orders about where I thought they would do the most good. Finally one of them took, and with no time even to say "thank you" to General Spaatz for his hospitality, I was squeezed into the fuselage of a B-17 between two airplane motors which were being flown to Foggia for replacements. The presence of these engines was a fortunate thing for me, because they were so heavy that no one paid any attention to the additional weight of seven cameras and all the rest of my gear.

From Foggia to Naples there was so much traffic that hitchhiking was easy. It was more difficult in Naples to find myself a room. Most of the fine water-front hotels had been blown up either by our bombing or by German demolition. I finally got a room on the top floor of a hotel which was still intact on the summit of one of Naples' highest hills. The view from my bedroom was one of the "See-Naples-and-die" variety; which is the way I usually felt when I got there, because to reach it I had to climb five flights of stairs.

For three weeks I went around photographing the reconstruction of the harbor and the ruins of the city. Then one day in one of the main city squares, working with my head under a camera cloth, I was just reaching for a lens hood when it was passed conveniently into my hand. Next I groped for a filter, and a hand passed it into my fumbling fingers. The picture was ready now, and as I reached for a film-pack holder, it was slipped into its place in the camera. Only after the photograph was taken did I realize that the preceding steps had been a bit unusual.

I looked behind me and there stood the only person it could have been: Corporal Padgitt. "So you made it," I said.

"I slept on a bench at that airport," he said, "except one night when I got into a six-by-six to get out of the wind; but I woke up when they started to drive the truck away with me in it. When I couldn't get into a troop transport, I even tried to hitchhike piggyback on a P-38. Finally, after I was just going to write my congressman about getting another bench, on account of the one I was on had wore clear through, there was a C-54 due to take off, with room for just one more passenger. It was between me and a captain. Seeing as we both had number-three priorities, I sneaked my barracks bag on the plane while they were gassing up. When the plane was ready for the take-off they started to bounce me for the captain. But my barracks bag was under so many sacks of mail by that time that I stuck.'

It was weeks before I heard Corporal Padgitt utter another speech as long as this one: not until after we had been bombed, strafed, and repeatedly shelled together.

CHAPTER 3

Nothing Ever Happens in Naples

ENGINEERING HISTORY was made in Naples Harbor. When Allied armies arrived they faced one of the most fantastic jobs of demolition the world had ever seen. This colossal destruction had been started by our own forces, bombing the enemy-held seaport; it had been completed by the Germans before they withdrew. The harbor had to be rebuilt again by us for our troops to advance. It was an unintentional partnership entered into by both sides, which produced the greatest tangle of blown-up docks, smashed warehouses, sunken ships, and snarled loading gear that American GIs and bulldozers had ever had to deal with.

Our bombers were responsible only for the broad pattern of destruction. The picture was filled in by the enemy with diabolical artistry. It was not sufficient for the retreating Germans to sink all ships that Allied air raids had left afloat. They sank them scientifically, placing each sunken ship where it would have the greatest nuisance value. Sometimes they sank one ship on top of another, chaining the two together so that the dock obstruction would be as difficult to clear as possible.

It was not enough for them to mine or dynamite all buildings lining the harbor which had escaped Allied bomb loads. Blowing them up would have made things too simple for our side. They set very carefully and delicately placed charges which blasted out only the floors and left the walls precariously standing. This made the buildings useless, but left the dangerous walls for us to level before the area was safe.

It always sounded uncanny to me when I listened to American engineers speak almost admiringly of the "beautiful job of demolition" done by the Germans, but this was an expression I was to hear often during my work on Naples Harbor. The science of demolition has progressed to incredible refinements in this war. No doubt the enemy mixed imagination with destruction, but our American engineers used just as much if not more imagination in their task of reconstruction. Many of their new devices and new tools will not be made known until after the war.

Each time a power shovel pushed over a tottering wall, as a child might push down blocks, the wreckage was put to immediate use in filling up gaps and potholes in the harbor. It was always interesting to me that we could use the rubble directly from a bombed building on the water front—load it into a dump truck, take it a few yards away, pour it into the quayside, and continue construction, basing it on a bed of destruction.

Sunken ships were ingeniously put back to work. Exposed hulls were fitted with rails and runways so they could be used in unloading troops. Bombed ships blocking the docks were simply leveled off, their smokestacks and superstructures cut away, and then reinforced to be used for docks themselves. Oil tankers clogging the harbor were bridged with prefabricated metal parts and employed as piers for unloading Liberty ships.

And over this reconstructed destruction of war, a never-ending stream of C rations, ammunition, GI boots, blankets, tentage, jeeps, bake ovens, delousing units, and blood plasma was being unloaded and rushed frontward.

Some of the most dramatic work in the harbor was invisible. Under the surface of the water divers bit away with cutting tools at the snarled debris, dismembered sunken wreckage which blocked the fairways, blasted the obstructions with which the retreating enemy had hoped to interrupt our vital stream of supplies.

It was one set of wits against another when it came to neutralizing mines in Naples. The Germans were increasing in subtlety with each new region they left behind. Early in the Italian campaign, some American boys entering the courthouse of a small town saw a picture of Hitler on the wall. It was a natural action for one of them to snatch it off the wall. He was instantly killed and his companions were maimed by a mine wired to the picture frame. Another group found a piano in a house, and one of the boys sat down to play. As soon as he touched the keys all the soldiers in the room were killed.

There were four types of booby traps, those touched off by

pressure, by release of pressure, or by pull, and the chemical-mechanical type. Experts found all four as they combed through Naples buildings. Any building left fairly intact was in itself suspect and had to be elaborately checked. Every doorknob, chair, and floorboard had to be tested. With all this care, an occasional time bomb inevitably escaped detection, as in the case of the Naples post office which blew up in a sector where there were many Army offices.

A week after the post-office disaster, one of my friends, an American infantry major, had his life saved by a prostitute. He was walking through the Santa Lucia district, passing the row of once fashionable hotels lining the water front. He was about to walk into one of them, when a streetwalker accosted him. He noticed her wistful face and how starved she looked. Instead of brushing past her, as he would ordinarily have done, he paused and declined her courteously in the few words of Italian he knew. He had just started on, when the whole pavement seemed to rush up toward him. Before his eyes, the hotel folded, floor after floor, like a giant accordion, and the concussion threw him into the middle of the street. His footbones were fractured, but that brief stop on the sidewalk had saved his life.

It was almost a month before engineers dared to turn on the electricity in the city. Meanwhile, people had been without light, and without water, too, because the Germans had blown up the water pipes and they had to be repaired.

The engineers had to be certain that as thorough a job of mine clearance as possible had been done before turning on the electricity. There was danger that when the main switch was thrown, any number of hidden mines or time bombs might be activated and more buildings blown up.

Before the light was going to be turned on, the city had been ordered evacuated except by MP's, fire-fighting squads, and medical personnel. A radio truck had toured the city the day before, warning civilians to take to the hills. From early morning on, a flood of ragged Italians carrying chairs, food, and babies on their shoulders had swept toward the hills.

The power was to be switched on at noon. There were small knots of officers in front of each building, because it was going to be the job of each little group of soldiers and officers to go in after the main switch had been thrown and turn on one light after another. I did a lot of planning to decide where to be at the crucial moment. Padgitt and I toured the city in the jeep and consulted with the engineers as to which were the most suspected blocks of buildings. Finally we picked a spot near the Aquarium on Via Caracciolo, where we could face several streets, principally Riviera di Chiaia and Via Partenope, where occasional groups of comparatively intact buildings were considered particularly suspicious. I had a whole battery of cameras, each fitted with a different focal lens, set and ready in the jeep so we could rush to any part of the city which might start to blow.

I remember how the same major who had been saved the week before by the streetwalker limped into his headquarters with two of his men. Turning on the light switches was a dangerous job, and he didn't want to send his men anywhere he would not go first.

The headquarters was in an old apartment house requisitioned from a countess. It would have taken only a small mine to send her paneled walls and marble stairways toppling down. I felt like a ghoul with my camera focused on the building which, if it blew, would make a fine photograph but would spell the end of the major and his men.

The power went on. One after another, lights appeared in the countess' apartment, in the naval and Air Force headquarters down the street, in the British officers' mess, in the whole row of buildings along Santa Lucia, in the buildings on the hills rising above Naples Harbor. Everything was lighted up—and not a building was blown. The entire city blazing at once was testimony to the thoroughness with which our engineers had done their job. There would be need for watchfulness for another twenty days, because chemical bombs activated by the power would still have to be guarded against. But, with care, the city would be safe. The civilians flowed back again into Naples with their chairs, their bedrolls, and their babies.

CHAPTER 4

Life Goes Underground

ONE NIGHT during a raid over Naples, a group of guards on a hilltop hurried into an orchard for cover from dive bombers. One of the soldiers jumped into a convenient hole. When the raid was over, his companions found that he had vanished. The men lowered a soldier on a rope and kept on working him down the hole until the end of the rope was reached, after paying out fifty feet, and they had to pull him up again.

They searched until morning, when an Italian peasant led them to the bottom of the hill and took them through a crevice massed with hanging ivy. They found they were in a long subterranean passage. Finally the tunnel opened into an enormous cavern. A slender beam of daylight leaked through from a hole 150 feet above their heads. It as through this shaft that the American guard had fallen. His crushed body lay on the rocky floor.

This was no ordinary cave. It was filled with industrial machinery. The soldiers went from chamber to chamber, and everywhere they found scenes of wreckage such as none of them had ever seen before. When the Germans had had to flee from Naples they had evidently torn through these caverns, blowing up all the heavier machinery with dynamite and shooting up the more delicate equipment with pistols.

The searchers found wrecked lathes and drill presses, and smaller caves fitted up as photographic laboratories with metallurgical testing equipment for making microphotographs. One small chamber was piled to its rocky ceiling with stacks of aluminum pigs. The contents of the cave were requisitioned by a committee of Allied engineers, and the material eventually went to the British to be used for salvage.

This was the beginning of the discovery of many caves. One of the most dramatic of these was an immense series of high-arched caverns overhanging the sea and housing a complete airplane factory. For two years this plant had operated with 400 workers, 100 of whom were women. When I visited it there were still twisted frames of double-decked beds lining the walls of several caverns, where the workers had slept safe from bomb raids.

When Allied armies were drawing closer, the Germans did so thorough a job of demolition here that the rocky floors were a mass of crumpled fuselages, radio parts, propellers, and mangled bodies of aircraft. It was on September 27, when the Germans knew their days in Naples were numbered, that they set off 250 demolition bombs.

The chief engineer, Professor Raffaele Polispermi—a professor of mechanical engineering at Regia University in Naples, who had also been responsible for the design of the airplane models—managed to smuggle some of the more precious instruments out of the cavern and bury them at the bottom of the cliff. Then the professor stole to the deep recesses of one of the caverns and pulled down a lot of cabinets, so that the Germans would ignore that portion of the cavern, believing it already wrecked. He hid himself under the pile of wreckage. When they had gone on to another cave, he was able to slip out and save some of the pattern-making machinery, piling debris over it so the Germans would pass it by.

Then the Germans started pouring gasoline and benzene over the equipment, setting fire to it. Civilians had been ordered out of a strip of land 300 feet from the sea and all roads had been blocked and guarded. The professor stole through the woods to round up a few of his workmen. Twice he had to cross roads, where each time he overpowered and killed two German guards.

He and his small group of men, who had equipped themselves with blankets, made their way back to the sea wall. There they found that fire and smoke were pouring out of the mouth of the cavern. They waited until the sentry was at the far end of his beat and then, covering themselves with their blankets, which they had dipped into the sea, they ducked into the factory. They saved a complete set of the pattern- and die-making machinery, so that after the Germans moved on they were able to set up sufficient equipment to start a new factory.

During the three days of destruction by fire, a few Italians managed each night to get into the cavern for a short time. With the aid of fire extinguishers and pails of sand they contrived to save considerable material. They knew they could count on a few hours to work, for the Germans would not come into the cave because of the flames.

When I arrived to take pictures, I found an angry knot of Italian workers. They were friendly toward us but enraged at the Germans for wrecking their factory. They started begging me to put them back to work at once, not realizing that putting Italians back to work is a province over which a war correspondent has not the faintest jurisdiction.

During the transition period while this factory and others were being requisitioned by the British, the workers could not understand why there were so many delays in getting back into production. They needed their wages, for they were short of food and felt keenly the fact that their children were underfed.

This was the first of many protests about food that I was to hear on all sides from Italian civilians. And only a few days later I came upon a food riot in the streets. The people were storming a shop whose owner had been selling flour at black-market prices. I witnessed real starvation, however, the next time I ventured into a cavern.

Beginning with the first raid of Allied bombers over Nazi-held Naples in late 1942, vast numbers of Neapolitans had started moving underground. Some of them had not seen the light of day for more than a year. In one enormous cavern, originally a quarry, which had housed stores for the Italian Royal Navy, hundreds of families had assumed squatter rights. There in the dim cavernous recesses of the cliffs overhanging the city, these families gathered together the chips and scraps for a "house" and settled down to a cave dweller's existence.

Occasionally, after a heavy raid, a few of the bolder ones would steal out and rifle the bomb wreckage, coming back with perhaps a door, a bedstead, a couple of kettles, a birdcage, or even sometimes a donkey or two or three chickens. And life would go on. The more enterprising built shacks within their rocky vaults. Sometimes whole caverns took on the look of shanty towns; but the majority of the wretched inhabitants lay on piles of rags with no protection against the dampness and cold.

Never did I visit one of these caverns without being led by weak, protesting parents to the side of at least one dying child. More often there would be several in each subterranean refuge who were literally perishing from hunger.

In the face of death going on before my eyes, I felt hopelessly inadequate each time we went to photograph these caves. Crowds of children stormed around the Corporal and me, calling out what has become the familiar chant of Italian children—*caramelle, caramelle*. Padgitt and I were nearly swept off our feet each time we reached into our pockets and brought out the handfuls of hard candies we always carried. The destitution of the children seemed even more bitter to me when they laughed and shouted happily over the candies, as children always will.

It is easier to satisfy a child with a caramel than to answer some of the grownups who were frankly puzzled at the food situation.

It is not easy to administer justly an occupied city, to prevent the growth of a black market, and to see that our supplies are properly distributed. Still, our failure to do this may have serious effects on the future. I observed that the friendship with which we were greeted when we landed in Naples rapidly cooled during my stay there.

Another complication was the typhus epidemic which spread rapidly, first carried by lice and then intensified by lack of resistance caused by undernourishment. The epidemic ran unchecked for two months before corrective measures were taken. Only when it grew to frightening proportions in early January was something done. Then the Medical Department was called in and, with the assistance of the United States Typhus Commission, civilians were treated with lice powder and given medical care, and military personnel was quarantined from entering Naples except on urgent business.

Fortunately, we had not a single case of typhus in our Army. This is a testimony to the excellent care given our soldiers, who are superbly fed, given antityphus injections, and helped by every possible facility for cleanliness—even delousing units placed close behind the front lines.

Life in Naples had taken on some extraordinary aspects. One day I visited an old cistern where I had to go down for some hundred steps below the surface of the earth. People were living there who had made their way down those steps fourteen months before and were determined not to climb up out of the cistern until the war was over. It made little difference to them that the city was held by Americans and British instead of by Nazis. They were as terrified of the German bombs falling on us as they had previously been of Allied bombs falling on the Germans, and their resolution held firm not to show their faces to the light of day until the world was at peace.

Even the traffic tunnels which run through Naples were crowded with human beings. Our jeeps, trucks, and ducks passed in a never-ending stream along these traffic routes which connect various parts of the city, and on each side, crouched upon the sidewalk, were dozens of Italian families who had settled down to live there permanently. Sometimes they had succeeded in setting up a few boards to divide them from the family next door and to give them some slight protection against the wind which constantly swept through the tunnels. Some of the men in these families went out periodically to get work in the harbor, since many civilians were being employed there; but the women and children, wrapped in rags and crouched against the tunnel walls, had settled down to a life of lethargy.

Not only had the poor fled from Allied and German bombs, but also the rich, although, as usual, the rich were able to hide in greater comfort. High above one of the main thoroughfares of Naples rises a cliff of soft rock. A number of exquisite little modernistic houses had been chiseled out of the face of this rock, and these gave their wealthy inhabitants not only complete protection against the heaviest air raids, but also a magnificent view of one of the most spectacular harbors in Europe. Those elaborate hideaways were eventually requisitioned as American military offices.

CHAPTER 5

Hot Spot

"JERRY'S BEEN up on that mountain looking at us down the barrels of his guns for a long time," said the engineering officer from the front of the jeep. He was on his way to a demolished road where his gang were breaking through a German-made barrier. I had been told that I might come along. With us in the jeep were Corporal Padgitt, superintending the cameras, and Captain Deutschle. Bighearted Joe Deutschle accompanied me on many of these trips. He was an ex-newspaperman, now PRO with the Army Service Forces.

"Our men have sure taken a beating on these jobs," remarked the engineer, "with the Blonds in their OP's up there hanging over each spot where we stopped to work."

We were weaving our way between the knife-edged peaks of the Colli pass, through which engineers had thrown a chain of bridges across ravines too deep for sunlight to reach. But German binoculars could probe into most of them, and enemy observers could deliberately choose which half-track, jeep, or road gang to shoot at. This was a war for high ground. The side which could see the most had the advantage. The fighting in Italy was slow and costly because for so long the enemy held the highest peaks.

The entire Fifth Army battlefield throughout the winter of 1943–44 was enclosed within a snow-tipped mountain triangle, formed by the Cassino corridor, the hills behind Venafro, and the rugged terrain backing the little town of Colli. Struggling toward the lofty edges of this triangle, soldiers and mules made their dizzy way. Running through the enclosed central area was the road to Rome, where our troops moved a few feet forward, a few inches back. Through monotonous and costly months, few but the wounded or the fallen had a chance to rest. Small wonder that in GI terminology this was Purple Heart Valley.

Today I was seeing for the first time the upper point of this triangle.

We drove over an unspectacular trestle crossing, the kind you would scarcely notice if you were driving through the Poconos. "We named this 'Hot Spot Bridge,'" said the engineering officer, "because we lost eight of our engineers here last week. Really a bad break. Jerry started laying them in just five minutes before the bridge was finished."

I studied my companion's profile under his helmet. His features gave a hint of his Polish ancestry, and he had that strong-jawed resolute look which is so typically American. Lieutenant Colonel Stanley Walter Dziuban was young for his rank, only twenty-nine, and had graduated as Number One Cadet from his class at West Point. I had heard about his outstanding record with the Combat Engineers.

During the Sicilian campaign an armored car in which he was riding had struck a land mine, overturned, and caught fire. He was badly lacerated and his wrist was broken, but he was thrown free, and at the same time enemy machine-gun fire opened up on his men who were escaping from the burning car. One wounded soldier could not get free because his crushed arm was caught beneath the car. Lieutenant Colonel Dziuban ran back, amputated the man's arm with his field knife, and dragged him to safety just the instant before the car exploded. The lad he saved recovered, and Lieutenant Colonel Dziuban was awarded the Soldier's Medal.

During our journey forward I picked up a good deal of information from the engineer. I found that everybody was talking about the new mines. The Germans used to set them with time fuses which gave the discoverer, if he were quick, from two to four seconds to run a few yards and throw himself flat. Now they were often set to explode instantaneously. This gave you two choices: throw yourself flat and hope for the best, or keep one foot firmly rooted to the mine, which would cost a leg but might save some lives. I remarked that that would take incredible presence of mind.

"Some of our boys have done it," Dziuban replied, "and it protected the rest of the gang."

Then he instructed me that if I had to step off the road at any time, I should be very careful to place my feet in the footprints of someone who had gone before. Or I could walk in a jeep track, stepping right in the wheel marks. But never take a step off the road otherwise.

The German mine layers were getting craftier, he told me. They were even booby-trapping unexploded charges. And it was an old story about trapping dead bodies. Only that week a couple of his men had found a dead German soldier in the middle of this very road. They checked the body, and after ascertaining that no tripwires were attached, they lifted the dead soldier and looked around for a spot where they could give him a decent burial. A little clump of shrubs by the roadside seemed just the right place. Evidently the Germans had figured this out in advance, because although the body wasn't booby-trapped, the bushes had been. "That cost us two good engineers," the young colonel commented bitterly.

We crossed a new structural (Bailey) bridge just completed near the high-walled town of Montaquila, turned into a little rocky side road, and passed the ruins of a thoroughly demolished power plant. Retreating Germans had blown the generators off their foundations and wrecked the large aqueduct intakes along a several-hundred-foot span, making repair impossible and leaving nothing but a hillside of scrap metal and concrete.

Then around a curve of road we saw a mine-sweeping crew, clearing an area by the roadside so it could be used to park repair machinery and 'dozers. With the men advancing in couples, it looked almost like a stately dance. The sweeper went first, walking with a peculiar swinging motion, sweeping from side to side his iron pancake on its long instrument-set handle. Following close behind was his partner, carrying a rifle to protect the sweeper from snipers, and holding a tasseled marker to plant on any suspicious spot where the indicator showed buried metal.

"The demolition boys sometimes send a herd of goats in," said the engineering officer. "But up in these hills there are more mines than goats."

Just beyond the sweepers, the road shrank to a mere shelf carved into the sides of the precipice. The whole riverbank here was one sheer cliff towering above us and falling to the Volturno a hundred feet below. Long ago, Italian laborers had reinforced this tortuous highway with arched abutments, but German demolition squads had made a shambles of the ancient masonry blocks. Just ahead of us the thoroughfare was completely blocked by a boulder as large and compact as a small bank building.

"The Blonds did a clever job on that one," commented Colonel Dziuban, as our jeep came to a stop. "Quite a trick to lay a charge just heavy enough to topple that big boulder over so it would come to rest right in the middle of the road."

The men had been working for two days, chipping away at the boulder with TNT charges, which they set delicately so as not to cause a landslide.

As I began focusing cameras, I took off my helmet, which kept getting in the way. "I ought to make you keep your helmet on," said Colonel Dziuban. "It's not a good idea to go around here without one. But it certainly is good to see a woman's hair again."

I think it was a few minutes before most of the road gang realized they were being photographed by a woman, because my regulation leggings, trousers, boots, and field jacket were exactly like the clothes they wore. They didn't have much to say, but they certainly gave me plenty of help.

"We're opening up the road one way only," the officer of the demolition squad explained to me. "They need to put Long Toms on that plateau just beyond. It's so rugged up here there's hardly room for your own heavy guns. We'll certainly be getting action up here when a battalion of infantry is supported by two battalions of artillery. That will be the setup beginning with tomorrow. That's eight times the normal amount."

Each time the engineers were ready to set off a charge, they notified me in time to set two cameras, one for Corporal Padgitt to operate and one for me, so we could catch the blast from different angles. Then the men set charges in a "beehive"—a device used to give downward force to the explosion—and shouted a warning for everyone to get out of the range of flying rocks. A great black cloud rose up with a roar, and after the hail of rocks subsided, they wired TNT blocks, and off went another great black burst. At intervals, an angle dozer pushed the rubble aside; it would be used later as gravel, for gravel, I was informed, is a precious commodity in war.

"After the armistice they ought to carve the bulldozer in marble," said Lieutenant Colonel Dziuban. "If they're making statues of heroes, it's been a hero all right."

We were having mess of K rations under a camouflaged tent half when we heard an air burst coming into the gorge behind us. An air burst is an antipersonnel shell, set to explode not on impact but a certain distance above the ground, possibly twenty or fifty feet, to wound or kill whatever men may be below. In ravines like those we were in, it has a second objective. It acts as a placer shell, for since its burst is visible to the enemy observers, their aim can be adjusted on targets too deep in the cliffs for observation of a direct hit.

"They're after that new Bailey bridge," said the Colonel. The long bridge we had crossed shortly before we reached the road block was in a gorge deep enough so that the Germans, even from the tops of their mountain peaks, couldn't see it. But they could aim an air burst above it—which they could see —work out their mathematical corrections, and adjust their fire accordingly.

I knew that this was a strategic bridge because it was carrying a constant flow of supplies for the same push which the new plateauful of artillery was intended to support.

When we heard the next air burst sail in, Colonel Dziuban jumped up. "I'm going down there to see what's going on," he said. "You can come along if you want to."

I didn't have to ask Padgitt if he wanted to come. He had loaded the cameras and himself into the back of the jeep in a single motion, and we took off around the bend.

We rounded the base of the mountain, circled the ruins of the power plant, and then were out in the open part of the gorge facing the new bridge. A wisp of greasy black smoke was rising over the road in front of us.

I noticed something strange about the road. This was the first time I was to see it, but I was to meet it many times again. In a peculiar way the road had suddenly gone dead. Where just before you would have seen soldiers all over the place, engineers working, people cleaning out the ditches, men driving trucks and jeeps, suddenly the road has become perfectly quiet.

This is what happens to a road during a shelling. I think if you had your eyes closed you would smell it. It wasn't that there were not people there. There were many people—soldiers lining the ditches and crouched behind big rocks, some lying flat behind the ruined fragments of an old stone wall. They looked up at us curiously as we drove past. Several deserted trucks were in the road. I remember a motorcycle turned over on its side with the engine still running, and I recall seeing a jeep—or rather it was part of a jeep; the rear wheels were there but the front was missing.

Just then another shell sailed in and made a direct hit on a "protective truck" which was mounted with a .50-caliber machine gun and had been drawn up near the new bridge to defend the men working there against strafing planes. The truck burst into flames, its gas tanks caught fire, and the ammunition it carried for its ack-ack gun began exploding in all directions. As Colonel Dziuban stopped the jeep, giving me a chance to take pictures of it, a tall column of dirty yellow-orange smoke began rising up and curling over the Volturno River valley.

The Germans were very kind to me that day, because they gave me just time to take the two pictures I wanted before we heard another scream overhead, and made for the nearest ditch. It was a muddy ditch, but suitable for our purpose, as it had a high mudbank in back of us, which gave a certain amount of protection, and it afforded a clear view of the bridge the Germans were trying to hit. The shells were landing on the road opposite us, directly across the narrow bend of the Volturno, and Padgitt kept handing me film packs and reloading cameras as fast as I could shoot with them.

In a curious succession we could hear the sounds of the shelling. First would be the screaming whistle overhead, then a lapse of time which seemed like minutes but could only have been a split second, and we would see the shell bursting on the road opposite us. Then after a lapse of time—because light travels faster than sound—which again seemed like minutes but must have been less than a second, the roar of the exploding shell would come back to us.

Immediately we would hear another whistle, this time a little higher-pitched or lower-pitched than the one before—you can't help wondering whether the changed pitch means it is coming closer or farther away—then we would see the burst and hear the explosion.

Colonel Dziuban had it worked out to a science. We would hear the scream, and he would say, "You can stand up now for a second," I would pop up and take my picture, and then we would duck before the next shell came.

Finally there was a letup. "That was thirty-two rounds in eight minutes," said Corporal Padgitt, and we made for the jeep.

"I guess we can consider the subject covered," I remarked, thinking that if the Corporal could sound so matter-of-fact, I would try to sound nonchalant, too.

We had just started climbing into the jeep when we heard another whooshing sound overhead, and we hurried back to our ditch. The shells were falling closer to the bridge now, and, incidentally, closer to us. Then one shell hit the bridge but only struck a corner of the abutment, knocking off a bit of masonry. I don't know whether Corporal Padgitt was still counting rounds at this point. But I do know he was handing me equipment as I needed it with all the *savoir-faire* of a portrait assistant in a Fifth Avenue studio.

The Germans had bracketed their target now, and they switched from smoke shells to HE. The high explosives sent dull coils of black smoke rising from each hit; it was a very unphotogenic type of shell.

At last a shell fell directly under the bridge, where it could have done a great deal of damage. It made a great splash of water, but that shell was a dud. It would have cost us the whole central span if it hadn't been.

At this point a Piper Cub flew overhead and hedgehopped its way toward the enemy. I could see why foot soldiers have such affection for these Grasshoppers. The Cub seemed like a brave little friend up there, and it turned out later that it was.

"This is a good time to go forward," said Colonel Dziuban. "The Germans will probably hold fire for a little while; they won't want that Cub to spot their gun positions."

We jumped into our jeep and drove away from the river crossing, and had reached the base of the mountain when the shelling started again. Looking back, we saw the Germans had shortened their gun range just enough so that the shells were falling in the road right where we had been sitting. I always felt that that Piper Cub had saved my life.

All the rest of the afternoon I photographed where the engineers were removing the boulder from the road. While the man blasted away we could still hear the shells coming in and dropping behind us—we were more or less protected behind the mountain. The Germans were evidently determined to knock out that new bridge. The rocky walls of the ravine picked up the echoes in a horrible way. Every time a shell came in, it sounded like a baby wailing through the gorge.

I kept thinking, "Well, of course, we're going to have to go back over that bridge in order to get home." It became a sort of obsession with me, but I decided I might as well go on taking pictures. However, I couldn't keep the idea from turning over in my mind. I thought there must be some other way to go home, but I knew there wasn't. In about an hour we would start traveling along that same road where we had been pinned to the ditch; we would go over the bridge where the Germans were aiming, along the stretch of road where we had watched the shells falling. For one brief minute we would drive behind a hill where we would have protection from direct enemy observation, and then we would have a long stretch of road, above which the enemy sat in his OP and looked down at us.

At last it was almost dusk and time to go home. It is important for all extra traffic to get off the roads before nightfall, to leave the highways clear for the heavy convoys bringing up supplies to the front. A very businesslike, gray-haired engineer came to call for us, according to our prearranged plan. He was the Commanding Officer of the Engineering Corps, Colonel Dziuban's immediate superior, and was to be my host during my stay with the engineers. Even then, preoccupied as I was, I noticed how the expression on his face amusingly matched the expression of the eagles on his shoulders.

We piled into the Colonel's command car, Corporal Padgitt with the driver in front, the Colonel, Captain Deutschle, and I in back. "Don't fasten that door too tight," the Colonel directed, and we started toward·the opening in the gorge.

As we rounded the mountain and again came out on open road, once more we saw a little greasy smoke escaping into the air just in front of us. Once more the road had that lifeless look.

As many soldiers were there, but they were somewhat rear-ranged by that time. I suppose they had been in and out of their ditches a dozen times that afternoon, trying to get their work done in between.

The driver pulled the command car to a full stop before turning into the bridge. The Colonel turned to the Captain and said, "All right with you, Captain?"

The Captain answered, "It's up to you, Colonel."

"No, I want to consult you first," said the Colonel. "How do you feel about it?"

"Colonel, it's up to you," the Captain replied.

Nobody asked me how I felt about it.

The Colonel said, "Well, if it's got your number on it, it's got your number on it. Let's go ahead." And ahead we went.

We were just turning into the bridge when I heard a whistle. It was a long whistle, and I thought it would never stop. Suddenly I realized it was our driver whistling to keep his courage up.

On the far side of the bridge stood a white-faced MP; his essential job was to keep traffic spaced widely as it crossed the bridge. "That's a mean post he's had today," said the Colonel to us, and leaning out he shouted, "Good boy. You're doing a fine job."

Once over the bridge we swung into the part of road on which I had watched the shell falling; then for one blessed moment we were hidden from enemy view behind the hill—and again were out in the open, traveling over the long stretch where the Germans had direct observation.

We were about to cross the Hot-Spot Bridge when we ran into a traffic jam—a very bad thing in wartime. The MP's who do our police duty are very efficient and usually are able to prevent road congestion. But the Hot-Spot Bridge had become a bottleneck, and there was nothing to do but sit and wait.

While we were waiting, an air burst sailed in ahead of us. We couldn't see whether or not any damage had been done. Then at last the traffic started and rolled on slowly but steadily, and we were swept on with it.

We crossed the Hot-Spot Bridge, and on the other side I saw two boys lying there so quietly they looked as though they were asleep. One was on one side of the road and one on the other.

There hadn't been time to move them, and the traffic flowed on in a slow, steady stream between them. These soldiers lay there quite peacefully, and in such natural positions it seemed almost as though they must be resting by the roadside. As we drove on I glanced back and saw that one boy had lost half his head and the other had lost all of his face.

It was dark when we reached the Engineers' Command Post. The colonel went to the phone at once; he was in constant contact with all parts of the front where his men were working.

From the reports we found out that just after we had left the area the Germans had hit our Bailey bridge, but only managed to land a shell on one corner of it. Two panels were knocked off, but within eight minutes the engineers had patched it together and traffic was flowing on again.

CHAPTER 6

Monks and Engineers

MY LIFE while working with the engineers more nearly approached a routine existence than any other I lived while covering the war. This was largely because I had regular quarters instead of living like a gypsy with my bedroll in fox-holes and dugouts. By contrast, my billet seemed quite normal. I lived in a monastery with fifty monks and I slept in a cell.

This was a happy solution to what had at first seemed a bit of a problem. When I arrived, the hospitable engineers were eager to make me as comfortable as possible, but there was no room to give me private accommodations in the cluster of tents where they had their quarters. Within walking distance, however, was a fourteenth-century monastery. The engineers, having struck up something of a friendship with the monks, prevailed upon their Father Superior to put me up.

My cell opened out on an echoing, vaulted corridor, lining which were scores of identical cells inhabited by the holy fathers. Often at night I could hear them pattering back and forth to visit each other, chattering loudly among themselves, and unexpectedly breaking into gales of laughter like youngsters in boarding school.

The plumpest monk was Fra Mario: to the engineers he was "Friar Tuck." The smallest monk was Fra Antonio, called "The KP." Friar Tuck's amazing girth was so disproportionate to his height that the neighboring engineers, who should know about matters like pedal locomotion, never figured out how his legs under his black frock managed to carry him so easily about the corridors. The KP was a surprise to all of us, because although we had not given the matter much previous thought, we had never realized that monks could come so small.

The KP was so named because he spent hours tagging about the skirts of Friar Tuck in the stone-paved kitchen. There in the midst of whirling steam, looking like a fattened-up witch over

his caldrons, the friar sometimes turned out miraculous concoc-
tions for his friends, the *Americanos*. His most frequent dish was
something resembling Southern spoonbread, which appeared
with countless varieties of trimming and sauces and was known
as *pasta*. Even more popular than *pasta* was Friar Tuck's
spinach. It was hard to tell whether there was more spinach or
more garlic in the big wooden bowls that emerged from the
kitchen.

The hours which Friar Tuck spent away from his bowls and
kettles were largely taken up with his embroidery. He had a
flair for roses. I believe that only on the floor of heaven, into
which undoubtedly the good father had been granted special
insight, could roses like his grow. Certainly no earthly blooms
ever possessed such an intricacy of unfolding petals, such a
blinding brilliance of vermilion and scarlet.

But the obliging friar was always ready to lay these fascinating embroideries aside for more drab needlework. Every time
one of the *Americanos* came over with a shirt or a field jacket that
needed mending, Friar Tuck set to work. He had a sewing
machine in his cell. He was very good with patches and
reinforcements, and he was outstanding with insignia, which he
appliquéd in place by means of a double cross-stitch.

Since the monastery had been continuously inhabited by the
same religious order since the fourteenth century, I suppose the
monks had grown accustomed, in their worshipful way, to the
presence of the relic of a saint which reclined full length in a
deep stone niche behind Gothic pointed doors at the foot of the
main staircase. But our engineers—and there were a number
who liked to come over and visit—never got used to being on
visiting terms with a mummy. They were inordinately impressed with it, and I think the monks were rather pleased at the way
the engineers peeped between the pointed doors whenever they
came over, as if they wanted to see how the mummy was getting
along.

The central courtyard of the monastery was a pleasant place
in the mornings. The sun (when it shone—which was by no
means always in "sunny Italy") marked the hour on an ancient
sundial and cast endless arched shadows from the colonnaded
porch which surrounded the court in a perfect square.

Often a handful of engineers came down to get hot water to

shave. I would see them with their helmets full of soapy water propped up on the balustrade. The friars filed by, filling their pails and kettles from the central well. *"Buon giorno!"* each friar would say. *"Buon giorno!"* each lather-covered engineer would reply. Tiny Fra Antonio, the KP, always lingered in the kitchen doorway, unable to take his eyes off the *Americanos* while they scrubbed and shaved.

My early-morning ablutions were conducted not in the courtyard, but in a large stone cell, down the hall from my tiny one, which the monks had fitted with certain primitive attempts at plumbing. The Commanding Officer of the Engineering Corps, the Colonel who had picked us up in the gorge, came over early each morning to help me plan my day and made a practice of knocking at my door to awaken me. Then he would precede me into this dark cavern with its plumbing, make a preliminary investigation, and emerge with the words, "Coast's all clear." While I scrubbed, the CO stood guard outside the door to make sure I was not interrupted by monks, who might also wish to use their plumbing facilities.

The Colonel in command was one of those dignified, martial personages, with iron-gray hair, a clipped mustache, and an inflexible insistence on discipline, the type that even a layman instantly recognizes as "old Army." For reasons of censorship I may not mention him by name, but since a day came when he remarked, "Call me Tommy," we shall call him Tommy.

Tommy followed a regular routine of leaving me at the Senior Officers' Mess tent while he climbed the slippery hill through the olive grove for his morning conference with a still more exalted individual, the brigadier general in command of the corps. The general lived in a trailer which was reached by teetering over scattered boards loosely laid in a sea of mud.

There was nothing remarkable about the Senior Officers' Mess tent where I was deposited for breakfast, except the table top, which someone had rescued almost intact from the ruins of a demolished village. It was a thick slab of Carrara marble as white as the counter of a soda fountain. Once I had been invited to dinner at the general's mess. There was nothing remarkable about his mess tent either, except the tablecloth, a large one of fine linen left behind by some Italian general retreating with the German army.

Tommy returned from the corps officers' conference at about the time I finished my coffee and powdered eggs, which had been quite palatably scrambled by a most competent mess sergeant. (In the Army you rate the mess sergeant according to how well he disguises the powdered eggs or Spam he feeds you.)

Both the Colonel and I would take some of the lifesavers and hard candies which always stood in a bowl in the middle of the table, and put them into our pockets, not only for ourselves, but as handouts to the Italian children who were always crying for *caramelle*. Then we walked up the road to the Corps Command Post, which was on the second floor of a cracked plaster farmhouse in a room with leaded casement windows hung with flypaper. The walls were covered with maps and charts. A small area in the center of the room was raised to volcanic heat by a tiny brazier, a prized item which somebody had picked up. One yard away from the coals everybody shivered.

The Colonel took his field telephone off its hook on the wall and began checking his many forward installations. During these conversations Tommy, nursing his various bridges which were growing along the front, always reminded me of a gardener watching his flowers bloom. He inquired about rainfall, flood conditions, and the previous night's shell damage. Then he consulted a miraculous set of aerial photographs through a stereoscope. The pictures were pieced together, mosaic fashion, over a sheet of illuminated glass in such a way that when you looked through the stereoscope the peaks and rims of the gorges jumped at you, and the demolition which had to be repaired fell into three-dimensional perspective. Through this device, the engineers estimated the width and depth of the gorges to be bridged, and calculated the type and amount of materials needed.

Weaving his eyes over this luminous sheet of glass, like a crystalgazer, Colonel Tommy could plot the enemy's destruction in advance. In the twelve-mile stretch of Colli-Atina road, the Colonel knew that thirty-eight acts of demolition would occur by the time the Germans were pushed completely out of this area. In the case of those most imminent, he already had the bridge parts loaded up on trucks, ready to rush to the front the instant they were needed, so that our infantry could press ahead with almost no loss of time.

The Colonel picked several installations to inspect and arranged for me to go along to take pictures. When the locations for the day's work had been selected, we piled into the Colonel's command car, Corporal Padgitt in front with the driver, Colonel Tommy and I in the rear. Later on we made other trips and often one of the captains came along. Usually it was good-natured Captain Joe Deutschle, with whom I worked a great deal. Sometimes it would be Captain Harry Morris, whose experience in civilian life as an architect of low-cost modern housing projects in Detroit made him a competent officer with the engineers. I was always amused at the way the youthful but scholarly face of Captain Morris, with his silver-rimmed spectacles, nearly disappeared from sight when he put on his helmet.

This trip was typical, however; we settled into the back seat of the command car with our knees up to our chins, because the floor had been piled deep with sandbags to break the force of the explosion in case we ran over a mine.

Once we had swung out into the open and started down into the Volturno valley, the benign atmosphere of my monastery fell away like a dream.

"This valley has always been bad news," said Tommy.

Along the tops of the ridges above Venafro, we could see sporadic white smoke bursts where our shells were striking at enemy gun positions. Every so often, black puffs mottled the sky from ack-ack guns shooting toward enemy reconnaissance planes too high for us to see. Once a brief dogfight took place over our heads, and we leaned out to watch, following the course of the fight, as though in skywriting, until the thready vapor trails of the planes disappeared over the mountain.

As we drove along I was fascinated by the road signs. At every turn and crossroad clusters of them pointed to ordnance repair depots, water points, field hospitals, and ammo dumps. The installation of these signs is included in the multiple functions of the engineers. Near a one-way bridge a new sign was being put up for the French troops, PONT À SENS UNIQUE. Just beyond a water point another sign, POINT D'EAU was being installed. "For the Goums," said Colonel Tommy. The most frequent signs had to do with dispersal of traffic. A traffic jam can be murder near the front if the congested stretch of road gets a plastering from shells, or a burst of machine-gun bullets from a strafing plane. Every short distance there was a warning sign, 50-YARD INTERVAL, which if kept usually guarantees that a strafer will not get more than one vehicle per attack.

Evidently some of the Engineering Corps sign painters got tired of the similarity of wording, for we began passing rhymed series, strung out "Burma Shave" fashion along the highway. One such sequence of five signs, decorated with drawings of a bespectacled soldier being dive-bombed by a frightening plane with swastikas, read:

> there was a gi near venafro
> who couldn't read signs by golly
> jerry planes were overhead
> and now he is dead
> so solly my boy so solly

Tommy was somewhat irritated that members of his Engineering Corps were wasting paint, but finally as we kept passing more jingles he was moved to little rhymed recollections of his own. "Have you heard this one?" he asked, and recited:

> Lives of engineers remind us
> We could write our names in blood;
> And departing leave behind us
> Half our faces in the mud.

This poetic interval was brought to a halt by our running into a real traffic jam. "That's a fine way to get bombed and shelled," said the Colonel, "with everybody getting all jammed up bumper to bumper," and leaping out he started directing traffic himself.

"Spread out!" he shouted. "You're fine targets for Jerry; all lined up like turkeys in a ditch." He began ordering the traffic about with such terrifying authority that I suspected that when he was a little boy he had wanted to be a traffic cop. We could hear him talking savagely in a monotone to himself. "Let a few of them get scattered around so they can't get up again, and they'll learn."

"That's telling 'em," said Padgitt from the front seat, and then started shaking with stifled laughter at the faces of a few incautious jeep drivers who were trying to sneak ahead of the line and were startled out of their wits to see the Old Man himself directing traffic.

"Enough of those Jerries killing us without our trying to kill ourselves," roared the Colonel, sending the offenders back to the very end of the line.

Finally the traffic began slowly to roll on again; we went with it, and Tommy hopped back into the command car in such a cheerful mood that I suspected I was right and he enjoyed these chances to play policeman.

As we came out into the flood plains of the Volturno, I caught my first glimpse of the "Delirium Tremens Bridge."

"That's a beautiful bridge," I exclaimed.

"That's what Jerry thinks," said the Colonel. "Jerry keeps going after that bridge like a duck after a June bug."

Jerry had indeed, we found, been after the bridge that very morning. There had been a dive-bombing attack, but a patrol of Spitfires had driven off the raiders. Just before daylight there had been an attempt at sabotage. Four Germans loaded with dynamite had slipped through the lines at midnight, wearing their summer uniforms which are so similar in color to those of our paratroopers that they had almost reached the bridge undetected. Only when some Italians asked them for cigarettes was their insignia noticed, and they were turned over to some American Negro troops for arrest. Since the saboteurs came in uniform they would be, according to international law, held as prisoners of war, not shot as spies. But the engineering bridge gang, who were discussing the incident excitedly, felt that the spy line was dangerously close.

This double-triple Bailey, the "DT" as it was called, had had a strenuous war history. Three times it had been rebuilt. Twice the floating pontoon crossings, which had preceded the present structure, had been swept away by floods. Then the engineers put in a double-single Bailey (double span wide; single span high). This, too, began washing away when wreckage accumulating against the remains of the old Italian piers began forming a dam. Overnight the fierce, pent-up stream began forcing its way out, cutting into the banks like a spade, and actually changing the course of the river.

Engineers working up to their waists in water and paddling

around in rubber boats rescued the sections of the double-single Bailey, and began reinforcing it into a double-double. When I arrived with the Colonel, the engineers were adding still a third tier for strength, converting the double-double into a double-triple, or "DT." Small wonder that it was nicknamed "Delirium Tremens."

Much of the incredible speed with which the engineers rebuild demolished bridges and span shell gaps in roads is due to the portable design of the Bailey, the most remarkable bridge in the history of military operations. It can cross any gap up to 240 feet without pontoons, and with pontoons the stretch is almost limitless.

The bridge parts are interchangeable and light, the heaviest requiring only six men to lift it. The prefabricated sections are ten feet long, and only one steel pin is needed for each joint. The Bailey fits together like a gigantic Meccano toy and, after being built on rollers on the edge of a river, can be pushed over by the building crew without mechanical aid.

Time schedule is everything in building bridges in a war area. While the double-triple over the Volturno was under construction, traffic was being carried temporarily over a floating trestle treadway that had been thrown across upstream. The new Bailey had to be finished in time to carry the heavy convoys that would start at dusk for the front.

"What's the time schedule?" Colonel Tommy inquired of the officer in charge.

"I'm phoning Traffic Control that we can take an uninterrupted load at four."

"Now you're cooking with gas," Tommy approved. "You sure of your load capacity?"

"The only thing is headroom, Colonel." And while the two officers discussed the requirements of a "class forty load," I began photographing the intricate latticed panels swarming with men. They were pinning together lateral stays and cribbing with such astonishing speed that I could watch the bridge growing before my eyes.

Under the center of the new span, but not touching it, was a broken masonry arch, the last remnant of the Italian bridge which had been blown up by the Germans. As it was clogging the stream it had to be blasted away.

The charges were placed by men in rubber boats, and when everything was ready for setting off the TNT, the men scrambled down off the bridge to be out of the way of flying rocks. There were two points of view I wanted, so I posted Padgitt at one of them, with the Rolleiflex, and occupied the other myself with a Linhof. Colonel Tommy called warning signals so we could both be ready to catch the blast. Then the Colonel gave the word to blow, and a ravishingly beautiful geyser rose high in the air and descended lazily in a shower of diamonds. I had time to snatch two separate pictures; the corporal had been quick enough to catch three.

"Jiminy, if *Life* should print one of my pictures instead of yours!" the Corporal exclaimed. "Just only one shot! Boy, won't you get the razz!"

Well, the censor had the last laugh on that one. The Corporal did get the best picture. Exposure right; filter right; focus perfect; composition marvelous. It was a honey! It was so good that it revealed the construction of the bridge, and was censored out.

After the explosion, the bridge gang scrambled back with their tools like monkeys up a trellis and several GIs took off in the rubber boats that are always around a bridge job. They were after the fish which floated to the top, stunned by the blast, and they paddled about until they had scooped up several helmetfuls.

It was 11:30 and mess lines had begun forming. We lined up at the rear end of the mess truck for hot C rations with canned peas and meatballs, which were all poured together with fruit-salad mixture into our mess kits. We were just making our way through the mud to sit down on a log when I found myself suddenly grabbed from behind and whirled off my feet. I was amazed when I realized it was the Colonel. Despite the fact that we were Tommy and Peggy to each other, he had until now been consistently formal in his behavior. "What's all this?" I gasped; but instead of answering he threw me down in a crevasse between two rock piles and crawled in beside me.

Then I knew what it was—a strafer. A rising, crunching sound was coming up the road. From under the rim of my helmet I could see the engineering gang who had been clinging all over the spans of the Bailey, working their way down like circus performers.

That's a rough place to be just now, I thought.

"Keep your head down," Tommy said.

As I ducked, I caught out of the corner of my eye a glimpse of the strafer with its painted swastika. Behind it were two more planes, a pair of Spitfires hot on its tail.

It was only another second before people were pulling themselves to their feet again. The Spits had chased the ME off, and we could watch all three racing away over the ridge above Venafro until the mountains blocked them from sight.

The relief was so great we were hilarious. The boys pulled my mess kit out of the mud. "Anyway, it's good eating mud," they said, and brought me another dose of C rations. "We engineers get so we can't enjoy a meal without eating some mud with it."

We were all excited by the close shave of the bulldozer operator, who came up during lunch to show us his helmet. He had been at the wheel of the dozer when the ME started up the road. Any vehicle is a bad place during a strafing, and he had streaked across the road in time to jump behind a low wall. He was just crouching down when he was thrown over on his back so violently that he thought for a minute his neck had been broken. When he pulled himself together he found that he was quite unhurt, but that a hit had creased his helmet down the middle like a Homburg.

So, while we finished our C rations and drank our canteen cups of cocoa, everybody began matching narrow escapes. The best story came from a second lieutenant who had gotten up during the night, and stepped out of his tent for the usual purpose, during which time a brief strafing of the tent area took place. After it was over, everybody visited around and made sure that no one had been hurt. When the excitement died down, the lieutenant crawled back into bed and was annoyed to find his cot wet. Evidently someone had dropped his canteen there with the cover unscrewed, he thought. In the morning he found that his canteen had a hole in it and a 20-mm. shell had passed through his mattress where his chest would have been and had buried itself unexploded under his cot.

CHAPTER 7

Foxhole Studio

I HAVE always been sorry I never got to know that Signal Corps photographer better. We shared the same ditch when we got caught between the two contestants during an artillery duel. As I learned later, he was a most interesting person.

It was hard to tell whose shells were passing closer to the tops of our heads, theirs or ours. Ours whooshed over with a sound we found comforting, as though someone were stroking a bolt of raw silk. Theirs came on like quick blasts on a police whistle. "Close enough to part your hair down the middle," said Corporal Padgitt. The effect was not comforting.

The Corporal was at my side handing me film packs as I needed them. There was nothing much to photograph—just those monotonous fountains of earth and rock rising across the road and coming a little closer each time, as the Germans tried to "bracket" the target. But I have discovered that it contributes to a healthier state of mind to keep on working at such a time. Nothing else you can do, anyway; you're pinned to your ditch.

The Signal Corps photographer evidently felt the same way. Things had been happening so fast that I had not even seen him join us until I tried to edge upditch a little, where there was a better viewpoint, equally well protected. I had half pushed my way in front of someone when I realized that he had a movie camera in his hands and was using it very busily to record the barrage; it seemed a great coincidence to find another photographer in the same ditch. I am not especially noted for politeness when getting pictures, and I doubt if anyone's manners are at their best during a shelling. However, there is a certain code of behavior, and even then my professional habits asserted themselves; I could not push another photographer out of the way.

We never had time to speak to each other. The exchange of shells ended as quickly as it had begun, the engineering gang swarmed out of the holes and gullies where they had thrown themselves, and the Signal Corps photographer somehow disappeared in the shuffle. Later I learned that he was Technical Sergeant Peter Ratoff, brother of Gregory Ratoff, the Hollywood director. And still later I learned about his final act of courage.

About two weeks later, and not far from the place where we had met, Sergeant Ratoff was working at a Chemical CP. This Command Post was located in one of those small pink plaster farmhouses which dot the Italian countryside. The Chemical Section, which comes under the engineers, has charge of throwing smoke screens and laying smoke pots for camouflage.

We know that Sergeant Ratoff tried to photograph that JU when it swooped out of the sky. We know, because of his camera. It wasn't the safest thing to do, but there is no safety, anyway, at such a time, and those fine action pictures always represent a narrow escape on the part of the photographer. Suddenly the dive-bomber headed right for the CP. In less than a minute it was over. The building had been wrecked; the colonel in command and his staff had been instantly killed, and not a trace was ever found of the sergeant again. But his movie camera was still turning freakishly, quite undamaged; a tribute to a brave man who died at his job. He was reported "missing in action" by the War Department.

On the day I encountered Sergeant Ratoff, Padgitt and I were visiting different types of bridges: the primitive bypass type, thrown hastily across streams and gullies for an infantry advance; the sturdier trestle crossing which is built as soon as the engineers can install a heavier job. These are replaced by Baileys as soon as it is not too hot to risk the materials.

There was a good deal of bridge building and road clearance going on that day, for the Goums were coming. For miles back the roads were lined with these French native troops. They sat by the roadside, waiting for darkness, the reddish-brown stripes of the burnooses they wore blending with the landscape. These Goums were seasoned troops, veterans of the North African and Sicilian campaigns. They looked sturdy and somewhat frightening, with their fierce knives in their belts. In addition to their primitive weapons, they carried our new Lend-Lease M-1 rifles.

Everyone hoped the Goums would do well. They were replacing a division of our American boys who had been in the lines for sixty-nine days and badly needed a rest. Truckfuls of weary, bearded soldiers were being brought to the rear that day. They would be taken to the fine delousing plant just out of shell range. This had been newly set up with shower baths and tentfuls of quartermaster supplies where the boys could exchange their filthy clothes for new boots and field jackets. After delousing they would be sent all clean and shaven to Naples or Sorrento for a short leave. After that, although we did not know it at the time, they would take part in the amphibious action of which we had already heard rumors, and which later materialized at Anzio.

Colonel Tommy was busy helping to get the French engineers and artillery sections installed. He had left us at one of his bridge projects, just before the artillery duel took place, and after it was over, the Corporal and I had tried to take a few pictures in the fading light. It was one of those cold, drizzling days so characteristic of winter in Italy. The bridge-building scene was as photogenic as gray blotting paper, a disadvantage we tried to overcome by the liberal use of peanut flash bulbs. The Corporal waded around in the shallow stream, stringing extension wires from my camera, which I tried to operate from a very wobbly rock.

Nobody minded the rain except Padgitt and me. Cloudy days are a protection against dive-bombers and strafers, and while they are no insurance against shelling, everybody was in a cheerful mood at the cessation of the barrage. It seemed a miracle that no shells had hit either the men or the bridge. In fact, there was a good deal of delighted comment on how many shells the Krauts could toss away without hitting anything. Also there had been a rather high percentage of duds. That always made everybody feel good. We never knew whether the duds were caused by hasty and faulty manufacture or by deliberate sabotage, but we always hoped it was the latter.

It was almost dusk when the Colonel came back to pick up Padgitt and me—and then all of us found to our horror that one of those enemy shells had not missed its mark. It had made a direct hit on a gun position just up the hill in back of us and killed the whole crew. "You could have carted the remains of that gun section away in a jeep," reported the Colonel.

To go home we had to pass through the same old bottleneck, over the Hot-Spot Bridge. This was a critical point. One of the most disturbing things about traveling to and from the front was the fact that there were only two main highways. Over both of them the enemy hung in his observation points, watching the traffic on the road below. Of the two main drags, the one we were on wound through Colli Pass; the other was the famous Highway Six, which supplied troops in the region of Cassino. As we started homeward, convoys of trucks were passing us with their loads of ammo and food for the front lines; but this evening we negotiated our journey through the tortuous pass without incident. Soon we were out in the clear and well on our way home.

I find it difficult to express the blessed relief, the quickening joy, with which you find yourself heading home from the front. Each mile in the road brings a lightening of the heart. Every day I had felt this surge of relief when I started homeward, and I was not proud of it.

What was happening to me, I wondered. For the last several years, as a war correspondent, I had been through my quota of bombings. I had been bombed in Barcelona, in Chungking, in Great Britain, North Africa, and Moscow. And, while nobody likes having bombs come too close, on the whole I had not minded it too much. You are a small target in a big place, and the chances are that you will pull through. You are willing to take your gambling chance in a city.

But shelling was different. Shelling was like a dentist with a drill. And with me, those shells had found the nerve.

Partly I think it was knowing how much science went into the aiming of those guns that made it so hard to take. The enemy was after a specific target. If you were unlucky enough to be at that target, from your point of view he was after you. It was intensely and horribly personal.

And another element came in. In many forms of danger you can do something about it, and that is your salvation. Even when we were chased in the cub by the four FW's, I was saved from fear by the fact that Captain Marinelli was doing something about it—and doing it so capably and swiftly that my confidence in him was instinctive and absolute. Also it happened so quickly that I hardly had time to think.

But with shelling, you simply can't do anything about it. You are pinned to your ditch, if you are lucky enough to get to a ditch, like a fox in a trap. You are at the will of the enemy. As a result, it is demoralizing.

As we drove homeward, I did a lot of wondering about how those boys felt who had to stay up there week after week, and sometimes month after month, without even the break of getting out of it for a night. Later I was to see the deathly strain on their faces, the growing numbness that enveloped them like a shroud. This numbness was their only defense against an anxiety that had become intolerable. To live in a state of mental paralysis was the only way they could stand it.

Even on that evening, which was early in my experience at the Fifth Army front, I felt somewhat guilty about being in as free a position as I was: to be able to go back even if only for a few hours and drink up that blessedness of being out of range. Later I came almost to regret my voluntary position. My decisions to go to the front depended on no one but myself and my desire to do a thorough and honest job. I used to wonder whether, if I were under orders, it wouldn't be easier.

I remember how one of the correspondents, an exceedingly brave and able man who has reported more wars than most of us will ever see, developed a peculiar apprehension just before he was due to return to America. He had previously charged ahead with the infantry every time a town was captured, and had exposed himself repeatedly to danger in his job of reporting from the front lines. Yet during his final ten days with the Fifth Army he made no trips to the front. He was sure that on his last trip he would get it.

I think it was that day at the trestle bridge when the shells had missed us, only to hit the gun crew who were answering the enemy, that I graduated. The school of thought I graduated from had been a soothing one as long as it lasted; I had had an irrational conviction that "nothing could ever happen to me." From then on, however, I never found myself in a foxhole without wondering whether I had tried my luck one too many times. After all, there is something to the law of averages.

The highway was thundering with convoys as we drove homeward, passing us as they carried their vital supplies to the front. Many of these trucks were driven by Negroes. The roads would be perfect hell as they got farther forward, where the danger from traffic accidents without lights was even greater than the menace of enemy artillery.

We grew drowsy. We napped a little, and when we woke up we sang a little: old standbys like *Carry Me Back to Old Virginny*, to which Tommy added a splendid tenor; *Juanita*, to which he sung a beautiful alto, and finally *O Sole Mio*, on which Padgitt surprisingly joined in from the front seat.

As we drove homeward the fine rain died away and the moon came up over the dark hills. We knew we would be late for mess, so we fished around in our pockets for those hard suckers supplied with our rations, candies which come in so handy at such times. Out of an unappetizing tangle of grubby notes, pencil stubs, and camera odds and ends, which I carried in my field jacket, I produced a prize: a Tootsie Roll I had bought at the PX. I divided the sticky mass as evenly as possible among the Colonel, the Corporal, and the sergant driver, and marveled at the things which take on value to adult men in war.

A red star rose over the mountain. It was an artillery wind guide, a lighted balloon sent up by the gun crews to compute deflection data. It hung like a kerosene lamp just above the horizon. The entire landscape was whitewashed by the moon.

"I've come to hate moonlight," commented Colonel Tommy, "ever since my best friend was killed on a moonlight night. Strafing pilots can see too much."

When we arrived at the CP, Tommy went up to his stereoscope and charts and I walked down the road to the monastery hoping that Friar Tuck would give me something to eat. I found that he was already giving the junior officers a feed in a great dungeonlike vault in the basement. From the walls a fresco of faded saints looked down on what must have been, in their centuries-long experience, a unique scene.

Friar Tuck sat on a chest in the middle of the room, surrounded by a group of officers shouting with laughter. They were teaching the friar to smoke his first cigar.

The inevitable bowl of garlic and spinach was there, and with it we had slabs of some wonderful honeydew melon someone had obtained in an obscure trade with the peasants. The native red wine which had been so plentiful when the Americans came in had grown hard to get. So we roared our welcome when "Suitcase Simpson" came into the dungeon, rolling a straw-covered bottle which must have held five gallons. "Drink up that vino," he said, "and you'll change your identity." "Suit-case Simpson" had earned his name because his feet were so big. Outside the junior officers group he was known as Captain Robert Darling, Supply Officer.

We drank vino from our canteen cups, and ate dripping melon slices with the spinach, while Friar Tuck made faces over his cigar.

It was always interesting to me how consumption of food of any kind at any time would start a conversation about beef-steaks. There was no limit to the variations that a discussion of steaks could take; endless consideration went into that eagerly anticipated event in the dim future—the first steak order when you got back in the good old U.S.A.

"Just pass a match under mine and hand it to me," said Harry Morris.

"I'll take mine medium with French-fried onions," was "Suitcase Simpson's" vote.

"I'll have to put a piece of mud on the edge of the plate and eat it like mustard," said Joe Deutschle.

"I'm going to order a sirloin four inches thick, with a piece of Spam on the side, and I'll just put that Spam on the floor and say, 'To hell with you,'" said Major Arrasmith.

Four-inch steaks and eggs with shells on them had become symbols of home.

Major Bill Arrasmith had many observations on the egg situation. "Funny thing," he remarked. "In Africa we could buy quantities of eggs. In Italy we can't buy eggs but we can get all the chickens we want. How did all the eggs get over there and all the chickens here? Who separated them?"

Major William Strudwick Arrasmith was a great hearty fellow. In civilian life he had been an architect for most of the Greyhound Bus Stations throughout the country; now he served as Corps Planning Officer. "Arrow" came, he told me, from "the South, where men are men and women are oh, so happy about it."

It was a lot of fun to be with the engineers. They had great *esprit de corps* and worked together like brothers. The combat engineers enjoy enormous prestige in the Army; in the unwritten social ledger they are rated close to pilots as glamour boys. This prestige is a deserved tribute to their constant readiness to pave the way for infantry troops and artillery, no matter how hazardous the advance. Like all men in dangerous professions, they joked about it. During a break-through, they told me, "Jerry just sits up there and watches, and then aims at the one man who has a castle on his collar."

They had had their hands full during the recent floods, with banks and piers being washed away overnight, and the river changing its course every time the water rose. "We had a hard time," they said, "keeping the Volturno twisted around so it would go under our bridges."

"You know, those bridge parts by the time they get them shipped over here are worth more than their weight in gold," the engineers told me, "and they are very heavy."

And they let me in on their latest joke on themselves. It was about a span which hung in lonely grandeur across one of the wildest mountain gorges. No wheels would roll over it; no highway connected it with the world. It would hang there like a monument forever. When our troops made their first advance through these mountains, the engineers had thrown together a series of temporary bridges, which served to rush supplies over the gorges until a permanent road was opened. Then the front lines changed, and new bridges were needed in a hurry in forward areas, so they removed the chain, working from each end. When this job was done, they found one span left in the middle. It was impossible to move it; in fact, no one could reach it. "It's going to be there for a good long time," they chuckled, "so we named it The Engineers' Memorial Bridge."

It was bedtime, and the engineers went out to climb their muddy hill to their tents, and I went up to my cell. I had just arrived when there was a knock on the door. It was one of the draftsmen, an avid camera enthusiast, who volunteered each night for the kindest deed he could have done: he called for my boots and leggings, always unbelievably weighted down with mud, and had them washed and dried by morning.

Then Colonel Tommy knocked. He had come to perform his

last item on the day's agenda: to escort me as usual to the cave of plumbing, make sure it was clear of monks, and mount guard outside the door till I emerged from the murky depths. Then he saw me to my cell, said good night, and went back up the hill.

It was only during my last day at that station that I learned the enlisted personnel had somehow found out all about the Colonel's little chaperoning trips and were taking a delighted interest in these unprecedented activities of their commanding officer. During this ritual, anyone who asked for the CO was given the gleeful reply: "The Colonel's doing latrine duty."

As I climbed into my narrow cot, the walls of my equally narrow cell reverberated to the confused voices of the guns outside. Always I have been an incurable reader in bed; even war could not break me of the habit. Obeying the blackout, I made a kind of tent of my blankets, and in approved boarding-school fashion read under the covers by flashlight. My book was an appropriate one. Someone had given me a weighty volume called *The Tools of War*, by James R. Newman, which dealt with the development of firearms, siegecraft, and fortifications from the beginning of recorded history. It traveled with me throughout the Italian campaign until it became as worn as an old coat.

So, hunched under the covers, I tried to catch up on some of those things which girls are not brought up to know about guns. I read up on range and elevation capacity, muzzle velocity, and recoil mechanisms of rifles and howitzers, of 105's and 155's, while those same 105's and 155's carried on their barking and stamping and roaring through the night.

When finally the text became unintelligible to me, I switched off my light and lay watching the square of window blaze up and fade with each clatter of guns. It was a good deal like trying to sleep over a noisy street crossing in the corner room of a cheap hotel. With the artillery flashing on and off like a neon sign outside my window, I had to put my head back under the covers again before I could drop off to sleep.

CHAPTER 8

Salt of the Earth

"IT WON'T hurt much longer, Buddy," Lieutenant Colonel Sanger was saying as he adjusted the tube in the throat of the soldier who lay on the litter. Corporal Padgitt and I paused with the cameras near the operating table. We had come up from Naples to do a series on the work of the Medical Corps, which was one of the many varied activities coming under the Army Service Forces. The Corporal and I stood there watching the gentle and skillful movements of the surgeon, working on a boy who had been drowning in his own blood.

Colonel Sanger glanced up for an instant from his work. "Go right ahead and take pictures if you want to," he said. "It's not a pretty sight, but war is no pink tea party. It's important for people back home to have a chance to see what things over here are really like."

I found it hard at first to take photographs in the face of so much suffering, but with the operating surgeon so absorbed in his work, it became increasingly easier for me to become equally absorbed in mine. I realized that people at home wanted to know what their boys were going through. They had a right to know, and it was my assignment to portray the reality of war as I found it.

The soldier on the operating table had been brought in earlier that morning with a hole in his throat and chest and a wound in his stomach, caused when a shell had smashed into a stony ledge on Mt. Maggiore, flinging fragments behind a rock where he and his companions were snatching a little sleep.

To keep the boy from smothering, Colonel Sanger was siphoning out the blood from the lungs through a metal tracheotomy tube, and the soldier's own blood was being returned to him through intravenous injection. An additional injection needle carried plasma into his system.

The windpipe had been broken and the boy was breathing through the hole in his throat. As I started taking photographs, Colonel Sanger began probing through the same hole to patch up the tear in the boy's chest. At the foot of the litter, a cluster of white-capped, white-gowned surgical assistants incongruously wearing muddy boots leaned over the white-draped patient. They were removing a slug of steel from the small intestines and closing the rent in his abdomen.

"What causes that puffy look in his face?" I asked.

"That's due to the air that kept escaping when his windpipe was broken," the surgeon explained. "The air kept infiltrating under the skin during the whole time he was being transported back to the hospital."

That process of transportation had taken less than five hours. Because of the enormously shortened time which elapses between the time a man is wounded and the time he reaches the operating table many lives which would have been lost in the last war are being saved today. Evacuation and field hospitals are closer to the front than they have ever been before in the history of the American Army.

I noticed that a card, like a baggage check, was attached to the patient's arm and gave the detailed history of his trip to the hospital. It was at 3:15 in the morning that he was picked up by a couple of medical-aid stretcher-bearers who sprinkled sulfa on his wounds. It must have been a slippery trip for them carrying this boy on a litter down the rocky slopes of Mt. Maggiore, but by a quarter after five they made it to the medical-aid station situated in a cross-shaped trench at the foot of the mountain.

There the soldier was given plasma and morphine injections, and continued his bumpy way in a Medical Corps jeep. At 6:30, he was driven to a group of ambulances camouflaged under nets slung among the ruins of a stable. In one of these ambulances he continued his rough trip to the clearing station. At a quarter to seven he was carried into the receiving tent of the evacuation hospital, from there he was taken to the shock tent where he was given more plasma, from there to the X-ray room where photographs were made of his wounds, and from there the patient and the dripping X-ray negatives were carried to the operating tent.

By 8:12 Colonel Sanger had read the story which the still wet pictures had to tell, and begun the delicate task of pumping out the lungs to keep the boy from drowning in the leakage of his own blood.

The patient was moving his lips a little now but making no sound. Colonel Sanger, realizing that the boy wanted to talk and was finding it impossible because of the air escaping from the broken windpipe, placed his fingers over the hole in the trachea and said, "Try to talk now, Son." We heard the boy murmur feebly, "I'm thirsty." "That's fine, Buddy," said Colonel Sanger. "See, you can speak now."

He took a small sponge and laid it on the boy's lips to moisten them. Because of the stomach wound, I knew they could not give him water. With a look of great tenderness, as though he were teaching something to a child, the Colonel took the soldier's hand and gently placed it over the opening in his throat, thus forcing the air up against the larynx so the boy would be able to speak.

After several feeble tries, he found he could do it himself. It seemed to me that an expression almost of happiness came into the puffy face. The lad felt so much less helpless when he knew he could talk. To learn he could speak after all did a great deal to relieve the growing dread he must have felt before he discovered the extent of his wounds.

The Colonel was so absorbed and so earnest. It meant so much to him each time that boy managed to utter a feeble word. "Will he ever be normal again?" I asked. "Oh, yes, he'll recover all right. He'll be as good as new," said the Colonel.

Lieutenant Colonel Paul W. Sanger is one of the best thoracic surgeons in the Army. He is thirty-seven years old, has a narrow handsome face with precisely chiseled features, and a mind as sharp as his own surgical instruments. Dr. Sanger had been an instructor in surgery at Duke University Hospital for six years and it was during the time he was practicing in Charlotte, N.C., that the war broke out.

He was sharing an office with a brain surgeon, Dr. William R. Pitts, and he and Pitts, together with other surgeons from Charlotte, decided to volunteer as a unit for service in the American armed forces. It happened that General George Marshall was passing through Charlotte and Dr. Sanger broached the subject. It was with the blessing of General Marshall that the surgeons from Charlotte gathered up medical men and nurses from both the Carolinas and near-by regions. This group later became incorporated into the 38th Evacuation Hospital.

When they pitched their hundred tents and set up their 750 beds close behind Mignano, near the ridge of hills bordering Cassino Valley, the hospital had a staff of approximately three hundred. Since the officers, both nurses and doctors, were Southerners, and most of the enlisted personnel came from Pennsylvania and New York State, some wag put up a sign reading "Mason & Dixon Line" between the nurses' and enlisted men's tent areas.

The "38th Evac" had been in the field since D Day plus one in Africa, they had followed our Army through Sicily, and by the time I saw them in Italy they had become experts at adapting themselves to the most rigorous conditions. They had carried their own water pipes, their own water-storage tank, and their generator for light and power through these many months of war. Later, when they were to move on to Anzio, they picked up and relaid these pipes once more.

The surgeons had learned how to pitch their tents to suit the lay of the land each time they met a new set of field conditions. Their orthopedic surgeon, Captain Robert Augustine—who had worked from the tropics to the Arctic, in South America and in Alaska—plotted out each new hospital area so that patients could travel in a continuous line from receiving tent through shock ward, through X-ray into the operating tent at the front end and out the back tent flaps into a convalescent ward.

The nurses had learned to build small dams and mudbanks to keep their tent floors from flooding in the rain. They knew how to tighten their tent pegs to keep their shelters from sailing away in windstorms, and how to loosen their tent ropes again when the tentage dried out in the sun and shrank.

They had raised the process of bathing in a helmet to a high science. The helmet rests on an empty ration can so that it doesn't start tipping over when you get the water nice and soapy. You keep on your galoshes until you get down to the feet. Your tentmate helps you scrub your back.

The nurses gather up extra comforts for tent furnishings as they travel. Those I saw ranged from straw rugs which the girls purchased from the Arabs in Tunis to a gilt-edged, full-length mirror which they salvaged from a bombed palace they passed on their journey forward through Italy.

When I encountered the unit at their location by the side of Highway Six, First Lieutenant Hallie Almond was in charge of the sixty nurses. Pale eyes and pale hair gave her a look of fragility in sharp contrast to the rugged life for which she had volunteered. I saw Lieutenant Almond first when she was pushing her way out of a tent, carrying several pairs of mud-caked galoshes.

"I thought the girls might feel better if I washed off their boots for them. They have been crying."

"Why are they crying?" I asked.

"I wish I knew," she said. "They never answer me when I ask. It's a fatigue neurosis. They just can't help it, living in the mud and taking the same thing every day; but I have noticed that they only cry when the work is lightest. The minute we get a flow of badly wounded patients, they are back on their feet, smiling and telling little jokes to make the boys feel better. I'm trying to arrange some trips for them so that they can go to Naples to see the sights. Maybe some of them can get to Capri once in a while, or at least get to a dance or a movie now and then."

Naples was only two hours' drive away, and the Orange Club was its Mecca. I was always delighted when I recognized girls I had photographed leaning over hospital tables and tending desperately wounded soldiers, laughing and dancing like any bunch of nice American girls off for a good time. Such a transformation! It was hard to believe these were the same girls, jitterbugging around the crowded dance floor. It meant just as much to the nurses as to the soldiers to have this brief holiday from war.

These nurses surely earned the rare dances and movies. During the heaviest day of battle casualties, their hospital received 238 cases. It was a light day that produced as few as seventy. Often it was regular procedure for the nurses, doctors, and technicians to work the clock around with the nine operating tables occupied at all times.

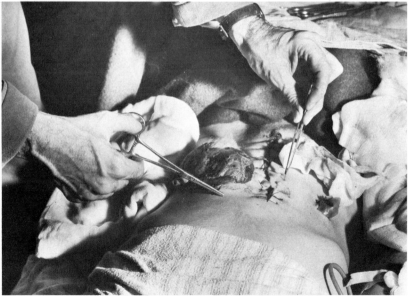

Above: Chinese war orphans, Chungking, China, June 1941.
Margaret Bourke-White, LIFE Magazine © 1941, Time Inc.
Below: Pvt. J.G.'s abdominal operation, Italy, 1943.
Margaret Bourke-White, LIFE Magazine © 1944, Time Inc.

Above: Shooting a Long Tom cannon, Italy, 1944.
Margaret Bourke-White, LIFE Magazine © 1944, Time Inc.
Below: Tattooed skin, Buchenwald, 1945.
Margaret Bourke-White, LIFE Magazine © 1980, Time Inc.

Above: Wurzburg, Germany, 1945,
Below: American infantrymen line up for chow, Italy, 1943

Above: German butcher and his wife, Berlin, 1945.
Below: Margaret Bourke-White, Naples Harbour, 1943.

Above: German pilot POW in Russia, 1941.
Margaret Bourke-White, LIFE Magazine © *1941, Time Inc.*
Below: Russians sitting in the Park of Culture and Rest,
billboard showing removal of incendiary device, Moscow, 1941.
Margaret Bourke-White, LIFE Magazine © *1941, Time Inc*

Above: Night Raid on the Kremlin, Moscow, 1941.
Margaret Bourke-White, LIFE Magazine © 1983, Time Inc.
Below: The Germans from Weimar whom Patton ordered to tour
Buchenwald, 1945.

Above: Alfried Krupp, Essen, 1945.
Below: Soldiers recuperating at military hospital, Italy, 1949.

Above: Margaret Bourke-White autographing a bomb, England, 1942.
Below: Margaret Bourke-White dressed up for her first bombing mission, North Africa, 1943.

The difficulties of the Medical Corps were increased many times by the Italian mud. The mud did much more than merely make matters inconvenient for them. It greatly increased the hazards of infection.

When our soldiers left North Africa for Italy, they met a new hazard, the danger of gas gangrene. The soil of Africa had been little touched by agriculture; but in Italy, the earth for generations had been fertilized with animal and human waste. Thus any foreign matter in a wound could give rise to the most serious infection.

To check this, drastic measures often had to be taken, such as the swift amputation of an arm or a leg. Surgeons were frequently faced with what is always a dreadful decision—to take the chance and treat a mangled leg, or to amputate. "In a gas-gangrene case, they are dead or on the mend within twenty-four hours," one of the surgeons told me. Antitetanus injections, given when the boys were picked up on the field, helped to combat the danger of infection.

Sulfa has proved invaluable. One of the first things the litter-bearer does when he picks up a wounded soldier on the battlefield is to scatter sulfa powder on the wounds. The soldiers themselves are issued both the powder and sulfa pills; many a wounded man has saved his own life when help was delayed in getting to him.

I was discussing this with Colonel Sanger and I was amazed to hear him say, "The boys, of course, are supposed to take sulfa pills by mouth as soon as they're wounded, but often they don't have any with them."

"Why don't they have them?" I asked.

"Because frequently they have already taken them surreptitiously," the Colonel replied.

"What do you mean, surreptitiously?" I inquired.

"The boys discovered very early in the war that it was a good idea to take their sulfa pills when they were afraid of gonorrhea, so they often get caught on the battlefield without them.

"Between sulfa and plasma," Colonel Sanger continued, "this is a very different war from the last one. Let me show you a case that has just come into the shock tent. We're fighting to keep him alive with plasma."

On a litter propped up on wooden sawhorses under the

slanting tent walls was a soldier with a shattered pelvis. He was surrounded by nurses and ward boys who were inserting an injection needle connected by a rubber tube to the amber-colored plasma bottle suspended above the patient's head. His face was cold and clammy and so pale that all blood seemed to have drained from him. This was almost literally the case.

"He has lost so much blood," said Colonel Sanger, "that even his wounds have stopped bleeding. It's what we call peripheral circulatory failure. There actually is not enough blood left to circulate through his veins and arteries. He is in a state of acute shock. This is a very close case; but he may live, and if he does, he will have plasma to thank for saving his life."

We went on into one of the convalescent wards and stopped by the side of a patient who was recuperating from ten hours on the operating table, during which he had been given six units of plasma and six units of whole blood. To feed him, Nurse Deborah De Shaw of Brooklyn was injecting a glucose solution into his veins. This soldier had received numerous intestinal wounds from the penetration of shell fragments from an air burst.

When the healing process was completed, he would have a few inches less of the amount of equipment which is allotted to the average human being, but he would heal and probably function quite normally for the rest of his life. In the meantime, his convalescence was painful.

He was still delirious. "Stop, that's enough," he kept telling the nurse, trying to shake himself free from the injection needle which was feeding him with glucose. She held his arm still and supported the needle steady. "That hurts," he murmured.

It touched my heart to see this soldier in such pain. I found it very hard to maintain a professional cameraman's attitude, but I tried to keep on working as well as I could. His discomfort would not last much longer, the doctors told me, as the healing was progressing satisfactorily.

The whole process seemed miraculous to me. The surgeons had performed an unusual operation on the boy and were justly proud of the results. Major Pat Imes of Louisville, Kentucky, stopped by and spoke to me in the midst of my work, repeating what Colonel Sanger had already said to me.

"I'm glad you're photographing some of these cases," he said. "They won't look very pretty to the folks back home, but we feel that there has been too much sugar-coating of this hospital business. We think the people back in the States should realize what their boys are going through." Colonel Sanger heartily endorsed the importance of carrying back a true picture of the realities of war, and we tiptoed out of the ward to another tent where he could show me some more cases.

He led me next to a boy who had lost half his upper lip. "He'll be all right, too," said Colonel Sanger. "That boy has a better chance than a lot of cases that come in. You see, we're born with more mouth than we really need. He has enough lip tissue left to do a good patchwork job."

We passed another patient at the end of the convalescent ward who was recuperating from leg and arm fractures. "He ate twelve pancakes when they brought him in two days ago," said Colonel Sanger. "He was the hungriest patient we ever had. All he said when we put him on the operating table was, 'I got the no-food cramps.'

"It's amazing how much good even a hot drink does when they are carried in here wondering if they are going to die. Simply washing his face does a lot for a lad when he is feeling pretty low. Then he sees a woman and knows that war can't be so bad if there are women nurses there. A little of that 'Eve' stuff does a lot of good for those boys when they are brought in from the front."

Padgitt picked up the photographic gear and we pushed our way out under the tent flaps and heard the chaplain starting up his victrola. Making our way through the mud, we passed a small grim pile of amputated legs which a ward attendant was covering with a piece of canvas. As we hurried on, the chaplain's music still reached us clearly. He was playing *Ah, Sweet Mystery of Life.*

Inside the operating tent, I found Major Pitts stooped over a soldier so completely covered with surgical drapes that nothing but a section of skull was visible. He had been given local anesthesia. Major Pitts was probing through a small hole into the soldier's brain.

As I worked, taking progress photographs, I watched the Major draw out thirteen splinters of bone that a shell blast had driven into the brain. The largest fragment was one inch long and half an inch wide. When he finally drew out the last and deepest piece, which lay two inches beneath the surface of the brain, exactly one hour had passed.

"Can he possibly live through all that?" I questioned.

"He has about a fifty-fifty chance," said the Major, "but he may be paralyzed." The soldier's right foot had been completely blown off, but the leg operation had to wait until the more essential work on the brain was completed. As always in the serious cases, an amber-colored plasma bottle hung above the operating table, and plasma was flowing through a rubber tube into his veins, to ward off shock.

After Major Pitts had worked to coagulate the blood, by means of an electric current, he was ready to repair the covering of the brain. To do this, he borrowed a piece of the temporal muscle from the side of the boy's own head, and the wound was closed.

I was astonished the next day to find that the brain patient was able to carry on a normal conversation with me. "How do you feel?" I asked.

"I feel better than I did the time I had my tooth knocked out playing baseball," he said. He smiled a one-sided smile at the Major and me. "That was the time I got my gold tooth," he added.

I questioned him about the type of work he had done before he entered the Army. Ironically, he had worked in a TNT plant.

"I bet you didn't know you were having your picture taken," I said.

"Yes, I did," he said. "I could tell that someone was flashing lights in my face." It seemed a little late to apologize for disturbing someone having his brain operated on, but needless to say, I did apologize—and very humbly, too. I had had no idea he was aware of what was going on around him.

Major Pitts was delighted with the progress the soldier was making and assured me that his recovery would be almost complete, that probably the only remaining trace of the paralysis would be a slightly crooked smile.

The next day I happened to be working up at the front lines, forward of the evacuation hospital. It had been a rough day with shells whooshing into the hillsides and whistling over the roads. When I returned to the hospital to spend the night, I was greeted with, "We expected to see you about now, but we thought they would be bringing you in on a stretcher."

"What made you think so?" I asked.

"They brought in another war correspondent a few hours ago."

I was led to the bedside of Richard Tregaskis, author of *Guadalcanal Diary*. He had been brought in with a skull wound which was almost identical to the one I had photographed, and he had been operated on by the same surgeon.

The skillful Major Pitts had drawn eight bone splinters out of the journalist's brain, and Tregaskis was doing very well indeed, but he doubtless owed his life to the speed with which he had been brought to the operating table. It was less than five hours after he had been wounded, while storming a mountaintop with the Rangers, until he was brought into the receiving ward of the hospital.

"I suppose you don't have to be six foot six to reach up and stop a shell," I told him, "but probably it helps."

"The thing that helped him the most," said Major Pitts, "is the fact that he has a scalp like a bulldog—all corrugated. It made a sweet closing, sort of fell together."

It was less than two months later that Tregaskis and I both left from the same North African airport. We were flying back to the United States. He had made a remarkable recovery and was wearing only a small bandage, about two inches across. "They're going to give me a nice silver plate to wear when I get home," he said. "Maybe you'll autograph it for me."

"What would be the use?" I replied. "Who is tall enough to read anything written on the top of your head?"

Among a group of battle-hardy correspondents, Dick was one of the bravest I knew. Newspapermen are not compelled to go storming mountaintops with Rangers. With Tregaskis, that inner desire to do truly firsthand reporting burned deep and clear.

Richard Tregaskis was one of the many patients who were evacuated by air. Many were moved in hospital ships.

The last thirty miles the patient traveled in Italy, before being transported away from the war zone by sea or air, was made in a hospital train. This was no ordinary train. There were many difficult problems for our engineers to conquer before that train could be set in motion.

First the entire length of track was repaired. Having seen from the air how every tie had been systematically cracked in two, I was able to understand the size of this job. In addition, every rail had been conscientiously broken by means of baby bombs the size of tomato cans placed at thirty-foot intervals.

Next—in all parts of southern Italy—first-, second-, and third-class coaches were gathered in from where they lay among the railroad wreckage the Germans had left behind them. The insides of the cars were stripped, and bunks for patients were built in. Leaky roofs were mended, broken wheels replaced, and shattered windows reglazed.

The reglazing presented difficulties. The engineers had lifted out unbroken panes of window glass wherever they were fortunate enough to find them in bombed buildings and houses, but they had no glass cutters to reduce the windowpanes to proper size. The problem was solved by going to local jewelers and borrowing diamonds with which to cut out new windows for the train.

The hospital train carried 350 patients a day and had a staff of six nurses, four doctors, four cooks, and twenty-nine enlisted men. It started from the Naples railroad yards every morning, gathered a load of wounded by noon, and by midafternoon it had brought them back to Naples, where they were either loaded on planes, swung up in their litters to a hospital ship, or carried to one of the large base hospitals for further recuperation.

The nurses, along with the hospital train staff, had their living quarters right on the train.

The train was actually a hospital on wheels, equipped to handle any medical emergency. The patients traveled in three decks of bunks graduated according to the severity of their wounds, with the most serious cases at the bottom.

It was a welcome sight to the boys to see a flock of pretty Red Cross girls come through the train, passing out candy, cigarettes, and copies of *The Stars and Stripes*. More than one GI was heard to say, "How long has this been going on?" En route they were given hot mess, but their greatest thrill was the discovery that for the first time in many months they found themselves between clean white sheets.

After traveling with the wounded on the hospital train, and recording their journey as far as the deck of the hospital ship which would carry them home, the Corporal and I started frontward again to photograph one of the small, compact field hospitals located directly behind the fighting lines.

During all this work with the wounded, Padgitt had been even more uncommunicative than usual. I thought I knew why. For I found myself deeply moved by what I had seen, by the care our Army takes of its soldiers, and by the immensity of the sacrifices made by so many of our fighting men. As citizens of America, I thought, the many of us who are not called upon to fight must be deserving of this contribution which has been made for us.

The Corporal evidently was thinking along the same lines because unexpectedly he volunteered: "If there's anybody back in America that don't realize what these guys are going through, well, all I say is they should go to the back door to cash their pay checks."

We drove on in silence for several miles, and then he went on, "Those boys we saw that lost a leg or an arm, you don't hear none of them complaining. I suppose they know how near they came to losing their lives. That's all part of the old war game and is to be expected.

"What gets me is there's plenty of us guys that get three hot meals every day, and happen to do a lot of our duties way back out of shell range. Us guys will go home as heroes. Plenty of those guys up front who do go home will go home as 'just another cripple.'"

Ahead of us, marking a muddy lane leading off from the right side of the highway, was a sign: 11TH. FIELD HOSP. RECEIVING. Padgitt swung the jeep into it, trying to avoid ruts cut as sharp as canyons, and as he cautiously piloted the jeep forward, he remarked, "That's one reason I'm glad to get the chance to work up forward with you, Peggy. You can't fool the public in pictures. And people should be shown just what those boys do to become a cripple."

CHAPTER 9

Fifth Army Field Hospital

Nurse Betty Cook was applying a coat of polish to her nails as carefully as though she were going to a party. Actually she was about to keep a date with a semiconscious boy who had a spray of shrapnel in his chest and face and had lost his left foot. She made an incongruous but pretty picture sitting on her bunk in her striped seersucker hospital dress and high muddy boots, her gentle oval face framed by soft dark hair.

"It's so nice to have a little scented soap and a bottle of nail polish out here," she said. "Yesterday when I was working with the Major, preparing for that traumatic amputation case, I was afraid he was going to scold me about my nails, but he only said, 'It looks good to see a woman with red-painted fingernails again.' "

Cordelia Elizabeth Cook, twenty-four-year-old Kentuckian, was one of ten surgical nurses in the 11th Field Hospital. These girls were working closer to the battle line than American women had ever worked before in this or any other war. Our troops, at this time, were fighting their way through the lowlands of Cassino corridor, and these ten nurses were stationed actually ahead of our own heavy guns. A short stroll in the wrong direction would bring one right into German territory.

This advanced position of the field hospital made it possible to save many of those desperately serious cases inevitably lost in the last war. Here the worst brain, chest, and abdominal cases, which could not stand the long trip to the rear, were taken off the ambulances and given immediate definitive surgery. The evening I arrived with Padgitt, two soldiers had been brought to the hospital within the same hour they were wounded. When strong enough, the patients would be moved back another five miles to the larger evacuation hospital.

The field hospital, marked with its red-painted crosses, was itself laid out in the form of a large cross whose arms were formed of big, continuous wall tents. A wounded soldier entering through the receiving ward could run the whole gamut of treatment without being carried out-of-doors. Near this central cross of canvas were the mess tent and clusters of smaller tents used as the staff's living quarters.

Towering above this small encampment on a mountain peak six miles away was a German observation post. From this height the Germans could survey a fifteen-mile length of Highway Six. If they turned their binoculars southeastward they looked down right into our little tent cluster; northwestward they overlooked Purple Heart Valley.

Whenever the girls had time to glance toward Jerry's mountaintop, they could watch columns of smoke rising from our shell hits, where we were attempting to blast the enemy out of his stubbornly held vantage point. The nurses were learning to ignore the deafening staccato of our guns during the day, but they could never grow accustomed to the way their beds trembled all through the night. Ours and the enemy's artillery crashed back and forth at each other, the two-way traffic of shells passing directly overhead.

Bedtime for the day staff came early in the blacked-out field hospital. I had arrived with Corporal Padgitt at dusk, which, during those winter months, came at five-thirty. The Corporal had gone off to find quarters in the enlisted men's area, and I went to a tent with five of the nurses, where I was to spend the night. It was only seven when blonde little Lieutenant Frances Mosher, of South Bend, Indiana, a coat thrown over her pajamas, stoked up the primitive little wood stove in the center of the muddy floor and heated bath water in an empty apple-butter can. Lieutenant Elsie Nichols began bathing in her helmet, finishing off her feet methodically with foot powder.

Nicky was from Melrose, Massachusetts, a good-natured girl, a bit on the plump side. "One of the first things you learn on this job," she explained to me, "is that even if you don't have time for anything else, you have to take care of your feet."

Tall, slender Lieutenant Ruth Hindman, her blonde hair glistening with rain, burst through the tent flaps. "The whole

Volturno is running through our powder room," she said. "We'll have to get out our shovels and deepen that irrigation ditch in the morning."

"That little floating tent you call a powder room is the most forlorn bit of architecture I've ever seen," I commented.

"Oh, it's so much nicer than the slit trench we used to have," replied Ruthie.

Ruthie Hindman was from Johnstown, Pennsylvania, and was one of those generous women who are always cooking something for somebody. She started making cocoa in a plasma can—not mixing cocoa with plasma, to be sure; but in a hospital there are a thousand uses for cast-off plasma cans. The cocoa had just come to a boil when there was a sound like a rising wind rushing out of the mountain toward us.

"Is that theirs or ours?" cried Nicky.

"Theirs," shouted Ruthie.

And instantly all that remained visible of the nurses were four pairs of legs sticking out from under the cots. By the time I had followed their example the sound had reached tornado proportions, when it suddenly came to an end in an abrupt thud.

"That's the first time they've ever aimed at the hospital," exclaimed Nicky, as the girls pulled themselves to their feet.

"Don't worry, honey, that was just a stray one," said Ruthie. "They're not after us; they're trying to knock out those guns beyond us. They aren't going to keep it up."

"There it comes again," shouted Fran, and we fell flat on our faces while a new sound carved a screaming path toward us until all sounds were lost in the deafening roar. It seemed as though the earth would never stop pelting against the tent walls, but at last it was over and we crawled to our feet. The lights had gone, but finally one of the girls found a flashlight and when she switched it on I remember noticing that three C-ration cans had blown through the door of the tent and wedged beween a couple of my camera cases.

Then I heard a voice from outside, "You all right, Peggy?" It was Padgitt, and with his help I gathered up some camera equipment and we started out into the darkness. Thirty feet from the tent we were stopped by a tangle of waist-high wires. This was why the lights had gone: the camp's improvised electrical circuit had been strung through the mess tent, adjoining the nurses' quarters.

The Corporal put on his flash, carefully dimming its beam with his hands, and we found that there was no more mess tent. We were standing on the brink of a neat, round shell hole, and strewn about were cans of rations, onions, benches, stoves flung in all directions, and slashed lengths of tent canvas. The CO, Major Bonham, was poking around the ruins, deeply relieved to find that no one was caught under the debris. Three of the hospital staff had been wounded by shrapnel, he told me. It seemed a miracle that no one had been killed, with the shell falling within less than fifteen yards of the operating tent. The mess sergeant had just stepped out of the tent flaps to get gasoline for his cookstove, and had been blown five yards off his feet. He landed on his face very much surprised, but not at all hurt. Ten minutes later the night staff of thirty-two would have been in the mess tent for coffee and pancakes.

Stumbling over wreckage to the hospital tent, Padgitt and I found the shock ward a gloomy cavern with no electric light. Over each litter hung a small knot of medics in muddy boots, and wearing helmets, diagnosing wounds with only the illumination furnished by their GI flashlights.

The largest group were leaning over a soldier whose thighs had been practically amputated by a high explosive shell. Only raw strips of flesh and skin held the legs to the mangled body, and his right forearm had compound fractures of both bones. The boy's lacerated face was only partially visible under the oxygen mask; from twin bottles, mounted on a standard over his litter, both plasma and whole blood flowed into his veins.

The clay-colored lips, ringed by the oxygen mask, started moving, and Nurse Wilma Barnes leaned over to listen.

"They're taking my blood," whispered the soldier.

"No, Clarence, they're not taking your blood," she said, "they're giving you something to make you stronger."

"Do you learn all their first names?" I asked.

"Always when they come from Texas," replied Wilma Barnes, who was a handsome, black-haired girl from Abilene. "The doctors just automatically call me every time they get a patient from Texas. It makes the boys pep up to know somebody from their home state is taking care of them."

It happened that the greater number of boys being brought in that night were from Texas, since the fiercest of the fighting at that time, on the outskirts of Cassino, was being carried on by the famous 36th Division, largely composed of Texans.

We had thought that first salvo of shells was an accident, but it was only the first of many that screamed over our hospital all through the night. Sometimes every few minutes, and often every few seconds, a warning whistle would sound overhead, and the entire hospital staff—accompanied by the Corporal and myself—would fall flat to the ground. But as soon as that shell landed, the surgeons, nurses, and ward attendants would rise instantly to their feet and continue their work of taking care of the wounded. There was so much changing and disinfecting of rubber gloves, so much sterilizing of instruments, that a vacant cot next to Clarence's litter filled up completely with gear.

Clarence had lost so much blood that the doctors were giving him whole blood and plasma in both wrists instead of one. They were fighting hard to sustain him through his state of acute shock, until he had rallied enough to be operated on.

The chief surgeon was applying a wire tourniquet around his torn thighs when a whooshlike sound swept over, closer than the rest. "Cross your fingers that it holds," he said as we all hit the dirt.

We had just regained our feet when a particularly loud scream came piercing toward us and we all fell flat. I noticed that Wilma, before she dropped down, took time to check the position of the blood and plasma needles in the boy's wrists. I heard her say, "Hold your arm still, Clarence," and she lay down on the ground beside his cot.

The instant we heard the bang of the exploding shell, Wilma was the first person back on her feet, making sure those transfusion needles had not been jarred out of place.

I remember thinking that it was a privilege to be with people like that.

As we all got off the muddy ground again, one of the surgeons commented, "Just a wee bit different from pounding the marble floors of a big hospital."

"Buy me a one-way ticket to New York," remarked one of the ward boys.

Occasionally a naked electric bulb hanging in the center of the tent blazed on as soldiers working in the ruins managed to make a temporary contact. But always before long the electricity failed again, and the surgeons went back to their flashlights.

A small and terrified dog came crawling in under the tent canvas. "Will somebody put Sad Sack out?" ordered Wilma.

The hours crawled on in their grotesque routine. The periodic whoosh overhead; the dive for the floor; up again and on with the work; the constant changing of blood and plasma bottles. Clarence was on his seventh unit of plasma, and 5000 cc.'s of whole blood had flowed into his veins, a record amount for that hospital.

So much blood was being used that night that the supply was running low. Members of the hospital staff began volunteering to give their blood. Then the truck drivers were called in from out-of-doors; they came, a few silent figures at a time, lying down on any available litter to give their pints of blood, and hurrying out again to work. At last the need of blood became so great that the gun crews from the artillery positions up the road came down in rotation, long enough to donate blood and then go back to their job of shelling the German mountain.

Once more Clarence moved his pasty-colored lips and Wilma leaned down to listen. "No, Son," she said in her soft Texas drawl, "you can't have a cigarette yet. Wait just a little while longer."

The little redheaded Commanding Officer, Major Bonham —"Bon for good in the French language and ham, good in any language," he had told me earlier—came up rolling a replacement oxygen tank. "Things are at their worst," he confided, while shifting the tank. "We're almost out of Type A blood. We're running out of blood citrates which we need for all these transfusions, and now the oxygen is giving out."

He checked the dials. "It's not working properly," he said. "There's only one tank left and that's being used in the operating room. We must keep that patient breathing. We'll have to move Clarence in there."

Clarence was without oxygen for four and one-half minutes while the little procession, headed by Major Bonham carrying the twin bottles on their standards, moved through connecting tents into the white-draped operating tent, where Clarence could again be connected with blood, plasma, and oxygen supply. He shared his new oxygen pressure tank with the patient on the operating table, a boy who had been brought in with multiple wounds of face and chest, and with one third of his thigh shot away.

While Clarence was being moved, Padgitt helped me transfer the camera into the operating ward. When he had me installed in the new location he said, "Can you get along without me for half an hour, Peggy?"

"Of course," I replied, but I was secretly a bit surprised, because never before had the Corporal left me during an emergency.

At the end of half an hour Padgitt came back, looking a little pale. It was only later that I found he had given a pint of his blood—his was Type A, the kind they were short of.

Clarence's breathing had grown so shallow by this time that the balloon at the base of his mask, which should inflate with each breath, lay almost flat on his chest. Captain Floyd Taylor (burly, able surgeon from Haskel, Texas, who helped rescue *Time* magazine's Jack Belden on Salerno beach) began pinching the nostrils under the mask and holding his hands over the mouth, trying to force Clarence to breathe deeper.

"He's getting everything for shock that the books have to offer," said Captain Taylor.

Meanwhile Wilma had recognized another Texan on the next table. "How do you feel, Chester?" she inquired.

"Not so good," Chester managed to reply.

The group of helmeted surgeons were now leaning over Chester, debating whether to amputate or try to save his wounded leg, thereby running the risk of gas gangrene. Having decided to try to save Chester's leg, they tied on gauze masks and, still wearing their helmets, began to operate.

It was two in the morning before Chester was moved to the adjoining ward. Meanwhile Clarence had received a total of 6000 cc.'s of blood. He was moving his lips again in their rubber frame, and Captain Taylor tried to catch the words.

"He's asking for watermelon," the Captain explained. "They often ask for their favorite foods when they're near death." Leaning over Clarence, he said, "They're not in season, Son."

"Cover up my feet," Clarence murmured. And then, whispering, "I'm so cold," he died.

I took a last picture of those feet, still in their muddy boots, and with the boy's own rifle strapped between them where it served as a splint for the crushed legs.

The corps men lifted the bloodstained gun away. "Be careful," one of them said, "it may be loaded."

Kindly Captain Taylor bade me good night. "The lad wouldn't have had much left to do with if he had lived," he said, "with both legs and one arm gone."

Wilma and I stumbled home together. Watching death so close before my eyes, I had forgotten the wholesale screaming death being hurled from the mountaintop. The enemy's mountain hung above us silhouetted as though against heat lighting. An occasional brilliant flash threw shadows like those from moonlight across our path.

Back in our tent we found Ruthie, Nicky, and Fran drinking more cocoa. "We just came from Betty's tent," said the girls. "An hour ago she was hit in the elbow by shrapnel, but she had her heavy coat on and the wound isn't serious."

It seemed blessedly normal to be back in the tent chatting with the girls. They were discussing how surprised German prisoners acted to see American nurses so close to the front, and how a captured German officer had said that German nurses do not work within a hundred miles of the lines.*

"It seems to do our boys good to hear a woman's voice," said Ruthie. "When Clarence was brought in today, he said, 'Tell that woman to come over here so we can look at her.'"

"Clarence died," Wilma reported.

"I always get a funny feeling," said Ruthie, "when I have to go through their pockets afterward and take out all the things. So many things they think they've got to have."

"What things?" I asked.

"Always a picture of their girl. That's the first and last thing they'll ask to look at."

I had just voiced a comment on how quiet it had become when the word "quiet" was drowned out by a sound as though

---

* After the opening of the Normandy beachhead, German nurses were found near the front lines.

the whole German mountain was rushing toward us, and we were back under our bunks again waiting for the sweeping terror to spend itself and die.

"I'm going to make my bed right under my cot," said Nicky, dragging all her bedding to the floor and covering her face with her helmet.

A series of short booms and coughs began echoing through the mountains. "Theirs or ours?" asked Nicky.

"Ours," said Frances. "When you hear the whizz first and the thump afterwards, it's theirs; and when you hear the thump first and the echo afterwards, it's ours."

Whizzes, echoes, and thumps began to intermingle so vigorously that our cots rocked. "Are you going to get under the bed?" Nicky called.

"I'm already under it," Ruthie answered.

It wasn't much longer before we had all dragged our blankets down in the mud and all of us stayed under our beds.

"I pity those poor boys up there," said Fran. "Look at us. We've got heat. And all the comforts. Those poor boys in the foxholes can't even put on a pair of dry socks. They can't even build a fire."

Then the noise of the guns drowned out the conversation again. In the next lull Ruthie spoke up. "I got a letter today that burned me up; 'I hope you send me some fine laces from one of those picturesque Italian towns.' Lord, when we get to those towns there's nothing left of them."

"I get letters saying 'Send me some souvenirs; I'll pay for them,'" said Fran. "The only souvenirs we can send are pieces of shrapnel."

I had been searching around during this temporary quiet spell for a safer place to put my cameras. Next to my bunk was a small table crowded underneath with barracks bags. I pushed away the barracks bags and placed my cameras there. Then it occurred to me that the spot I had picked for my cameras would be a good place for me. I had just shoved the cameras out and slid under the table with all my blankets when Jerry started in again.

"I'm really scared," said Nicky.

"Come over and get in bed with me," said Wilma. "Then if we die, we'll die together."

A new sound was growing out of the mountain now. It was like a giant stalking toward us over the hills. Closer and closer the giant feet came until the last three steps crashed around us with the loudest sound I had ever heard.

"It's a creeping barrage," said Ruthie.

"I'm worried about those poor boys in the hospital who are still in shock," said Wilma. "It's so much worse for them, because they can't understand how, if they're really in a hospital, it sounds as though they're still in the field."

"Can they tell?" I asked.

"Oh, yes. They lie there and call out the names of the guns."

The giant feet were marching toward us again, and when the last crash had died away Nicky commented, "It's worse than when they bombed our ship in Salerno Harbor."

"It seems as bad as when our ship caught on fire and those poor British nurses got burned to death and we had to leave in lifeboats," said Nicky.

A throaty reverberation began knocking through the hills. "Theirs or ours?" I asked.

"That's thunder," said the girls. It seemed such a benign sound, and, when the rain started pelting on our tent, I decided that the guns would have to stop. But the gun crews in the mountain had decided otherwise, and the pounding rain only made it more difficult for us to distinguish between their guns and ours.

We didn't know until the next morning that shortly after the beginning of the thunderstorm, two boys were killed across the road.

Hairlines of vivid light flashed under the tent flaps and all the pin-holes in the canvas began winking on and off. It was as though a brilliant torch flickered on and off through a sieve, each flash a burst from the muzzles of our own guns. Our 105's and 155's were booming repeatedly, and the deeper voice of the 240's was roaring out toward the German-held mountain peak.

"You know what I always think of," said Wilma, "every time they bring a boy in? My kid brother—especially if the soldier's about the same age. Doesn't it always remind you of your brother?"

And the girls began worrying about their brothers scattered throughout the various war theaters of the world. I wondered how these brothers would feel if they could see their brave sisters pancaked under their cots while a two-way barrage passed over their heads.

It was just grim waiting the rest of the night until all the crash and booming faded into tangled echoes beating through the hills. But all nights have to end, and finally we staggered stiffly out into a welcome rainy dawn.*

---

* Before the reader starts hunting for the photographs of Clarence and Chester, of Betty Cook and Wilma Barnes, and the other nurses described in this chapter, as well as the ambulance drivers and the exploding ammo dump described in the next, I must explain that due to the hazards of war, this entire group of films was lost in transit from Italy to Washington.

CHAPTER 10

We Move Toward the Front

IN THE morning, all over camp, people began digging trenches in their tents right beside their cots, so that the next time the hospital was shelled they could roll right out of bed into their foxholes. Nicky launched on a particularly ambitious excavation, designed to hold her whole cot and her barracks bag.

We had a stand-up breakfast, handed out from the rear end of a truck which had been rushed up with rations. The hospital's food stocks had been completely blown to pieces— although many of us picked up edible odds and ends that had been blasted into our tents. The truck had brought K rations, which are packed in flat, waterproof cans, each holding enough concentrated food for one person for one meal. We were given our choice of breakfast, dinner, or supper rations. The supper unit contains a can of cheese flavored with bacon, and breakfast and dinner units consist of varying degrees of blended egg yolk with chipped ham or sausage. The truck drivers had picked up a twenty-gallon can of hot coffee on the way, and Ruthie, always efficient on the food end, ladled it out in canteen cups and empty plasma cans.

We stood knee-deep in mud, in the drizzling rain, eating our cold K on crackers, and watching the GIs clear away the remains of the mess tent.

After breakfast I visited Chester in the ward tent. After having left him the night before with his face hidden by an oxygen mask, I did not recognize the spry, smiling patient, smoking a cigarette and talking to anybody who would listen.

"Who are you, and what do you do?" he asked me as I approached. This was a surprise, as usually it was I who did the interrogating, not the patients. Chester's normal occupation, I found, had been driving a bread truck in Texas, and he hoped the war would end as soon as possible so he could get back to his truck and his girl.

Nurse Betty Cook, her pretty face rather white and her wounded left arm in bandages, was back on duty. She was to be awarded the Purple Heart, as the first nurse to be wounded on Italian soil.*

We climbed into a jeep driven by a Medical Corps man with a red cross painted on the front of his helmet. He was going to take us forward to an ambulance relay point where he would pick up a load of wounded to bring back to the clearing station. As our jeep slithered out of the mud-churned hospital area, the sun broke through with that capriciousness so characteristic of Italian winter weather. We slid through steep carved ruts, while the sky swiftly cleared and the sun sparkled on a road as glossy as chocolate lacquer.

We turned into Highway Number Six and headed directly toward the German-held mountain. Jerry's lofty observation point was fog-bound and seemed to be rising from a bowl of milk. Everything was so still, so pure, that it seemed impossible that from this same mountain such hell could have gushed forth the night before.

As we drove toward the front, in this crystalline light, even the signs of war took on a softened character. The tanks and half-tracks and mules, crowded under olive groves so as to be screened from the air, seemed there for some peaceful purpose. The soldiers peeping out of caves and clustered in sheltered ravines might have been resting during a hiking trip planned by a tourist agency. Ancient villages, hanging like fairy castles in the cliffs, took on such magic in the slanting sun that one forgot that every wall was pockmarked and every roof had crashed into rubble. The Italian landscape became a picture-postcard background for war.

Only the road signs brought back the grim reality. Signs which read MINES CLEARED 20 FEET EACH SIDE gave way, as we drove forward, to signs reading WARNING: MINES NOT CLEARED BEYOND ROAD SHOULDERS. I reflected that it would be many

---

* A few weeks later, at Anzio, she became the first woman in the American Army to receive the Bronze Star, "for meritorious service . . . in direct support of combat troops." This made her also the first woman to wear two decorations.

years before Italian mothers could let their children out to play
in the fields without fearing for their lives, or before tourists or
lovers could wander carelessly through the hills.

But even on this tranquil morning, when it seemed there
could be no evil in the world, I kept two cameras open and
ready. My Rolleiflex always hung by a strap around my neck,
so that any sudden flight to a ditch could not separate me from
working equipment. A Speed Graphic with a telephoto lens
rode always on my knees, ready for instantaneous action. As we
drove along, I periodically checked the apertures and shutter
settings to conform to changing light values. If anything happens, it occurs with such speed that the extra second it takes to
open a camera may cost a picture. Both Padgitt and I always
kept our pockets filled with extra film, never knowing when the
rush of events might separate us from the jeep or when we might
come back from a foxhole to find our jeep no longer in existence.

We were driving parallel to a stretch of railroad track where a
squad of road engineers was busy clearing away the broken ties
and rails, transforming this railroad bed into a second highway
which would relieve Number Six of some of the pressure.

We were just crossing a small trestle the engineers had
constructed over the framework of the blown-up railroad
bridge when I saw, rising straight out of the mountaintop ahead
of us, an amazingly tall column shaped like a swiftly growing
poplar tree.

"Stop!" I called to the jeep driver. "I want a picture."

"Hold it!" he said. "Jerry's been aiming at this bridge every
day for a week now. We don't want to be on it when he starts
laying them in again."

By the time we had driven beyond the trestle, the smoke
column had vanished, but soon another, and then another grew
where the last had been. These ghostly poplars were being
planted from our side. We were trying to run Jerry out of his OP
with phosphorus shells. I wondered what it was like up there in
the little caves and foxholes where the Germans were hiding,
with the flaming explosions searing their flesh and setting fire to
their clothes, as the phosphorus from each burst kept running
into their dugouts like hot quicksilver.

Another mile of driving, and we reached an exquisite arch of
ancient masonry which led off Highway Number Six to the

right. A Red Cross flag hung over it, marking an ambulance relay point. Here casualties were brought in jeeps, when they could be reached by road, and in litters when they had to be carried directly down the steep mountainsides, to be relayed by ambulance to hospitals in the rear.

We drove through the archway, still miraculously intact, and behind it, as though it had been a Hollywood false front, we found an old stable laid in ruins. Camouflaged under low-hung nets was a cluster of ambulances. Sitting on the rubble piles was a group of badly shaken boys.

These were Medical Corps men, wearing the characteristic helmet painted with a red cross. They were stationed here on thirty-hour relays, and it was their job to go out in response to telephone calls from the front to bring back the wounded.

This had been a painful morning for them. A jeepful of them had just returned with a grim account of a shell hit that had taken place right before their eyes. While their jeep had escaped by a narrow margin, they had watched that shell land on another medical jeep that was crossing a road junction immediately ahead. In that jeep had been three of their gang, including their major. He had been a popular officer, and the boys took it hard.

Also it was disturbing the way Jerry kept concentrating on that particular road junction. These boys at the relay station had to cross that junction every time a phone call summoned them to the front.

It wasn't so much what the boys had to say as what they didn't say that gave me some insight into the way they felt. One of them kept turning the pages of a comic sheet he had received in the mail from home. Another reread old letters. The others sat doing nothing, and saying next to nothing, merely waiting for that phone call which would send them out to the front, over the road junction where they had lost their major, up to meet the litter-bearers at the battalion aid station, to get their load of wounded.

They didn't have to tell me that they were sitting there figuring out how they could outwit the next shell. I could see it written in their faces. It was like guessing heads or tails. If you speed up and cross that junction a little sooner, will you beat the shell there? Or if you go a little more slowly, will it hit the road before you arrive? And if it comes, is it going to be only a stray? Or will it be the first of a barrage?

You hear a lot of the philosophy, "The one that's got my name on it is the one that's going to get me." But I doubt if there is a soldier at the front who isn't trying to outthink that particular shell with his number on it.

The only way to bear the waiting, to endure the constant dread, is to develop a certain numbness which acts as a protective shell. This happens to the boys who must stay for weeks and sometimes months in the forward foxholes. The world around them becomes unreal. The days slip by with their overcurrent of strain and danger. But the Medical Corps men who are litter-bearers and jeep drivers see such concentrated results of each battle that even this merciful coat of numbness is impossible for them. Every day they carry casualties who are vivid reminders of what flying steel can do to soft human bodies.

Corporal Padgitt and I took pictures of the corps men as they sat there. Finally the boy who was reading his comic sheet glanced up and said, "It's time for mess. We've got all the K rations you want. Help yourselves. We don't get very hungry up here."

And he went back to his comic strips, reading and rereading the same four pages.

Padgitt and I had just finished a unit each of Dinner K and Breakfast K respectively (the Corporal liked the cheese ration —and no amount of danger could harm his appetite—and I always chose the egg-yolk concoction), when we heard a familiar sound rushing out of the mountain. It was that same crashing sequence we knew so well, like giant feet stalking in our direction. The medical boys grabbed us and rushed us into the ruins of the stable, where we lay in the straw as flat as we could.

Blast after blast sounded. As the echoes of each set of explosions died away, a new series of blasts began. We lay there pressed as tight to the ground as we could get. I remember feeling terribly long. Then I tried to figure out whether I would take up less space if I rolled up in a ball. But I made only a brief try at that, because it makes you feel uncomfortably high in the wrong places. Then I debated whether it was better to keep my helmet more over my face or farther over the back of my neck.

I tried to keep from wondering whether the one wall of the stable which was still standing would come crashing down on us. Then I began puzzling stupidly why the explosions kept on like that, one after another, instead of finally dying away as a barrage of shells usually does. I found that the others were wondering, too, and a few of us crept cautiously to the archway to look.

Fringing the road just opposite us was a curtain of rising gray smoke. "Why, they hit our small-arms ammunition dump!" one of the ambulance drivers exclaimed. The blasts we were listening to were from our own ammunition going up in smoke.

Somehow your own shrapnel doesn't seem so bad. The surprise element is lacking. Padgitt helped me set up shop behind a fragment of the ruined wall, handing me filters and extra film packs as I needed them, and we began photographing the scene ahead, framing it in the archway. It was a remarkable sight; we could get the results of enemy and Allied shelling in one picture. In the foreground were the blackish explosions from our ammo dump which the Germans had hit, and above rose the enemy's mountain with our phosphorus bursts still rising in graceful columns from the peak.

Our ammo dump kept on sputtering for an hour and a half, sending up ugly trails of smoke which stained the sky with a yellowish hue. At the same time, a high overcast began drifting over the sun, and with another of those fickle changes of weather a fine drizzle started sifting down.

The eruptions across the road were beginning to die away when the medical boys got a call to send a jeep forward for wounded. This was a good chance for Padgitt and me to hitchhike our way forward too, so we got into the jeep.

We negotiated the crucial junction quite quietly. Already the ever-present road gangs had filled the shell holes with rubble. At the side of the road, in addition to a few jeep fragments, were the twisted frames of two half-tracks and a 6 × 6 truck.

An eighth of a mile beyond the junction, our driver turned off Highway Six into a little byroad. We drove through an exquisite grove of evergreens until we reached a deep rockbound crevasse, where the heavy fir boughs created an artificial twilight. Almost invisible under their draperies of camouflage nets was a group of trailers, trucks, and pyramidal tents. This was a tank destroyer command post, the TD-CP, as the abbreviated terminology of the Army goes.

Our medical jeep dropped us here and went on. It was to continue another mile and a half up a steeply winding road to the cross-shaped foxhole which was the Battalion Aid Station, where it would pick up its load of casualties which had been carried on litters down from the lines. The Corporal hunted up somebody who would hunt for the CO.

The CO of the TD's was what is known as Quite a Character. Within my first ten minutes at the post I heard many stories about how his men had to hold him back, during each advance, to keep him from going in ahead of the infantry. In the eleventh minute I was told how he had captured a German single-handed and brought him back to the CP to interrogate him about German gun positions.

In the twelfth minute I was being introduced to the CO himself, a lively little barrel-shaped man with "old Army colonel" written all over him. It was less than a quarter of an hour before I had heard the CO's own account of what wonderful pioneer work was being done by his beloved tank destroyers.

"We had to make work for ourselves," he said, "figure out new ways for TD's to be useful." Tank destroyers were not mere machines to him. They were trail blazers.

A tank destroyer is not a tank, although to the layman it looks like one. It has armor, and carries a 105-mm. gun, which is used under normal battle conditions for destroying tanks. However, tanks would not be effectively employed by either side until the armies got farther out on the plains. So the TD's were being used as movable gun units.

"I had to figure out something to keep my boys from chewing their nails," the Colonel explained. "Come into the CP and I'll show you on the map."

He took me into the HQ trailer, which was suffocating from the heat of a tiny wood stove, and fitted up like an office, its walls lined with maps.

"We're reversing all the rules in this Italian campaign," he said. "Here we actually have artillery ahead of the infantry."

He pointed to a spot on the map, beyond Mignano, the road

leading toward Cassino. "See that little curve around Highway Six? It took weeks of fighting for us to work our way around that horseshoe. It's still so hot that it would be foolish to bring infantry along it."

He sketched out the front lines for me on the map. "Our artillery combed and searched and crisscrossed all the areas in front of the infantry. And now the troops have spread out into the hills to the right and left. But the horseshoe is being held by our tank destroyers."

I could understand why he was so proud: it was a kind of pioneering to use tank destroyers as mobile gun positions.

"The horseshoe gets so much plastering that we had to bring our TD's around it in the dark. That curve of Six is our most advanced position in the Fifth Army, as of today. At the end of the horseshoe is our most forward TD."

I could see the missionary gleam in his eye.

"My, I'd like to take a picture of that tank destroyer," I said.

"Well, that's really the front, you know," said the Colonel. "Beyond that lies no man's land."

"I've always wanted to take a picture of no man's land," I said, not quite truthfully, because until that moment the idea had never popped into my head.

"We'll see. We'll see," said the Colonel. "I have to go up there, anyway, tomorrow to make sure things are going all right. We'll see how the Heinies are laying them in."

While we were looking at the maps, a major of the armored division had taken down the field telephone which hung on its leather case on the wall of the trailer. Snatches of conversation drifted our way.

"Do you have any report from your forward platoons?" the Major was asking.

"He's getting all the dope from forward so we can make plans for sending out our night patrols," the Colonel explained.

"Here's the thing," the Major was saying. "The Colonel wants you to keep alerted, because last night there were two enemy patrols trying to infiltrate. Be sure to keep your people alerted."

"Ask them, how about artillery?" the Colonel broke in.

"Much stuff being dropped in there?" the Major questioned. "Can you make any guess as to the size of it? Is it direct fire?"

Evidently it was direct fire, for the Major replied, "That's tough!" The boys hate most the direct fire from the German high-velocity guns, for the shell lands before they can hear it scream. It's always the first high-velocity shell that gets some of our men because there is no warning for them to scatter into foxholes.

"Tell them to be prepared to move the battery," the Colonel broke in, and then added, "Tell them to talk to the Time and Space man."*

"The Colonel wants you to talk to the Time and Space man. Austin is the Time and Space man. Well, so long, pal. Be sure to keep us posted if the situation changes any up there."

The Major slipped the telephone back into its case.

I always admired these field telephones, in their smart tan leather cases. You held a button open with your finger while you talked, which snapped the circuit automatically closed when you finished, to conserve the batteries. Someone with imagination had picked the names of the telephone exchanges: words like Lightning, Rapid, Speedy.

"Time to put on the feedbag," said the Colonel, and we went out into the drizzling twilight and filed through a narrow fern-filled gorge to an open tent half which sheltered a board table. Mess was early; it was only five o'clock, but it was important to eat while we still had a little daylight, as we dared not use flashlights under the open canvas.

In the half-darkness several officers were seated around the plank table, laughing heartily. As we entered, I heard just enough of the conversation to know they were retelling the story of the celebrated buck private at Salerno, when they recognized me and stopped abruptly.

"Don't worry," I said, "I've heard that one before."

The tale, which had been gleefully related to me some weeks back by a second lieutenant claiming to be an eyewitness, was about a soldier who landed in the advance wave, and at the end of the first furious hour on the beachhead came up to ask where the prophylactic station was.

---

* The individual who calculates the complex problem of the time required for the specific movement of tank destroyers under existing conditions —"road net," availability of fuel, possible congestion.

For supper we had the usual choice of K: breakfast, dinner, or supper ration. We each took some of all three, making what looked like a cold stew in our mess kits, with the various egg-yolk compounds and baconized cheese, which we ate with the hard crackers that come in the K-ration tins.

During supper I heard more about tanks and tank destroyers. It was the tank boys, I was told, who were really "sweating it out." There had been occasional attempts to bring up tanks where they could be used effectively, like the one I had seen from the air when flying with Captain Marinelli, but the Jerries just sat up in their OP's and blasted them off the road as they came around the bend, like boys at a fair picking off mechanical ducks one at a time.

Our men had quite a time evacuating those tanks. Salvage squads brought them back for repair, but cleaning them out was the worst. "It is not much fun," I was told, "to climb into a tank and find the crew in such little bits you can't recognize them."

There was a good deal more along these lines, and some of it was pretty hard-boiled talk. But I realized that referring to death and wounds in the somewhat whimsical fashion these men frequently adopted did not mean that they had become calloused. On the contrary, each time more of their comrades were lost, they became angrier and more eager to punish the enemy. But the only way to bear the constant presence of danger seemed to be to talk about it lightly.

"I'll never forget the time they brought in those two fellows who had been shooting a bazooka," one of the officers continued. "One of them was hit in his pocket; and he had been carrying around his shaving brush. Did they have a swell time at the hospital picking out all those brush hairs!"

"That's what you call a close shave," contributed the Major, for which he got the razz from the whole table.

From this point the discussion reached that inevitable debate: do you hear the shell that hits you? As long as I traveled in heavy gun circles I was to hear this problem endlessly discussed. It was never solved to everybody's satisfaction, but it usually ended up with someone affirming positively, "Well, I claim that the one that gets you you never hear!"

After mess, I was conducted to a contrivance of which the

men were as proud as of their TD's. It was a shower bath, and it was being turned over to me for my exclusive use.

When we reached it, they pushed me through a small muddy hole in the side of a hill, and then went away politely and left me to my own devices. The hole was thickly surrounded with exquisite maidenhair ferns which hung over it like a fringe. Inside, a cavelike pit had been dug out of the earth, just deep enough so that to get my feet to the bottom I had to let myself down by my hands from tree roots. In its murky interior I propped up my GI flashlight, hung my clothes on a small root, and swung a five-gallon can from a larger tree root, where it had been filled with water and roped to a primitive swivel device. Insofar as my aim was correct, I would receive a complete shower bath. I aimed carefully and pulled. After negotiating this, I put on my clothes. I suppose I was technically cleaner. I was certainly muddier.

It was completely dark when I climbed out of the mudbank. I worked my way through the slippery gorge and, tripping over camouflage nets here and there, finally located the CP trailer. Inside it was bright and warm from the little wood stove.

The Colonel was on the telephone, directing the front patrols. "I don't believe those people down there are alive to the danger they're in. I think their line is out. Get a recon out. Be pretty hard to get them on the radio and tell them all the things you need to.

"It's a pretty wet night. Better send a combined patrol. Even as dark as it is, better not drive a jeep.

"Get past the junction, do some listening. Remain thirty minutes and come back. I want a report as soon as you return."

He replaced the telephone, which was immediately taken over by the Major, who phoned through to the head of the horseshoe to get in touch with the mule skinners. "How many mules have we got on the deadline?" he inquired. Meanwhile the CO turned to maps to explain to me about mules.

Mules are as valuable as guns in this mountainous warfare in Italy. Under cover of darkness, mule trains go up the rocky slopes to troops which cannot be reached by jeeps, carrying food and ammunition supplies. Sometimes the terrain is so rough that the men must even leave the mules behind, and carry up supplies on their shoulders. But always our soldiers are fed no matter how great the difficulties. The CO pointed out one spot on the map on a forward rocky slope where enemy fire was so heavy that one of his boys got pinned to a foxhole for eleven days. He was within sight of his comrades, but the intervening hundred-foot stretch was so hot, both day and night, that no one could carry him his rations. They solved the problem by tossing him a ration can every few hours, until on the twelfth day he was freed by an infantry advance.

These forward positions were pointed out to me on a remarkable series of maps. The maps, I knew, were turned out in a steady stream by the Engineering Corps, from small offset presses on trailers brought up close behind the lines and operated by the "Typo Unit." These typographical charts showed detailed elevation data, treeless and wooded areas, and the numerous mule trails. The maps interested me particularly because it happens that my father, who was an engineer and inventor of printing machinery, was responsible for designing the first eight small printing presses on trucks to be brought to the front lines with the American Army in France in World War I. These presses printed daily charts from photographs made by reconnaissance planes, and in the First World War this was considered revolutionary.

It was after midnight when the Colonel received the call for which he was waiting, from the returning patrols.

"Did they draw any fire during the movement?" we heard him ask. "That's very good."

And then he listened further. "Lantern or something burning in a house?" And then: "Have they reported any mines around that area? . . . Did they explode it? . . . Oh, I see, disarmed it. . . . Well, I think it's mighty fine work, pal. Glad you made those changes. Be sure and keep us posted if anything further happens up there." And he hung up.

"There were German patrols attempting to infiltrate past the horseshoe," the Colonel told us. "Some came past at ten and some after twelve. One of our boys heard them pass so close that he could hear them whispering in German. There's some reshuffling going on."

It was as hard for me to leave this direct wire to the front as to put down a detective story, but it was time to go to bed.

The Major led me out into the darkness and established me

in a trailer where I was to spend the night. The boys had outdone themselves with my "boudoir," just as they had with my private shower bath. They had lifted out the ammo, or whatever it had previously contained, and blown up an air mattress for the floor of the truck, and put my bedroll over it. One of the standard five-gallon water tins had been placed by my bedroll, so I could wash in my helmet.

I undressed in total darkness; even my small pencil flash could not be used in the truck because the camp must maintain complete blackout. As usual it was something of an achievement to pour water from the heavy GI can into my helmet without tipping it over. I assisted the operation by propping the helmet between my heavy GI boots.

I had spent nights in foxholes sleeping in my bedroll on the ground. Once in the bottom of a dugout I had been given a door to sleep on, salvaged from a ruined farmhouse near by; and that door had been a luxury. So my present quarters seemed very fine indeed.

I lay in the darkness and listened to the hoarse voices of the guns speaking to the enemy and echoing rhythmically through the hills. The sky brightened and darkened as the muzzle flashes from near-by artillery blazed forth periodically and then died away. At regular intervals I could hear the footsteps of the sentry, just beyond my trailer. Sometimes I could hear his low voice:

"Halt! Who's there?"

And the quiet answer, "An officer of the post."

"Come forward and be recognized," the guard would say.

And then I could just catch the exchange of passwords.

"Angus," said the sentry.

"Bull," replied the officer.

The night before the challenge had been "Jersey," and the response had been not "cow" as one might expect, but "Bounce."

The password is changed every night, and the selection is made on the basis of two words with enough connection to be easily remembered, but not so obvious that anyone can guess it. There is no fooling with passwords. The sentry is empowered to shoot at the feet of anyone who does not have the correct response.

I recalled a story about a recent password. An officer got out of a jeep at an armored division CP and approached the sentry in front of the headquarters tent. "Advance to be recognized!" said the sentry, and then spoke the challenge, "Pennsylvania."

"Railroad," answered the officer.

"Well, I guess that's close enough," said the sentry.

The correct password had been "Pennsylvania Station," but as the officer stepped forward, the sentry had recognized General Mark Clark.

CHAPTER 11

155-mm. Flash Bulb

EVEN IN the daytime the battery CP was always in a half twilight. It had been dug deep in the earth and was lighted by candles melted onto distinctive holders—jagged pieces of shrapnel. These were not just any flak fragments. Each piece, I was to learn, was one to which some crew member had a personal attachment because it had missed him.

When I crawled down into the dugout, the gun computer, a young lad who had grown an amazing mustache, looked up from his chart, his eyes popping.

"Jees," he exclaimed. "We'd heard that a lady had been seen taking pictures from foxholes, but we didn't believe it. Do my eyes deceive me?"

"Wake up," said another boy. "This is *Life* goes to a party with Long Toms. Isn't that the idea?" he asked, turning to me.

"Something like that," I replied. "I thought it might be nice to be at the sending end of artillery instead of the receiving end for a change."

"We can't guarantee that you'll see only the sending end of things tonight," they explained. "We never can tell when we'll get counterbattery."

Counterbattery is a matter of answering back at the enemy. Whenever you can spot his gun position you aim at his battery and try to wash him out. He does the same to you. Counterbattery is a game that both sides can play.

"We've been under a lucky star lately," said the battery executive. "It's a month since we've written any names on shells."

"What do you mean, writing names on shells?" I inquired.

"We have a custom in our battalion," the battery executive explained. "When the Krauts fire counterbattery, and we lose any men, we write the names of the men we have lost on the very next shell we fire."

Lieutenant Robert Maxwell, the battery executive, was a wide-browed young man with pleasant dark eyes. He was sitting in the midst of a mass of wiring and field telephones on a kind of earth bench which had been carved out of the ground and ran completely around the dugout.

"We have to have a telephone to each separate gun," he explained to me, "because the Long Toms are set so far apart that the crews can't hear shouted commands. With a battery of smaller guns, the commands come in direct to a phone by the guns and are shouted for all the crews to hear. Our CP here is a relay post from the Fire Direction Center to the guns."

He picked up a phone and started a kind of incantation into it. "Battery adjust. Shell HE. Charge Super. Fuse quick. Base deflection: left two-six-niner. On number two, close three; battery one round, quadrant five eight zero."

"Sounds like double talk," I said as he hung up.

"Those are the commands for Abel battery," said Lieutenant Maxwell. "Now we're just firing harassing fire at Highway Six toward the end of the Valley. But tonight, when you take pictures, we're going to be trying to knock out a certain bridge we've got designs on, just in front of Cassino."

I had met A for Abel before, in the word alphabet used by artillery. I knew that in the same battalion there would be a B for Baker and a C for Charlie battery, each with its four 155-mm. rifles.

"We'll have just time to show you around before mess," said the Lieutenant. "You'll be interested in seeing how the Fire Direction Center works."

The FDC, 500 yards away, was the nerve center for the big guns. The enemy was always trying to knock out your FDC, I was told, and you were always trying to do the same with his. But a Fire Direction Center was always hard to find.

This one was located in the deep cellar of a ruined farmhouse which, if seen by enemy air observers, would look like nothing more than a frozen splash of stone. Inside, the cellar had an academic look, in keeping with the higher mathematics employed there. Its scholarly appearance came from its furniture of little school desks which the boys had brought from a half-ruined school house just up the road.

One desk was shared by the Abel computer and the Baker

computer. At the next sat the Charlie and the ammunition computers. Opposite the computers, and facing them over a desk full of charts and transparent deflection fans, were two men carrying the august titles of Vertical Control Operator and Horizontal Control Operator. By an odd coincidence all the computers and control operators in this FDC came from Milwaukee except the Charlie computer, who was from Fort Wayne. Consulting a Fire Possibilities Chart this band of Milwaukeans and the lone Hoosier assigned the guns to each fire mission which could best reach the target. By the use of their computers, or deflection fans, as they were called, plus more mathematics than most of us ever had to learn in college, they worked out the vertical and horizontal shift of guns and tied in the guns for range.

By the time this tight little midwest group got through with their range and deflection calculations, a mere spot on the map where the Germans had a juicy target like a tank park, or a nest of mortars, was translated into a firing command for the Battery CP, and in no time at all a battery of Long Toms was blasting away at it.

"Almost time for chow," said Lieutenant Maxwell. "We'll have just enough time for a visit to the Counter-Battery Section."

We climbed out of the cellar and over the sandbags and piles of rubble and made our way up the side of a steep, rocky hill. Almost hidden in a thick olive grove near the summit was a dilapidated pink plaster farmhouse. An outside stairway led up to the second floor. We paused on the upper landing for a few moments to take in the superb view it afforded of Cassino valley.

Every little while a shell from guns emplaced behind us swept over our heads with a roar, and if we watched carefully for a full minute we could see something that looked like a ripe cotton boll disengaging itself from the far end of the valley floor and rising until it dissolved in the air.

"Routine harassing fire," said the Lieutenant. "Just enough shells on the highway to make things inconvenient for the Jerry supply lines." And we went indoors.

I was always amazed at the number of typewriters and filing cabinets that could be found in a combat zone. The Counter-

Battery Section looked like any well-run office, except that its personnel all worked with their helmets on. Also, a certain aura was lent to the filing room by the presence of the Family Willms.

Before the Americans pushed their way into this territory, the Germans had used this same pink farmhouse as an infantry CP. Some would-be artist had found the stretch of plaster wall irresistible, and the result had been a mural-size rendering in charcoal of Nazi home life. When the Germans were forced to retreat, they left the Family Willms behind.

Mama Willms (each figure was captioned) was large and terrifying. Papa Willms was so small and frightened that one wondered if he were a true representative of the Aryan home life which the boys had left behind. Baby Willms was any baby who needed to be housebroken. In the mural, which covered the whole Counter-Battery Section's wall, Mama was making Papa attend to a certain ritual which one usually considers the province of the distaff side. It made one wonder about home life among the Nazis.

Under this scene of Teutonic domesticity was stationed what the artillerymen called the Hostile Battery Historical File. Here, as neatly as though it had been filed in the Library of Congress, records were kept of everything that happened to every known battery of the enemy. For months back, and reaching to the present minute, reports were filed on every location we made of an enemy gun, every time we shot at it, every time it shot at us. Data were collected on enemy artillery all over the front lines. Information was turned in from forward observers, from Cub pilots in flying OP's, from Sound and Flash Battalions, who computed the distance of hostile guns by measuring on a tape the lapse of time from the instant the flash was spotted until the sound was heard. Our Counter-Battery Section co-operated with the British on their left and the French on their right to build their Historical File.

They examined all fragments of enemy shells they could collect. Doughboys were urged to turn in for analysis flak falling near them. By the width of the rotating band (the part that engages in the rifling and gives the shell its twist) they could get the range of the enemy gun and estimate its location.

This list of enemy guns is consulted before an attack, and

firing is done on the Counter-Battery Section's recommenda-
tions. Immediately before and during an attack, our artillery
attempts to silence these known enemy positions, so as to
protect advancing infantry as much as possible.

Through the Hostile File, we learned as much about the
enemy's firing habits as a diagnostician knows about his patients. The Germans are fond of using a roving gun, which they
shoot from one position and rush through a camouflaged road
to an alternate point, hoping we will waste a lot of shells on the
first location where it is spotted. They go to enormous trouble to
conceal this connecting road. Knowing through our files where
these positions are, we never waste shells on a roving gun unless
we actually see it in place.

But there is one type of hostile gun at which the Counter-
Battery Section advises our gunners not to shoot. Every once in
a while, through their cross-filing system, the Counter-Battery
experts discover that the enemy is firing inaccurately into an
area where we have no troops. Then they just let him go ahead
and shoot.

After this lesson in enemy-artillery psychology we went down
into the cellar of the pink farmhouse, which had been made into
a mess hall, and ate C rations, dehydrated potatoes and stewed
pears for supper. It was beginning to grow dark, and time to
load up cameras and guns. I had planned to work all night with
the heavy artillery, because I wanted to learn what a night in
the life of a gun crew was like.

"Hope you don't have an artillery duel," said the mess
sergeant as we started out of the cellar.

"Hope you're quick at getting into foxholes," wished the KP,
"or you'll get dents in your helmet."

When we reached Number 2 gun in Abel battery, the first
thing the Lieutenant did was to show me the nearest foxhole, in
case I should need it in a hurry, and then I was introduced to
the gun crew.

I had seldom seen people more thrilled about having their
pictures taken. It seemed to them too good to be true that their
own battery, for which they had an almost human affection,
had been selected for photographs. They had worked with these
155's throughout the whole Italian campaign, and had named
their battery Superman.

"How'd you come to pick our battery?" they asked. Usually these choices are the result of chance, but this time there had been a reason. It had been the idea of the Grasshopper pilots, who had been flying me from spot to spot during my work at the Italian front, to arrange for me to photograph the same battery whose smoke puffs I had caught in my pictures over Cassino valley. This was the battery with which Captain Marinelli had been in communication the day I had flown his mission with him, and it was these very Long Toms which had knocked out the German *Nebelwerfer*. Although Superman had moved periodically forward every time our troops had made an appreciable advance, Captain Marinelli was still air-liaison officer for the battalion.

As I ran around getting cameras ready, the boys warned me that there were two types of stakes I should stay away from. The first were aiming stakes, which the guns were "laid on" to put them on the "base point." The others were sticks marking small disturbed areas of ground. "What's in there?" I asked.

"We don't know exactly," I was told. "Possibly mines. But we don't like the looks of those spots, and there's been no chance yet to investigate. Healthier just to keep away."

The crew pushed back the camouflage net from the muzzle of the Long Tom. The heavy barrel, which had been depressed out of sight under the net, rose majestically into firing position. Squatting on the edge of the gulch, camouflage still blanketing its flanks, the great gun looked like some oversized mechanical giraffe sitting on its haunches, stretching out its long neck to survey the landscape.

The moon rose from behind a translucent rim of misty hills, and a thin line of silver slid along the gun tube like a sword. A red light drifted up above us; it was a lighted meteorological balloon. By following it with an instrument that measured its speed as it moved, it was possible to apply weather corrections on the flight of shells.

It seemed mysterious and extraordinary to me that a streamlined missile like a shell, making a journey faster than sound, could be blown off its course by the wind. But I had been told that in the projectile's fourteen-mile journey, even the earth's rotation would have time to affect its aim. Already the Abel computer whom I had seen in the Fire Direction Center had allowed for the world to turn fifty yards under the shell's swift path.

The crew helped me plot out camera positions. Each time the gun fired I wanted to get four different effects with four different cameras. It was hard to judge with the eye how far into space the flash from the gun extended, or how much photographic light it gave out. I was particularly eager to get one picture from as far toward the front as practical, to get the fullest possible effect of the muzzle flash. The men helped me choose a position where I would not be blown off my feet by the concussion, and they helped me ease into it gradually, trying it a little farther with each round until we had achieved the desired viewpoint. They gave me cotton for my ears so that I would not be deafened by the blast.

Each time the gun fired, the whole crew turned away from the flash and shut their eyes tight, and at the same time put their fingers in their ears and opened their mouths wide to protect their eardrums from the concussion. Getting the faces of the gun crew in action was an important picture in the series; Padgitt could be trusted to catch this as he had a quick trigger finger. I set his camera with one midget flash bulb to throw a slight illumination on the men's faces. The other two cameras I placed to catch other viewpoints, and the force of relief gunners divided into two groups to man each camera.

The crew chief called out his commands: *Load! Ready!! Fire!!!* The great gun let forth a roar, and each of us from our various locations tried to catch it at the exact instant of firing. Then I ran from my post at the side-forward angle of the gun, watching where I ran in the moonlight so as not to trip over the mine stakes, and changed the films and reset the cameras for the next round. Since there were several minutes between rounds, I had time to figure out new viewpoints, take measurements, and reset the focus between each firing of the gun.

There was so much interest in photography that night that relief crews from Baker and Charlie batteries came up to help during the hours they were off duty. Soon practically everyone not actually engaged in loading and firing a Long Tom was busy holding film packs, moving tripods, handling lens hoods and camera gadgets, helping me get the four cameras set up and synchronized in time for each round from the gun.

In order to catch each picture at the exact second of firing such close timing was needed, and we had so many signals to one another, that finally the boys said: "We think it would be easier if you would give the command to fire."

It isn't very often that a war correspondent gets the chance to command a Long Tom firing at a bridge by Cassino, and I was delighted. So each time the next round was due. I would yell *load—ready—fire* at the top of my lungs, and four pictures would be taken on four cameras while that 155-mm. shell crashed into space.

It was a little after midnight when the Brigadier General of the artillery brigade came along. He had heard that some pictures were being taken, and he dropped by to see what was going on. Everybody was so busy by that time, synchronizing the shooting of cameras with the firing of guns, that no one stopped for formalities with the Brigadier General.

So many camera gadgets were being passed from one man to another that soon the BG found his hands full of film-pack adapters, cable releases, and film slides. By that time the enthusiasm for photography had risen to such a pitch that it wasn't much longer before the General was operating my camera while I was giving the command to fire.

CHAPTER 12

Invitation to a Big Shoot

THE FIRING mission was completed just before dawn. There had been no counterbattery, and everybody was in a splendid mood. The gang started into the battery CP and told me to come along and have some cocoa. The BG was sitting inside with the computers, all of them holding steaming canteen cups of cocoa.

"I was ready to stop hours ago," he told the others, as I came in, "but I was too proud to quit."

I looked over my exalted assistant with a critical eye and decided that he was my favorite general. He had snow-white hair which stuck up above his ruddy face in sharp little points. He wore an expression as though he had been laughing at little private jokes all his life. Tied around his neck was a voluminous red and white scarf, which I had never seen worn with a uniform before. I asked him about it.

He took it off and showed it to me. It was a red cloth flag, somewhat torn, with a large white circle in the middle—an artillery sign used by the enemy, he explained, in signaling to their own guns whether the aim is short or over. He wore it as a souvenir of what was, to date, his closest call.

He had been with a group of his forward artillerymen during an attack. Affairs had taken a difficult and confused turn, and they were having to do some speedy diving into ditches. In the course of this he found himself cut off from the others and between his own forward artillery and the Germans. Just ahead of him was a group of Heinies, signaling to their own gunners with the red and white flag. The enemy artillery was "bracketing" to perfect their aim, and the General wondered whether he would ever see home again. Suddenly a high-explosive burst from a German gun fell short of its target, and hit right in the midst of the signalmen with the flag. So the General decided, in his words, that "they didn't need it any longer," and with his trophy he made his way back to his own side.

While Padgitt and I tidied up the unbelievably snarled extension wires, tripper cords, and cable releases, put the various lenses back in their individual leather boxes, folded up the cameras, counted and labeled the exposed film packs, and straightened up generally, the BG sat with the crew on the earth bench, batting the breeze as he called it.

They were discussing happily a recent decoration which three of their number had received. Three artillerymen had volunteered to go into a forward area and burn magnesium to make the Germans think we had a gun position there. The men had dug foxholes first, set off the magnesium, and crawled into their holes. The Germans showered the spot with lead, but the men managed to keep alive in their foxholes, and when the barrage quieted down they crept back to safety. Everyone was proud that this unit had thought up the feat and had accomplished it so successfully.

As the talk rambled on, becoming more and more technical, I was impressed with the constructive attitude of these men toward their jobs. Artillery to them was not a fixed science; the posts they filled were not mere jobs. They were always seeking new ways to employ their tools in the service of their country.

I have observed that in branches of the service where the men have this absorption in their work, the morale is correspondingly high. This was particularly noticeable with the tank-destroyer battalion, and with engineers and men in certain other jobs requiring a high degree of skill. With the artillery liaison pilots, who have the attitude of evangelists toward their calling, this creative spirit is outstanding. In these cases there is none of that fatal numbness which afflicts many soldiers.

Possibly the answer lies in being able to see the results of one's work. Even in civilian life, it is a blessed thing to see the purpose for which one works. But in battle, where the stake is life itself, I believe this is a spiritual necessity. It is inevitable that in war there must be thousands of soldiers fitting like chips into a vast mosaic whose pattern they cannot see. And, lacking that inner support which would rise from understanding the deeper purpose for which they serve, they take their hardships severely. But where men have the good fortune to be able to see their niche in the scheme as a whole, they can take a healthier stand against the ravages of danger. Certainly with these artillerymen, both morale and zeal were superb.

By the time the Corporal and I had the equipment neatly packed, and our caption notes in order, the men were too absorbed in their conversation to notice that daylight was streaming through the hole into the dugout. The Brigadier General was discussing the desirability of synchronizing their firing missions more closely with the Air Force. He wanted to get after the enemy antiaircraft installations which would threaten specific bombing missions. The afternoon before, eight B-26's had been shot down in full sight of the artillery CP. If he knew when the planes were going on a bombing mission in the area reached by his guns, he could concentrate on enemy flak batteries, timing his attack so the Germans would not have the chance to bring up fresh ack-ack guns before the mission was flown. Later that day he was having a group of air officers come up to work over the details.

While this discussion was going on, the firing officer was heating a remarkable object over the coals of a brazier. It was a shell fragment the size of a telephone book and almost too heavy to lift. "The night I heard that piece of flak coming my way I called on all the thirty-eight Apostles," he said. He had been sleeping soundly with it ever since, he told me, using it as a foot warmer.

At this point the General turned to me and asked, "How about some shut-eye?"

I was more than ready. Now that the long, exciting night was over I had suddenly folded up. The boys had arranged for me to have a dug-out to myself, and had equipped it with extra blankets. But the General decided that I should use his trailer, and insisted on swapping with me. I was too sleepy then to take in all the extraordinary features of his improvised home, but when I woke up several hours later I realized what a remarkable trailer it was. The entrance was designed like a refrigerator door in reverse. When you opened the door the light snapped off. No matter how absent-mindedly you might hurry out, it was impossible to break blackout regulations.

Over the built-in couch was a reading lamp, and in the ceiling was a blue night light, as in a Pullman car. The GI five-gallon can, which one sees in war areas by the million, had been fitted with a little spigot. You washed in your helmet, according to standard Army practice, but a little brace had been devised against that annoying tendency of helmets to tip over. Under the helmet rest, moreover, there was a drain.

At the right was a tiny electric coil for heating a small amount of shaving water, and at the left was a larger heater. Little drawback curtains of blackout fabric masked the windows; a built-in desk had compartments for V-mail blanks, air-mail stationery, maps and charts, lighter fluid, and the usual hard candies. The field telephones hung on neat hooks. A ventilator had been built in over the bed, and pictures of an extensive and charming family stood all about on tidy wooden shelves.

I had just finished observing these facilities, and using as many as a woman requires, when the General came to make sure I had everything I needed. "All the comforts of home is an understatement," I commented.

"I don't miss my girls at all," the General told me slyly. "When my aide and orderly get through I can't ever find anything. So I come in and start fishing around for what I want, and it's just like being home."

It was time for noonday mess, and while we ate scrambled powdered eggs in the cellar of Counter-Battery's pink farmhouse the General talked to me about flying OP's. Frequently he made surveys from the air to study the disposition of his guns, and to make sure the boys were on their toes with camouflage. On these flights Captain Marinelli was his pilot.

Recently the Cub pilots had flown a visiting commission of three Russian generals to various points along the front. Lieutenant Mike Strok, who speaks Russian, had acted as interpreter. The BG was impressed at the comprehensive knowledge the Russians had of artillery problems.

During their expedition, the Soviet delegation was taken to see a Prisoner of War camp. It happened that many of the Germans in the enclosure had also fought at Stalingrad. They were dumbfounded when they saw the Soviet generals, and they began muttering among themselves. A few minutes later, several of our Hawaiian Japanese soldiers came into the camp, and when the prisoners saw them their demoralization was complete. "We thought you were fighting on our side," they exclaimed.

"Might be a good idea to turn some of those Heinies loose so they could spread the glad tidings back in their own ranks," chuckled the General.

The word had traveled around the artillery post that I was going home soon, and when I finished mess a boy came up and shyly begged me to take four dollars to buy a dozen roses for his girl when I returned.

"Since you're going home so soon," said the General, "I wish you'd call my gal and tell her I'm quite alive and kicking."

"Of course," I said.

"I think a lot of my gal or I wouldn't trouble you to call. Tell her as far as you saw there were no signs of senility or premature decay."

"I'll give her an eyewitness account," I promised.

Then I told the General there was one more thing I wanted to do before I went back to America. I had photographed incoming enemy shells and outgoing "friendly" shells. Before I left I wanted to photograph "friendly" shells landing on enemy territory. Was that possible?

"Yes, that's possible," replied the General. "But it's not always healthy."

However, he consented to arrange it. Within the next few days there was to be a "big shoot." D-Day and H-Hour were of course secret. In fact, they had not yet been precisely set as the date depended on the infantry's reaching certain positions. But it would have to come soon. It was absolutely essential to capture Mt. Trocchio.

Mt. Trocchio was the last razorback peak guarding Highway Six at the end of Cassino valley. As long as the enemy had their OP's on the mountain where they could direct fire on every jeep, tank, and half-track that came through the valley, it was impossible for our infantry to advance into Cassino. A heavy night barrage was planned in the hope that it would win us the mountain.

Already large stores of extra ammunition were making their way to the front. All the guns in the countryside would be trained on that one mountain.

"I've never seen a photograph of that sort taken," said the General. "I don't know whether you'll be able to get anything. But it will really be something to see. I'll send my aide along to help you. Stay alerted so you can leave at a minute's notice. You'll be notified at the proper time."

CHAPTER 13

Box Seat for a Battle

D-DAY FOR Mount Trocchio was postponed and postponed. I had already obtained my travel orders in quadruplicate, with their BRITISH CONFIDENTIAL EQUALS US SECRET designation. Everything except the equipment I would need for the big barrage was packed and ready to go home.

The rains had been steadily pouring down, clogging all operations at the front. The artillery officer at headquarters, with whom I had been told to keep in contact, kept saying, "We feel like a bunch of snails. Come back again tomorrow." And when I came back I would hear more about the weather, and more about the habits of snails. "Snails thrive in moisture," he would tell me. "Maybe we'll get a break and get our firing orders tomorrow. All I know is we'll *have* to make that attack soon, because as long as the Krauts have those OP's, the infantry cannot get into Cassino."

I obtained an extension on my travel orders, and passed the days trying to imitate a snail. Meanwhile the weather brought my faithful Padgitt down with such a severe sore throat that he was confined to his barracks. Then one day at noon the sun came out and I received a cryptic telephone call suggesting that I get my cameras into a jeep within the next twenty minutes and start forward. There was no time to collect Padgitt, and no use upsetting him anyway, since he was probably still too ill to go—though I knew it would be a great disappointment for him to find he had missed out on the big show.

On my way to the front I was joined by the artillery general's aide, Lieutenant Harold Halstead Park, Jr. Lieutenant Park had the tall-dark-and-handsome type of good looks. He was a pleasant young man from Katonah, New York, son of the animal sculptress, Madeleine Park. "H-Hour will be five o'clock in the morning," he told me.

His general had arranged for me to watch the barrage from a forward OP on the top of a mountain that overhung Trocchio and, since we would have a steep climb ahead of us, had also delegated some men to help with equipment. He timed our arrival so as to climb the mountain after dark. The mountainside was under direct enemy observation, and if we had gone up by daylight, the signs of activity on our part would have drawn fire. There was no way the Germans watching through their binoculars could be expected to recognize that I was just a harmless photographer.

The plan was to get me to the top of the mountain first, a climb which would take about an hour. We were to carry only a portion of our equipment with us. Once we were sure that the position gave us the outlook we needed, the men would go back and carry up the rest of the cameras, films, and food supplies.

They would also carry up an artillery "zoot suit" for me—a heavily lined whipcord zipper suit which hung from suspenders like a pair of overalls. This would go on over all my heavy field clothes, which already consisted of two sets of GI long underwear, two sweaters worn under a heavy wool shirt, a field jacket, and a trench coat. My companions were afraid I would have a hard enough job pulling myself up the mountain in all those clothes; the zoot suit could be added later to keep me warm during the long cold hours of the night.

We made our way up the steep crags in the darkness, pulling ourselves up sometimes by our hands and knees, and then staggering on without even the aid of the usual red-lensed blackout flashlight. Even this feeble beam, it seemed, might draw fire.

We had to follow a white tape just faintly visible in the dark. The mountain had been so newly captured that our sappers had had a chance only to clear mines out of a slender pathway. The white tape was the characteristic marking indicating mine clearance. We took extraordinary care never to take a step even slightly to the left or right—rather difficult with the amount of crawling and sliding that our rocky climb involved—because we could never tell when a misstep might land us on a mine.

When we reached the top of the mountain, we found ourselves in a grove of ghostlike olive trees clinging to the rocky slopes. It took a good deal of searching to locate our OP, but at last we found it, a perfect little cave with excellent observation toward Mt. Trocchio and across the valley to Cassino.

In the dugout we found a surprising object—a delicate little, antique, gilded Italian chair. I don't know who could have brought it there, or when. It was an astonishing thing, especially since there were only completely wrecked villages for miles around.

Now that I was established in the observation point the boys prepared to go back down the mountain to get the equipment and the food, and Lieutenant Park said to me, "You know, I suppose I ought to leave one of these fellows with you. You wouldn't want to stay here all alone."

I knew there was a great deal to carry, and it was a hard climb, so I didn't feel right about having someone stay behind just for escort duty. I said so.

"Are you sure?" asked the general's aide.

"Oh, no, I don't mind staying alone," I assured him, and he started with my crew down the mountain.

I sat in the dugout and listened. I had been told that there would be only light firing until time for the barrage, as we were only going to be shooting counterbattery. If the Germans shot at us, and thereby revealed a gun position, we would of course chunk back at them. But otherwise our crews would hold their fire until H-Hour.

Perhaps to an artilleryman this was a light night, and maybe our crews were only firing counterbattery, but as I sat there in the coal-black dugout it sounded like a lot of shooting. So I decided to go out and watch. I took the little antique furniture piece, climbed out of the cave, sat it on the edge of the cliff, and sat down on my gilded chair to watch the shooting.

Right beneath my feet, at the foot of the cliff, was a row of howitzers sending out sporadic darts of flame. Since I was so high up and so far forward, most of our heavies were in back of me, and I could look over the hills from which we had come and see the muzzle flashes of friendly guns, looking as if people were lighting cigarettes all over the landscape.

The whole valley was clanging with our fire. I could hear our shells, coming from a distance of six to possibly fifteen miles, rushing like locomotives past me toward the enemy. Some of them seemed to be passing actually below the level of my mountaintop, sounding like subway trains rumbling beneath my feet. The rocky slopes picked up the echoes until the mountainsides seemed to be filled with slamming doors. Occasionally I would hear the whoosh of an incoming shell, but the Germans were aiming less toward the mountaintop than at our troop concentrations below.

As I sat there in my gilded chair I began remembering all the stories I had heard of enemy infantry attempting to infiltrate, and German patrols slipping through the lines at night. I remembered how they sometimes tried to overpower gun crews or capture forward observers. If they happen my way, I thought, they're going to be pretty surprised to find they've captured a woman.

Once I thought I heard voices, but the sounds died away. Another hour passed. This time I was sure I heard voices. They were coming closer. I wondered briefly what I would do if I heard them talking German. But soon they were near enough so that I knew they were speaking English. My crew had brought back not only our food and equipment, but a tiny oil stove to heat our supper. The general's aide had even carried a portable radio up the mountain so we could listen to the news broadcasts.

It was very cozy in our little cave. We blacked out the door and the observation holes with blankets while we heated our supper. We turned on our radio, and for a long time could get nothing but swing music. When this was interspersed with German we knew we were listening to a Nazi propaganda broadcast. The Germans, knowing our boys are hungry for popular American music, make recordings of our favorite swing orchestras and feed them back to the Fifth Army front. They play a great deal of cowboy music, and they specialize particularly in the latest song hits. The first time many of our boys heard *Pistol-Packin' Mama* it was beamed from Berlin.

Then a woman's voice, speaking perfect Manhattanese, broke into the program. "That's Sally," said Lieutenant Park.

"Hello, Suckers," said Sally. "How would you like to be in good old Wisconsin tonight? It would be nice going out to a dance with your best girl, wouldn't it? But don't worry about your sweethearts. They're having a good time. There are plenty of men who stayed back in America who can take your girls to dances tonight." And then the German radio gave us a little Harry James.

Finally we managed to tune in on a B.B.C. news broadcast. We could hear the clipped British accents of the announcer giving us news of various war fronts—Russia, the Pacific, and finally our own battle front—and we heard him say: "Fighting is severe in the Cassino Corridor. The Germans are strongly counterattacking."

"I hope that was last night," Lieutenant Park remarked.

The night crawled on with sporadic firing from both sides. We slipped out to watch it at frequent intervals. At 2.30 we heard the faint hum of a plane overhead. "Piper Cub," said Lieutenant Park. "That's Captain Marinelli dropping propaganda leaflets over the lines."

Clouds were drifting over the stars, and I grew increasingly worried. The moon was due to rise in half an hour, and I was counting heavily on that moonlight for my photographs. But it was much more than photography at stake; I knew our infantry were counting on that moonlight, too.

At half-past four the clouds began breaking and the flattened disk of a three-quarter moon sailed out into clear sky. The pale light gleamed on the white rocky slopes of our mountain and, for the first time, I could distinguish clearly the gnarled shapes of the ancient olive trees which clung so tenaciously to the slope. Their trunks were scarred and battered from frequent shell hits. Many trees were split in two, and the wreckage of broken branches was strewn on the ground.

I set up four cameras on tripods, focused them at infinity (pointing at the moon to do this, for the moon furnishes a convenient check for infinity), and then directed them toward the valley. The general's aide had helped me plot the camera range on charts, back in the dugout. We had to figure out our bearings carefully to make sure that we were including the proper field on each camera. I wanted everything set in advance so I could catch the very first shell burst of the barrage.

Next we took olive branches and set up a low camouflage screen in front of the tripods. I didn't want anybody mistaking them for machine guns. By that time it was five o'clock, and we kept our eyes glued to our watches and waited.

Everything had become so quiet that it seemed impossible

that a whole army had crept into position in the valley below us, awaiting the signal to go. Both the enemy batteries and our counterbattery had quieted down. At 5:29 the earth was deadly still.

And on the second of 5:30, the whole world seemed to open up with a roar. We could hear our shells swooping by like railroad trains. We watched Mt. Trocchio suddenly transformed into a Christmas tree lighted up with candles. Shells were crashing on it in a hail of falling stars.

These star showers fell in gusts like a thunderstorm sweeping along in waves of rain. We would see a cluster scattering over the western base, then a cluster crashing among the central slopes, then a handful sparkling against the northeast crags, and then a dazzling splatter toward the mountaintop.

There was nothing casual about the spacing of these star bursts. Watching the entire barrage, we could observe that each area in turn was being thoroughly blanketed with shells. Each acre of the mountainside had been parceled out among the batteries. Each gun was aiming at the specific area allocated to it.

Some of the shells winked on and off like fireflies as they hit, and some flowered into expanding red smoke plumes. I had heard men in artillery circles refer to covering a certain zone by "firing a serenade," and here it was: this unearthly serenade strumming against the mountain.

As we watched there was a progression of climbing stars spaced, we knew, so as to give our infantry a chance to advance. There could be nothing hit-or-miss about a sequence like this because the barrage had been planned to co-ordinate with the infantry. The battle plan had been laid by the infantry, and the artillery was supporting them in their specific plan of attack.

Toward the end of the hour the shells began crowding closer to the top. Finally there was a constellation of air bursts timed to fling their whirling fragments on the enemy troops below. They shone briefly like red planets hanging over the mountaintop, and then the barrage stopped as suddenly as it had begun.

We glanced at our watches. It was precisely 6:30.

"We've got several of our men in there with the infantry," said Lieutenant Park. "Some of our artillery officers go along with walkie-talkies so if the infantry ask for more fire in some specific spot we can give it to them."

Such a message must have been sent, because after a few minutes there was a new burst of shells on the extreme eastern tip of the mountain, where there must have been a nest of Germans still to be "neutralized."

Again things were quiet, and the valley was lighted only by the moonlight gleaming along shelves of mist.

"The Old Man's down in there somewhere, too," said the general's aide. 'You couldn't keep him away from a big show like this."

At dawn we watched something new. Our guns began firing a barrage of smoke shells directed in an even row along the mountaintop. They were throwing a smoke screen to mask our infantry as it stormed forward. It gave a most extraordinary effect. For a time the smoke shells were spaced so regularly along the curved summit of the ridge that Mt. Trocchio took on the appearance of an old-fashioned feather fan, with its row of ostrich plumes curling from the top.

Lieutenant Park heated some coffee. We sat on our clifftop, drinking it from canteen cups and watching the valley grow lighter. The whole battle area was spread below us like a map. As the sun rose, the light touched with blood red the wrecked houses of San Vittore and Cassino. We could pick out the hairpin turns of the road leading from Cassino to the Benedictine monastery just above, and rising over all was the snowcapped peak of Mt. Cairo, looking for a few minutes like a freshly chilled raspberry ice.

A little later the sky suddenly became spotted with dirty black puffs. "Whose ack-ack?" I asked.

"That's Jerry ack-ack," said Lieutenant Park. We could see fighter planes on two levels, but none of them were hit. And below, a little Cub was circling about tirelessly on its lonely mission.

Then the sky was quiet until mid-morning, when we heard a drone overhead and saw what looked like a long, thin line of geese flying toward the mountain. These were our fighter bombers coming to lend their support to the battle for Mt. Trocchio. Suddenly the first one peeled off, and then the next and the next. As they dropped their bombs, the mountaintop began gushing forth gray mottled columns like a smoking volcano.

Then smoke spread over the mountain until the whole scene became so obscured that it was impossible for me to take pictures any longer. We worked our way down the mountain, passed a line of pack mules picking their way along a gorge, reached our jeep, and drove back to the artillery Command Post.

At the CP the staff were hanging on the telephones, getting reports from forward. "They shot their last screaming shoot at us last night," the executive officer told me. "Some 170's came whistling overhead just before we started our barrage."

The artillery staff was in a jubilant mood because the attack had gone precisely according to the time schedule. I was told that during the hour-long barrage we had watched, they had shot five thousand rounds. All but a portion of the farthest slope of Mt. Trocchio had been captured. The men were calling it a mop-up action.

The staff officers began receiving reports from reconnaissance planes that German traffic was heavy in the region of San Angelo. Evidently there was a strong enemy movement toward the rear. Two dams had been blown up by the enemy as they pulled out, and the land between Trocchio and Cassino was flooding.

One serious setback had taken some of the joy out of victory. During the first five minutes of the attack, two direct shell hits had been scored by the Germans which wiped out both of our battalion aid stations. Fifteen medical officers were killed, and almost the entire medical staff was either killed or severely wounded. This cost us more than the lives of the medical personnel. Many soldiers died who would have lived if there had been somebody to take care of them during the attack. Purple Heart Valley had taken even more than its customary toll.

We went to mess in the pink plaster cellar, and during lunch the executive officer was called to the phone. When he came back he announced, "I just talked to WigWag, and they confirmed that all of Mt. Trocchio is ours."

During mess, Corporal Padgitt arrived. He had checked with my billet and, finding that I had left, had dragged himself out of bed and hurried forward, hoping to be in time for the barrage. He took it stoically that he was just in time to pack my cameras.

As I said my good-byes to the general's aide and the rest of the staff, the phones were ringing again. "It's the Old Man," relayed one of the officers. "He says we're going to have an artillery CP up there in no time at all."

Then the officer turned to me. "He's asking if you've been heard from," he said. "He wanted to make sure you hadn't been hurt, and that you got what you wanted."

"Tell him everything went marvelously," I said. "Tell him I'll never forget him for arranging it for me."

When the staff officer hung up he turned to me. "The Old Man says you must come back to us again. He says to tell you that we regard you as one of us now."

Padgitt and I had a long drive back to Naples, and on the way the Corporal, who was always getting hungry, placed a couple of C-ration cans on the motor under the hood. When we had driven far enough so they were hot we stopped at the side of the road for chow. The Corporal had the whole procedure worked out to a science. With each C-ration can of stew comes a second can of hard crackers. By emptying his cracker can and mine and filling them with gasoline, the two cans set side by side would support a canteen cup of water without tipping and the gasoline when lighted would burn just long enough to burn water for coffee. A small can containing the powdered coffee came packed with the ration.

"When I land in New York," said the Corporal, "I'm going to the Automat with a pocketful of nickels and play it like a jukebox."

"I'll drop in a few nickels for you," I promised.

"How does it feel to be going back to the U.S.A.?"

"Oh, I don't know. When you're a correspondent you get a sort of disease. Always afraid you might miss something."

"Well, I've seen you miss some things you were lucky to miss. When I think back to the jams we were in together and came out of without a scratch! That's one reason I liked to stay near you when Jerry was laying them in. I think you were born part horseshoe."

It is funny how you *do* feel safe with some people and unsafe with others. I had felt very secure with certain people, and unsafe with others who showed that they were frightened. And I had always had a feeling of great confidence with the Corporal. He had never given an inkling that an incoming shell was any more to him than just an incident in a busy day.

For dessert the Corporal brought out an apple and a *cochi* from the fruit supply we kept cached in the back of the jeep. Apples were Padgitt's favorite delicacy and he would bargain for them loudly and strenuously whenever we passed through a town in the rear areas where we could find a fruit stand. His business deals with fruit vendors were the only times I ever heard him noisy. But nobody seemed to like *cochis* but me. They looked like overgrown persimmons and tasted like a cross between honeydew melon and peaches. The riper and messier they were the more I enjoyed them.

"After you leave, they'll send me back to guard that same old door in Africa again," said Padgitt.

He reached for a second apple, and selected another *cochi* for me, so soft it barely held together.

"It's going to feel damn cheap to be sitting way back there where it's warm and dry, and where you have a warm bed every night and are fairly sure you're going to wake up in the morning.

"I'll be thinking of the time I put in up here, trying to sleep through that incoming and outgoing mail, not knowing when one of those letters postmarked 'Berlin' was addressed to me. And I'll be remembering those kids we saw up there who —well, I'll feel that I'm not doing a thing to help those guys up here," he concluded.

I wiped the *cochi* off my face and hands. The Corporal continued, "It sure will feel funny to be out of range."

This was the longest I ever heard Padgitt talk during the five months we worked together.

As we drove back to Naples I said, "Would you like me to look up those Army correspondence courses for you when I get back? The Army must have a law course."

"Gosh, that would be keen," said the Corporal. "I'd sure like to have something on hand to study."

When we arrived in Naples and started unloading the gear, Padgitt asked, "Peggy, when you go home, would you call my mom?"

"Why, I'd love to," I said.

Then I had to refuse a ten-dollar bill he tried to push into my hand. "Listen," I said. "When somebody does something for you every day for five months, the least you can do in return is make a long-distance call."

I was mystified when, without another word, the Corporal dashed off down a little side street. I sat rather impatiently in the jeep, wondering what on earth he had gone to do in such an unexpected manner. Finally he returned with a large package wrapped in coarse paper and string. "A going-away present for you, Peggy," he announced.

I opened it and a coral-pink counterpane of enormous proportions, elaborately machine-stitched in light-blue thread, overflowed the jeep. "Thank you," I said. "I'll take it home to my house in Connecticut and shall always keep it."

"I sure thank you plenty for telephoning my mom," said Corporal Padgitt.

DEAR FATHERLAND
REST QUIETLY

CHAPTER I

"Hitler Never Told a Lie"

THERE WAS one girl in Germany I never expected to find outside a concentration camp. She was Fräulein Hildegarde Roselius. I remembered her from her student days, when she came to New York to study journalism at Columbia University. I had not known her very well, but I had retained an impression of her energetic, outspoken personality. She was a big, vivid girl with long, powerful arms, a loud, bright laugh, and a habit of expressing her opinions on any subject that came up, volubly, in almost perfect English. I had considered it pleasantly, even amusingly, symbolic of what I supposed were her progressive ideas that, after having been graduated from Columbia, she carried back across the ocean the first gasoline filling station ever to be installed in her home town of Bremen.

It was through this gas pump that I got on Hildegarde's track again. In the oldest section of Bremen, near the Rathaus and the wonderful old market, her father, who was the Kaffee-Hag king of Germany, had rebuilt an ancient street in faithful conformity with the rare twelfth-century buildings which stood nearby. Returning with her American diploma, his enthusiastic young daughter had set up her corner gas pump smack in the midst of this genuine and simulated medieval architecture.

When our armies occupied Bremen in the spring of '45, and I was able to get through to the ruined center of the town, by dint of constant searching and by orienting myself with the remains of the Rathaus and the Börse I located Böttscher Strasse. I had been there in peacetime to visit Hildegarde and her Bauhaus artist friends. Now I found little that was recognizable in the street that Kaffee-Hag had built. But on the third floor of what had been the artists' "Club zu Bremen," in the cloakroom, I found Hildegarde herself. She had changed from the apple-cheeked fräulein I had known in New York into a large raw-boned woman with a loud imperious voice.

Hildegarde was fortunate in her cloakroom, which contained the only set of windows in the entire building. By hanging white lace curtains at the leaded glass panes, and digging up other odds and ends of furnishings, she had converted the place into a reasonably comfortable sleeping-and-sitting room. But she was less lucky in her kitchen: the corner room (formerly the washroom) she was using for that purpose had lost its two outside walls, leaving the once wealthy heiress to do her cooking on a kind of open shelf hanging over the ruins below.

It is hard to tell who was the more surprised, she to see me there, or I to succeed in actually finding her in the midst of such difficult circumstances. She was overjoyed to meet an old college friend from America, and I was particularly happy to find a German with whom I could talk frankly. I had found the German character unbelievably baffling, and Hildegarde should be able to help. She did, indeed.

Throughout the Allied advance into Germany, all the Americans I knew were discussing how surprisingly few Germans were willing to accept any responsibility for either the rise of Nazism or the launching of war. Brought up as we had been in the democratic tradition, we found it hard to comprehend the way Germans divorced themselves from any responsibility for their government. The American GI, who had traveled through England, Africa, Italy and France without any notable effort to understand the people of those countries, adopted a more thoughtful attitude as soon as he entered Germany. I heard many serious discussions in which our soldiers really tried to figure out the Germans. This more analytical approach was due, I suppose, to an interest in what this creature was like who so recently had been shooting at us, and to a desire to find out what had induced him to start shooting in the first place. Countless times I heard our men say, after seeing the fertile fields and orchards so reminiscent of our own country, "Why did the Germans go to war when they had so much already?"

An American Major expressed the bewilderment of all of us at the general disclaimers of connection with Nazism when he commented, "The Germans act as though the Nazis were a strange race of Eskimos who came down from the North Pole and somehow invaded Germany." Therefore, it was natural for me to remark to my old college acquaintance, "I have yet to find a German who will admit to being a Nazi."

Hildegarde's unexpected reply was: "You are now talking to a German who admits to being one."

Well, there it was! I had at last found what I was looking for: a real Nazi who would admit it and, what was more, would talk openly and even proudly about it.

It was not always easy for me to keep silent, while we sat in that little lace-curtained room and Hildegarde told me of her worship of Adolf Hitler and her unquestioning acceptance of all his views. But I could gain more, I knew, by listening to her ideas than by interrupting with my own opposing opinions.

"The Führer had a strong manly handshake," Hildegarde began, "the sort of handshake you like. A really *good* handshake. Everyone who met him liked him. He was very sincere, very frank. He believed in what he said. Adolf Hitler never knowingly told a lie."

At least, I observed to myself, Hildegarde has picked up one Americanism, if it is no more than the species of laurel we bestow upon a national hero.

She had met Hitler first at a tea party at Winifred Wagner's, but she had already heard a great deal about him from her father—"He knew my father well," she said. Herr Roselius had met Hitler at an earlier tea party given by Cosima Wagner in 1929, and, impressed by the man's "personality and sincerity," had come home and announced to his daughter, "I think this man will play a very important rôle in Germany. I like him. He makes a very good impression on me."

"Hitler tried hard to avoid war," continued Hildegarde. "Every German knows that we are not guilty of starting the war."

"Have they read *Mein Kampf?*" I broke in. "What about Hitler's expansionist aims?"

"Expansionist aims are all right as long as they can be carried out on a fair basis: fair trade, and fair commercial relations."

I checked my impulse to argue back and tell her the things I had seen with my own eyes in Czechoslovakia when the Germans marched in and appropriated that little democracy. Hildegarde went on to speak bitterly about the corrupting effect of foreign propaganda.

"Too many people have been listening to the foreign radio," she said. "Radio propaganda raises doubts among the German people."

This was a fine bouquet to hand our Allied propaganda radio, and I was eager to hear more. I had been associating with too many of our own cynical correspondents, I supposed, who were over-ready to be skeptical of our Allied propaganda efforts; the comments of a German graduate of the Columbia School of Journalism should be valuable. So I asked how our broadcasts had sounded to her.

"Why, I never listened to the American radio," she replied indignantly. "It would not have been fair or square to the Führer!"

If this voluntary abstinence from sources of information seems remarkable in a student of journalism, her next comment was even more so.

"And even if I had listened, I wouldn't have believed it. I know too much about propaganda. During World War I, Papa was in charge of German propaganda, so I know all about it. And I know America; I know how they handle advertising and all those things there. After all, I'm a journalist, I know those publicity techniques. No, if I had listened to the American radio, I wouldn't have believed it anyway."

"But it happens that it was the truth," I interposed.

"You mean to say our radio didn't tell the truth? Nonsense! Our German radio always gave the true news."

It was an easy step to lead her into talking about who caused the war. "Oh, England actually started the war," said Hildegarde. "England dropped the first bomb. Hitler made a very fair offer in regard to Poland. It was a silly thing in the first place for England to go to war about Poland. It was a very modest demand on the part of Germany—very modest. As to the ultimate responsibility, I don't know which country was *really* at the back of starting the war: whether it was England, or whether it was Poland, or whether it was Russia who was really behind it."

But anyway, not Germany, I noted, according to Hildegarde.

And then, expressing what I suppose was wishful thinking on the part of many Germans, she continued: "We always thought you didn't really want to bomb us. We always had the impression you wanted us to fight Russia and weaken the Russians before they crushed us. You were shifting about from one viewpoint to another, so it was hard to be sure. But I always thought your bombings stopped for a while when the Russians had too much success."

I was to meet this kind of thinking in one form or another again and again in Germany; even in defeat the Germans refused to give up the hope that sometime we would be fighting Russia for them.

"Why do you think America came into the war?" I asked.

"I think mostly for business reasons," she replied. "Many of our people asked the same thing: why is America interested in a war in Europe? Our business men think America wanted more markets in Europe, and of course behind it all were the Jews. The Jew pushed America into the war out of a revenge feeling."

It was when Hildegarde's discussion reached the subject of the Jews that I found her remarks the most revealing. I had not realized how simply—and adroitly—Hitler had stretched his hand into the past to pluck out the prejudice that would serve him best.

"Well, it is quite reasonable," Hildegarde said of anti-Semitism. "We felt the same way for seven or eight hundred years. We had no Jewish problem in Bremen. Up to 1880 the city had a law that no Jew was allowed to stay overnight. Even in recent years, out of four hundred thousand inhabitants, if we had two hundred Jewish families, it was much. The Jews were treated in a friendly way here, but we didn't mix with them. This was the tradition of centuries. Of course, for a large city like Berlin there was a problem; there the Jews had to be dealt with." And then Hildegarde smiled. "Here in Bremen we didn't take the Jews so seriously. Our two hundred families didn't have much of a chance anyway," she paused, and added with a laugh, "*if* they didn't behave the way the Bremen merchants wanted. So you see we had Nazism, practically speaking, always," she concluded. "We have believed in the Party principles for centuries."

Her creed given thus neatly, Hildegarde decided it was time for tea, and we went out into the kitchen to make it. It was not usual for a German to have either tea or fuel for cooking it, but Bremen was more fortunate than many other German cities. Here, where the Americans had put many people to work on the docks, coffee and tea were often obtainable from our men. Also, the fuel situation had been eased by an Army ruling permitting civilians to cut down every second tree.

Stoking her tiny stove with wood she had chopped herself, Hildegarde, in her substantial dress of navy blue wool, stood out incongruously against the background of devastation. Her kitchen, hanging insecurely, open to a panorama of wildly tossed ruins just beyond, gave the feeling of a small stage against which someone had lowered the wrong backdrop. Only the battered tower of the Martini-Kirche—church steeples somehow usually proved durable—was recognizable as the building it had once been.

Looking up for a moment, to say she hoped I would not be cold in her drafty kitchen, Hildegarde broke into a little laugh. "I don't mean to be impolite," she joked, "but it's your own damn fault if you *are* cold."

I did not retort, as I suppose I might have done, that my photographic flights over Bremen only that morning had yielded pictures of U-boats in all stages of completion, as well as a bombed airplane plant and some enormous submarine-assembly installations. Nor did I add that I had a particularly personal feeling about submarines, having been torpedoed myself earlier in the war by a German U-boat which undoubtedly had received its final assembly in this section of Germany. My memory was full of the many friends I had had among Allied fliers who had lost their liberty or lives through the necessity of knocking out just such war industries as the ones around Bremen.

Almost as though she had followed my thoughts, Hildegarde said, "You see that smashed house over there? A funny thing happened; everybody in Bremen was laughing about it. A tank full of water was left at the top. A parachutist came down. This poor fellow went right into it and had to be taken out by the Fire Company. It was last winter, and I think it was a rather cold bath for him."

We carried our tea back into the cloakroom and Hildegarde set out two silver-edged cups, one chipped and one intact. "You will get our best cup," she said merrily, and then she became serious as she told me another story about American airmen.

"There was one thing that raised resentment. That was the 'Murder, Inc.' business. Some of the parachute boys had on their slickers, 'Murder, Inc.' To the German people it meant that this was an American organization to murder. I was often asked about it. People would come to me and say 'What do they mean by it? You have been to America, tell us.' They were very angry. I said it must be some college joke. That raised lots of ill feeling; the people didn't understand it. I knew from college they might do it for fun, but people would say, 'Well, they shouldn't joke about things like that.' "

Those poor unlucky fliers, I thought. The cards must certainly have been stacked against them, after that ill-advised gag.

"It has been a great blow to the young boys of Bremen that we lost the city. You must remember they were all in the Hitler Jugend. One of the bridges was held by five boys. To them it is a terrible shock that Hitler has lost the war. Probably we can't convince other people of our ideas. But I have been a member of the Nazi Women's League through it all, and I would do it over again."

Here we are, I thought, moving into Germany with our well-equipped army, with service units for everything that rolls, flies, or breaks down. But we have no replacement parts for that philosophy which we set out to destroy. What are we bringing those Hitler Jugend who have lost their bridge and these women who have lost their hypnotic Führer? By what naïve arrogance can we assume that the liberated will automatically and conveniently love and adopt the democratic way of life, simply because their liberators love it?

"I believe that Germany could not have lost if it had not been for treachery somewhere," said Hildegarde as I rose to leave. "There were too many Poles and foreigners, and too many people listening to the foreign radio. After all, democracy may be all right for Americans, but it is a very questionable thing for Germany." I have seen much of this war and many times, in positions of hazard and peril, I have been badly frightened. But the terror that came to me after talking with this German girl was deeper and more lasting than anything to which I have yet been exposed. It is with me still.

CHAPTER 2

Champagne Is a Military Necessity

THE SPIRE of Cologne Cathedral was a wonderful spot from which to take pictures. I was a little breathless after the stiff climb, as I peered out of the chinks in the masonry; but perhaps I would have been a little breathless anyway, for far below me, rippling against the edge of Greater Germany, flowed the Rhine. The river was still dangerous: its bank was thick with German soldiers, hidden, waiting, killing—keeping the watch on the Rhine.

Our progress toward the heart of Germany during the spring of '45 had been so swift that it took on increasingly the characteristics of a journey deep into the land beyond the Looking Glass—until, during the final weeks of the war, we reached that blurred greenish region beyond even the reflection of the lives we had known. Victors and vanquished were behaving in ways strange, unfamiliar, and upside-down, and the world seemed flowing with champagne. Champagne, as any GI will tell you, is a military necessity. Perhaps the necessity had never been so urgent before.

When I met the three GIs celebrating outside the rubble-piled cathedral it was early March, and Cologne was ours as far as the river. From across the Rhine bands of fanatical Hitler Jugend still manned the ack-ack guns, even after many of their elders had fled, and mortar shells still whistled past the headless gargoyles to fall in Cathedral Square.

The chipped apostles over the west portal looked down placidly on a sign which had just been tacked up on the cathedral door: "YOU ARE NOW IN COLOGNE, COMPLIMENTS 1st. Bn. 36th Armd. Inf. Reg., Texas Spearhead." There was some dispute about that credit line between the 104th, the "Timberwolf" Division, and the 3rd Armored Division, which had entered Cologne simultaneously. There was also considerable irritation exhibited by the Air Force which, after smashing Cologne flat, was learning that the ground forces now tended to consider the bomber boys strictly rear echelon. But to the imperturbable saints over the Gothic arched portals, even though some had lost noses and chins and several had dropped stone wing feathers, it was all the same. Bombers by the thousand had come and gone. A Kaiser and a Führer had come and gone. An army of occupation was coming; that would go, too. But in the deep vaults under the cathedral, Mass had been celebrated with regularity through the bombings and throughout all the long dark time.

The three soldiers on the unsteady rubble were, according to the sign on the door, my hosts. Just as any good host would do, catching sight of me with my camera and of Sergeant Asch who was helping me carry equipment, they called out, "Have some champagne."

"We've got so much champagne we're brushing our teeth in it," said one of the soldiers. They actually were. The water system had been destroyed, and the champagne came in very handy.

"Come along with us," invited another soldier. "We were just about to go and blow up a safe."

"Bring her along," cried the others.

All right, I thought. I'm through the looking glass now. I'm in a country where you brush your teeth in champagne. Anything can happen here.

We ran across Cathedral Square, passed the skeleton of the 4711 Cologne building, stooping low as we hurried through the open portion of the square, for the Germans had direct vision on us once we left the cathedral and were likely to drop in a mortar shell or two if they saw signs of life. As we dodged into the comparative shelter of Wallrath Platz one of the boys stopped dead in his tracks and exclaimed in a tone of exasperation, "Dynamite!"

"Dynamite?" I asked.

"For blowing up the safe," he said. "We forgot to bring dynamite."

The nearest place to get dynamite, they decided, was at the company CP where the demolition squad would surely be willing to lend some. While the soldier went off to the command post, which was somewhere under the ruins of the Dom Hotel, the rest of us sat on the edge of a small bomb crater beside what remained of the Deutsche–Amerika Travel Agency. One soldier wrestled with a cork; the foaming fountain he released gushed out with a strange and lovely pink. It turned out not to be champagne at all, but a sparkling red moselle, which none of us had ever tasted.

While we waited for dynamite, I had a chance to look around me and try to recall Wallrath Platz as I remembered it from my first trip to Europe. Groups of tourists had rested their cathedral-weary feet under the little tables in front of what was now the charred husk of the Café Monopol, while they gathered strength for a shopping expedition along Hohe Strasse. The sign marking Hohe Strasse still hung on the corner, but its fashionable shops had slid into rock-piles and dust. Now it was a hunting ground for soldiers after souvenirs and booty. I have never read of a war in which soldiers didn't do some looting, and certainly this one was no exception. Cologne was the first great German city to be captured, and perhaps some of the looting that went on was due to curiosity. The GIs wanted to see what the houses looked like, how the enemy lived, what he had in his home. It was the land of the enemy and had been won from him by men who had hazarded their lives every foot of the way from Omaha Beach. They wanted some tangible evidence of their success. A man who has been bombed, shot at, and sniped at is not likely to have a very high regard for enemy property rights, especially if he suspects the property has been stolen from others in the first place. After the passion for "souvenirs" burned out, normal behavior toward property reasserted itself to a considerable degree.

"There's vaults and vaults full of stuff under that street," said one of the soldiers, in a slow Texas drawl. "There's everything there that a person might want. We haven't had a chance to go through the half of it yet."

This was "new rubble" that surrounded us. After the early bombings of '42 and '43 the débris had been cleared away and the city had managed some kind of return to life. It was only the week before, during the last great raids of March 2 and 3, when Cologne was being "softened" for invasion, that most of the buildings still standing had slipped down into the streets, sweeping some four hundred Germans with them. It was then that the cathedral, hitherto relatively untouched, had received the three direct hits which choked the nave with rubble.

"You didn't need to bomb the city again," the people had told us when we entered Cologne. "We wanted to surrender, anyway. We were just waiting for the Americans to come in."

The docility of the people puzzled us. The big-time Nazis had fled across the Rhine, and the civilians who remained were eager to please their new masters.

As we started again along the pathless waste of Hohe Strasse, equipped this time with dynamite, I decided that it took an infantryman, trained in finding his way on patrols by almost imperceptible signs, to guide us to the target. When we reached it, a stone pile looking exactly like any other stone pile, our leader stopped quite still and said in quiet desperation: "String!"

"Jeez. Yes, string," chorused the others. "We forgot string."

I wondered how string could help with the rubble problem. While one soldier went off on a string hunt, I learned that our amateur safe-crackers needed it to make a fuse.

At last, outfitted with string, dynamite, my cameras, flashbulbs, and a couple of torches, we let ourselves through a hole, down a ladder, through another hole, and down a precarious stairway, until we found ourselves in the third sub-basement below the street. By the illumination of our flashlights we discovered that we were in something that seemed a cross between Bloomingdale's on bargain day and your grandmother's attic. There were piles of folded lace curtains, boxes of damask tablecloths and napkins, chests of flat silver, suitcases of new and old clothes, and heaps of neatly folded, cheap red cotton flags with swastikas machine-stitched on in black.

Under and amidst all the linens and swastikas were rows of sleek dark bottles in crisp straw jackets. One of the handsomest bottles turned out to be fruit juice. Not enough of the cases contained champagne, the exasperated GIs complained, but Sergeant Asch, who knew wines, observed that many of the wines were really fine vintages of the great wine years. This made everyone feel better.

"My wife would go for a set like this," said the boy from

Texas, holding up a lustrous yellow rayon luncheon-cloth embroidered lavishly with bluebirds. Next he unearthed a mammoth Nazi flag in heavy silk, ornately bordered with white fringed cord. He offered it to me and I accepted it willingly, as it was the only "souvenir" I saw that I wanted.

By now the place bore no resemblance to your grandmother's attic. Each blaze of my flashbulbs showed weird glimpses of GIs searching through the confusion, uncorking bottles, poking their way from one cavelike chamber to the next. The boy from Texas led me through a hole in the wall into a fur vault hung with coats of seal and muskrat, moleskin jackets, fox capes. This was evidently a storage vault where townspeople brought their clothes for safety during the bombings.

"These are just old second-hand clothes," said the soldier, dismissing the fur coats promptly. "Come through this hole —there's another vault beyond. There are better furs there."

As I squeezed my way through the hole I set my Rolleiflex at an approximate focus and took a shot into darkness. By the flare of the bulb I could see the GI standing up to his knees in bundles of white furs. I couldn't tell whether they were fox or rabbit.

"You could pick up three thousand dollars here, easy," said the boy. And, as I shot off another flashbulb, he added uneasily, "Or maybe you don't need three thousand dollars."

By that time the others had scrambled through the hole in the wall after us, and it was just a matter of minutes before the vault was churned up into a blizzard of furs as they embarked on a search for mink. They never found any, but one soldier held up one of those scrappy, nondescript little pieces that some women wear over evening gowns, and asked me if I wanted it. I was completely uninterested. As it weighed only about an ounce, he tucked it under his arm. (Months later, in Paris, I learned that it was platinum fox, appraised at two thousand dollars, and that the soldier had given it to a French actress for reasons which were quite clear in his mind at the time.)

It was confusing going through vault after vault in the darkness, and finally we all lost our way. When at last we saw a gap of light above us and climbed up toward it, we found we were coming out into an enclosed court at some little distance from the hole through which we had entered. The Texan had climbed out ahead of the rest of us, and he was already laying his piece of string over the rubble and running it toward the far end of the court. "Stand back of that stairway," he called, and I realized that he was about to blow up the safe, which had been tumbled into the courtyard by bombings. Under other circumstances I might have had more confidence in his ability to handle dynamite; but with things as they were I was sure he would send us all crashing down into the whirlpool of drygoods below.

We had just time to flatten ourselves against the gate when the center of the courtyard rose with a roar and bricks and rubble dust flew in all directions. When the smoke cleared, the GIs were sitting flat on the ground, quite surprised; two of them were badly bruised, one had his cheek cut, but nobody was seriously hurt. When the boys examined the wreckage, they found nothing of any consequence. Whatever the safe may have contained had probably been carried across the river by fleeing Nazis.

While two of us were folding up the big banner in the middle of the Platz, the way people will fold a large tablecloth, a soft little "zing" hit the ground not far away. Then came a second "zing," closer. The soldier said, "Snipers!" and pulled me under a jeep. It was almost one motion, almost a reflex, very quiet, very fast, very professional. I felt my head to make sure my helmet was on firmly. I was thoroughly tangled up in the big flag and wondered uncomfortably if the sight of our souvenir swastika had caught the sniper's eye.

My companion had switched instantly to the habits of a trained infantryman. "Do what I do," he ordered. "Run when I run." He crawled out warily, crouched behind the jeep, dragged me out after him; and we ran full speed to the shelter of the battered arches of the Café Monopol.

"They'll be throwing mortars in soon," he remarked quite calmly. I noticed with some astonishment that he still carried a champagne bottle under his arm, and had begun automatically to tug at the cork.

But I had had enough champagne. And I was greatly disturbed because, if the Germans started mortaring the square, as they had a habit of doing late in the afternoon at about this time, they would catch Sergeant Asch and the other soldiers just as they were coming out. I was much relieved, therefore, when at last they appeared. We shouted a warning to them, and all of us piled into the jeep and left Wallrath Platz and Cathedral Square behind. But fast!

A few weeks later my huge Nazi flag, by that time elaborately autographed by war correspondents, famous pilots, and assorted notables, disappeared from my barracks bag, and I learned a fundamental lesson about loot: it is almost inevitably stolen from you.

CHAPTER 3

A Last Look at George Patton

THE SLENDER, natty figure standing in the midst of the billowing red parachute silk was the awesome General Patton, whom I had come to photograph. Patton was at the peak of his dashing career then, and when I saw him he was dividing up a captured German artillery 'chute in the hallway of his Luxembourg house at 3rd Army Headquarters, his kindly, rugged face looking out quizzically from the masses of scarlet silk.

"What's this stuff good for? What can my wife and daughter do with it? Do you think it will make a dress?"

I thought it would make nice sofa pillows, and as I went into a little detail about how they might be made, the General cut out a couple of panels from the enormous 'chute for me.

"Take as much as you want," he urged. "And some of this white parachute cord. What can you do with that?" Well, you could edge the pillows with it, or make a cord for a bathrobe or housecoat, I suggested.

"Take some more. Isn't it pretty stuff? The Germans have pretty good materials after all."

This was an historic evening on which I found the General tangled up in the parachute silk for his family. It was March 24, 1945, the night of one of the early Rhine crossings; infantry and tanks which had reached the east bank in the initial crossing were beginning to push their way toward the heart of Germany. Shrouded by the longest fog screen ever laid by man, more crossings were due to support the first. Under the cover of darkness tanks and trucks were rolling up to the western banks, assault boats were gathering, and combat engineers were bringing up pontoons and bridge parts for the longest floating Bailey ever to be built during combat. While the acrid smoke settled into the hollows and gorges of the Rhine, and the men waited

for the signal for that first fearsome plunge, their General
—dividing up the red silk—was glancing frequently at his
watch.

"Things have been going too smoothly," said General Patton. "It makes me jittery when things go too well."

As we walked from the hall into the living room, carrying in
my cameras and flash equipment, the General's aide was
rolling up a movie screen and putting away the reels of the
moving picture that had been shown that evening. Having an
after-dinner movie is a regular custom with many American
generals, and tonight General Patton had been seeing Betty
Grable in technicolor.

Exactly like many less notable persons about to have their
pictures taken, General Patton began consulting me earnestly
about what he should wear. If I could have known that the
General was going to be so concerned about his clothes, I would
have been less worried about my own. The strictness of General
Patton was legendary in regard to regulation attire for all men
and officers under his command and it had distressed me
considerably that the skirt to my uniform was two hundred
miles away in the Paris *Life* office. I had nothing in which to
visit the General except the slacks and field jacket in which I
had been sleeping for several nights. They looked slept in, and I
knew it.

Should the General wear his dress blouse, or his old battle
jacket, he wondered. The battle jacket, of course, I decided
unhesitatingly. In that case, I must promise not to shoot down
far enough to show that his pants didn't match, or he would have
to run upstairs and change them. Should he be photographed
in his steel helmet—the one he wore at the front—or this new
shiny thing the boys had fixed up for him? I selected the helmet,
since he wore it in battle, not guessing that the shiny helmet
liner was soon to become famous, that special lacquer was to be
flown in regularly for it, that soon there were to be three liners
with two of them periodically parked at rival ordnance com-
panies for maintenance and fresh varnishing. In fact, by the
time the General reached Berlin for the Victory Parade (where
he stood beside an even more resplendent Marshal Zhukov,
dazzlingly hung with medals), one ordnance company boasted
of having applied seventeen layers of lacquer, but was oversha-

dowed by the claim of the second, which had applied thirty-
eight coats.

At last, attired to the satisfaction of everyone present, General Patton leaned against the mantel in front of my camera and
turned his face away just enough so that his favorite profile, the
left, would show. I watched to be careful that he turned his face
away not too much, for I wanted the newly acquired third star
on his helmet to show also.

It is always helpful when photographing a temperamental
individual to have someone in the room to keep him absorbed in
conversation. In this respect General Weyland, who had
brought me there, proved of great assistance. Genial, talented
General O. P. Weyland, head of the 19th Tactical Air Command, was one of General Patton's warmest friends and his
closest working partner. Both officers believed passionately in
integrated ground and air support, and carried out this collaboration with outstanding success. I was making no effort to
listen to their conversation, particularly since the discussion of
two leading generals on the eve of one of the greatest break-
throughs in history might well be a matter of extreme confidence. Still, I could not help catching an occasional remark. The
gist of Patton's comments seemed to be: "All those 4th and 6th
Armored boys need is to get across and have enough space to
get into high gear." There was a good deal about how his boys
were to "keep high-tailing it forward," and after each remark
he glanced down at his watch.

"It will be in eight minutes now," he said, and then suddenly, startling me out of my wits, he cried, "Put that camera
higher up! Don't show my jowls!"

And not waiting for me to raise the tripod, he plopped down
in a chair, took off his helmet and leaned his cheek on his hand.
Then squinting up goblinwise at me, he announced, "Now you
can't photograph my jowls." It was a very hard position in
which to photograph him at all, but I have learned that
photographers get what they want faster if they don't argue
with generals.

"And don't show the creases in my neck," he added, after
which he took up his discussion once more with General
Weyland. This time it concerned the proposed junction between the 3rd and 7th Armies. "Now we're going to surround

one of our own armies again," said General Patton, laughing at what was evidently one of his favorite little jokes. When he laughed his expression was lively and charming, and I took another picture.

"Stop taking pictures of my teeth," he scolded. "Why are photographers always taking pictures of my teeth?" After eyeing me for a while to make sure that I was devoting myself to serious and therefore toothless expressions, he turned to his watch once more.

"Only three minutes now," he said, and resumed his talk with General Weyland.

Having firmly decided that a low camera angle with a long focus lens would be the best way to photograph the General, I had been sneaking my tripod lower, inch by inch, hoping he wouldn't notice and start worrying about his jowls again. Suddenly he looked at me and tucked his chin against his chest. "This is the only angle at which the little hair I have will show," he said. Then, "The new crossing is due to start." Glancing at his watch, "It has started!"

It was one minute past twelve. The three of us in that room in Luxembourg were silent, wondering how our men were faring up forward, in the smoke-filled darkness. We knew how those boys would be hopping into boat after boat, with no dramatics about it, no volunteering to be first or hanging back to be last. We knew how the reconnaissance units would be seeking out cellars closest to the river for first-aid stations, how the engineers would be floating pontoon sections for bridges, how the navy seamen, 250 miles from the nearest ocean, would be helping to ferry over the infantry, working as though sailors and soldiers had been functioning together all their lives.

General Patton had been puffing thoughtfully at his cigar. "They are crossing at a special place," he said. "They are going over at the Lorelei Rock. I was always fascinated by the idea of that Rhine maiden sitting there singing to sailors; I always liked the legend. I thought it was a nice idea to have the men cross where the Lorelei sat on the rock and sang." He devoted himself to the cigar once more. "And then," he added, "there was another reason. I picked a cliff that everybody would think unscalable. No one will expect our men to be able to climb the Lorelei Rock." Catching the enemy off balance was General

Patton's fabulous talent, as General Weyland explained to me later.

Our men must have been scaling that cliff even while he was telling me about it, for it worked out as he had planned. No German thought that foot soldiers could climb the Lorelei Rock. But what we could not know until later was that during the first crucial moments an unlucky spluttering of machine guns—apt to take place at any time at the front—had caught and sunk the first three boats. All the men in them were drowned; the Lorelei had fulfilled tradition and claimed her own.

"You can't go home yet," exclaimed General Patton, as I started to move my equipment toward the door. "I won't be able to go to sleep anyway. Things are going well, and I can't sleep when things are going well."

And, carrying my cameras back, he asked me, of all things, to give him a lesson in photography. He wanted to know why I kept changing lenses while I worked. So, setting up my baby Linhof on a tripod, I inserted a short-focus lens, tucked the General's head under the camera cloth, and demonstrated how a wide angle conveniently included a lot of territory but makes the scene look dizzy. Then, working him through the intermediate focal lengths, I ended with the telephoto, explaining how this lens magnifies distant objects and has its uses for portraiture as well, for it magnifies the subject's features also. "Making them look nobler," I emphasized. And adding in a stage whisper, "In spite of jowls," I started to pack up the cameras again.

"Oh, you can't go," protested the General. "I'm having fun." Bringing out a bottle of Bourbon, he poured drinks for the three of us.

"If I ran out of Bourbon and cigars," he said, "I'd be a healthier man."

"What will you do after the war?" I asked.

"Go back to my yacht. She's a lovely boat." She was called, I found, the *When and If*.

When General Weyland and I rose to leave, with finality this time, General Patton began begging General Weyland to let him fly a mission over the front the next morning. He wanted to go piggy-back in a P47, that is, ride as an extra man in a one-passenger plane.

"You can't go on any mission, General," General Weyland said firmly. "That's one thing we won't let you do."

But on the way home I found to my delight that I was to be allowed to go on one. "If it clears, we'll have an L5 for you," said General Weyland, "and you ought to be able to get some good pictures."

At ten in the morning it cleared, and the L5 was ready. We had only meager reports of the Lorelei crossing, but the earlier push just downstream at Oppenheim was going remarkably well. Flowing over the bridge, which was not much more than forty-eight hours old, armored traffic and infantry had penetrated in a narrow tongue toward Frankfurt to a depth of forty miles. This was to be a day of spectacular advances along the whole Rhine front. General Patton's instincts had been right when he was too elated to sleep. There was an electric excitement in the troops, and I felt it even at the airfield while the boys were gassing up the plane and strapping me into the observer's seat in the little L5.

"You won't have to worry too much about Jerry ack-ack," the boys said.

"It's our own ack-ack I'm worrying about," replied my pilot. "Through all that smoke, when the boys hear any airplane motor, they're pretty easy on the trigger-finger."

We flew over the vineyard-covered hills that flank the curving Moselle Valley. It was this course which the 3rd Army ground troops had followed only shortly before, going northward along the river channel and then turning south and following the left bank of the Rhine, preparing for the breakthrough at Worms and Ludwigshafen. Below us, staggered in sharp white lines across the dark hills, were ranks of concrete dragon's teeth, the Siegfried Line tank traps which had failed to stop Patton's tanks. We flew over the bomb-stippled rail junction at Bad Münster, where our medium bombers had hammered through the winter at the key to the rail system into the Saar Palatinate. Then we saw below us the delicate kite shapes of three Piper Cubs on the edge of a plowed field.

"That's the 8th Corps cub strip," said my pilot. "How about going down to get the latest poop before we stick our necks out?"

As we rolled to a stop, the Sergeant in charge of the strip ran up. "We came to inquire what is the current attitude up forward toward friendly L5s," said my pilot.

"They got a couple of our own 47s up there this morning," said the Sergeant. "The pilots jumped out and didn't pull their 'chutes." Indicating two areas on our map showing our own artillery, he commented, "These two spots are hotter than firecrackers."

My pilot ringed in red the areas to be avoided. "Been getting any enemy air?"

"Got eight Jerries in there this morning. Lost one of our fliers doing it. Oppenheim got attacked by 174 planes last night."

"Been getting resistance on the ground?"

"It's stiffening up now, sir," replied the Sergeant; and we took off.

As we flew forward, we saw ahead of us a long feathered plume resting lightly between the hills. It was a minute before I realised that it was the smoke shroud over the Rhine. This was the historic fog screen it took so many tons of chemicals to make. Directly in front of us the smoke was coming up solidly, bouncing upward like a succession of cotton bundles. "That's the new crossing," called my pilot over his shoulder, as he spun me for a couple of turns directly above it.

Whatever might be going on below the smoke remained a mystery to us, for there was little wind. The Lorelei preserved her secret. For one brief moment a breeze lifted the edge of the veil, and we caught a glimpse of a castle on a cliff, looking exactly as castles on the Rhine are supposed to look; and then the whole gorge was sealed from sight.

"Maybe we'll have better luck at Oppenheim," suggested the pilot, and we headed south toward the older crossing.

We cut our way over broad flat fields which were being used for colossal motor pools. To the left and right of the great highway it was possible to pick out all the component parts of a division: everything from supply trains to mobile guns, from medical jeeps to small aircraft, distributed in an even dotted pattern as far as the eye could reach. Flowing below us toward the Rhine were the endless traffic columns of the 4th and 6th Armored Divisions.

Just as we approached the town of Oppenheim—where, we

had been told, the astonished inhabitants had simply stood in their front yards and stared, heedless of falling shells, at the incredible spectacle of the enemy crossing their uncrossable Rhine—the wind rose and blew the smoke away from the water. Below us, beautifully spaced between perpendicular smoke columns, were four bridges over the Rhine. Farthest downstream was the original bridge demolished by the Germans, next the two pontoons which the engineers had thrown together for the infantry's rush crossing, farther upstream the floating Bailey, and above all, threaded like big beads through the water, was the mine net designed to catch and explode at a safe distance any mines which might be floated downstream toward the new bridges. Scurrying from one bank to the other were power launches and motorized ducks, each trailed by a widening golden feather which caught the dull sunbeams sifting through the smoke. This ferry service used its return trip to carry back the ever-increasing horde of prisoners. One of the ducks had capsized that morning, we learned later, when its load of German soldiers rushed in unison to one side of the barge to keep from getting wet in the spray of a passing launch. Our men had sent out boats to pick them up, but most of the panic-stricken prisoners were drowned.

This 11,000-foot Bailey, over which my pilot began flying in a series of slow rolls so I could catch it between the smoke columns, was a remarkable bridge. Part of it had been constructed on the shore as soon as the first toehold of a bridgehead was established. At the start of the crossing, simultaneously with the ferrying of men in assault boats, the Navy began towing armor over on the bridge parts, each Bailey section carrying a tank, which could roll into enemy territory at once. The 178th Engineers sent their A Company over in the remnants of the forward infantry; they set up covering machine guns on the opposite bank and began immediately to build toward the center. On the near bank, B Company was building, and farther upstream C Company constructed the middle section which, when it was finished, was floated down the current into place. Thus at no time was the whole battalion in one spot where it could be wiped out by a single strafing; and the world's longest floating Bailey was completed in two nights and a day.

We had time for two full swings around the crossing, one at low and one at higher altitude, with several smaller turns in between, before the wind flattened the smoke over the river and the bridges with their moving armored traffic were blotted out.

"We're living on the roads these days," a Corporal in the 178th Engineer Combat Battalion told me later that day, after I got down on the ground. "Soon as we get through with one job and get back to our CP, they say 'Here we go on another bridge.' Our boys are just dropping from exhaustion.

"But the whole idea is to get so many crossings that the enemy can't push them all back. While the infantry has the danger of going across once, we've had it twice already, with more to come—and most of our battalion are settled men with children. We get moved to all the hot spots: we're a mobile unit. Our direct superior is Patton, and we believe we're his favorite engineering battalion. We're proud as blazes because we've got the reputation of always being on the spot."

It was from this Engineering Corporal that I was able to reconstruct some of the details of the Lorelei crossing. "I never saw anything like the way planes came over in mass all day yesterday," said the Corporal. "They seemed to be just skimming the earth. Those big jobs, C47s, coming up with supplies. It was a beautiful job of coordination. It was really rough for those pilots, flying missions over and over all day. I never heard a guy in the Engineers but said he was glad he wasn't in the Air Force yesterday.

"And then that airplane crashed: there was a big flame and an explosion, and three men fell. They fell near our mess. We were all eating evening chow at six o'clock. Of course everybody lost his appetite right away. Up until that time it was all a sort of dream. And then these three men . . . it was a terrible thing. That plane had six men in it—only three landed safely. I went over to get them. I asked them to come over and eat. We had a little wine for them, and asked how the opposition was. They said 'Pretty heavy.' They made us realize we were really going into something."

It was later that afternoon, when I joined a mess line filing toward a mobile field kitchen, that I picked up some details about General Patton in the Bulge. I had known that he had spent his odd moments during the previous winter reading

Caesar's *Commentaries*, knowing he would be fighting through the territory where Caesar had fought, but I had never before heard the story of his Christmas card. It was sent to all the troops in the Bulge while things were at their worst, when the weather was so bad that air support was impossible.

"It is useless to wish you a Merry Christmas," began the message on the card. "I can only hope you will have a better 1945."

"Of course that hit every man just right," explained one of the boys to me. "Here we were, on Christmas Eve. Our packages had not come through, and then this little card arrived. It was sent down through the message center, one for each man; it came down like the order of the day, and it asked the men to pray for sunshine. Everybody had a lump in his throat when he got that thing. The prayer for sunshine was printed on a little card that you could put in your billfold.

"The weather had been so thick in the Bulge that even the birds were walking. You'd be surprised how these very cynical guys prayed like they had never prayed before. And then we had six swell days running, and of course the planes just came over in swarms all day long.

"But you had to be there to feel it. You just can't talk about it."

I asked these boys about the famed hospital-slapping incident. "The time we saw him in a hospital it wasn't anything like that," they said, and one of them went on to tell me about how General Patton had visited a gang of them in the 12th Evacuation Hospital during the drive on Metz.

"We had been putting up a road block, laying strings of mines; someone dropped a mine, and several of us were injured. Old Blood and Guts comes to the hospital and he wants to account for everybody. One boy had been hit by a grenade. 'Well,' says the General, 'anybody who gets close enough to be hit by a hand grenade, that's something.' And another boy had been hit by a sniper, and the General bawls him out, and says it was his own fault for not ducking in time. Then he walks to the middle of the hospital tent and stands there—so erect, the way he always is—and says, 'I want to get you boys home alive,' and the men all have tears in their eyes. And everybody was proud, proud as Punch because he talked to every one of them.

"When he left the hospital, he took that shiny helmet liner off and said, 'I take my hat off to the nation that produced such men as these.' Well, it was a fine exit speech, good second-act curtain stuff. Whether he's really sincere or whether it's for publicity, we don't know. But I never knew a man who worked under him and didn't swear by him. He could knock *me* half silly, and I'd still think he was a swell guy."

This day of historic advances, which had begun so dramatically for me with hearing from General Patton himself about the Lorelei Rock plan, ended for me somewhat as it had begun, in another encounter with the General. After my flight over the Rhine, I met my party in a jeep and began riding toward Darmstadt over the main highway, which by now was carrying swift moving columns of 3rd Army traffic forward. A total advance of thirty-eight miles had been made on this great day. Many areas had been crossed which there had not been time to occupy thoroughly; Germans were drifting back into some, trying to set up installations. Nobody seemed to know exactly where the front lines were, so it was a good idea to check now and then. At one of these check points I went into 8th Corps Command Post (it had moved ahead many miles since my pilot had landed at the Corps cub strip only that morning). The CP, known in army telephonese as ICEBERG, had been set up in temporary quarters in one of those overstuffed little German front parlors which were always being turned into "war rooms" with maps draped over the stiff Teutonic pictures, and field telephones hung over the edges of ponderous desks and armchairs.

I was making my inquiries in the vestibule when someone inside called my name. I went into the little parlor, and there stood General Patton, very neat and smart in boots and breeches, and wearing the helmet and battle jacket in which I had photographed him.

"We own the world up to here," he said proudly, indicating the front on the map. Then he turned back to the officer with whom he had been consulting, and as I slipped out I heard him say. "Tell those boys just to go hightailing along. You see, I think this war is over now. I want my men to be up front, to share the glory."

CHAPTER 4

A Reporter's Lot Is Not a Happy One

"CHOOSE A camp to end all press camps," said Colonel Boyd. "Choose a camp to end all war correspondents. Remember the rule: pick your location between a couple of artillery positions and within at least 600 yards of the primary enemy objectives."

These directions were intended as a sarcastic illustration of exactly what Sergeant Asch and I were supposed not to do. But we did not realize, until the Colonel was flying back for more war correspondents, how closely we had followed them.

When we returned to our camp from the Frankfurt airport we found our front porch and lawn covered with plaster which had been blown off the house by concussion, and discovered a single tank-tread in our front yard, the only recognizable fragment of the tank which had been parked there. We got out our chart of the city and figured out exactly where we were. We had followed Colonel Boyd's directive to the letter: 600 yards from our kitchen stoop was the new bridge over the Main River, across which our infantry had been fighting for several days in an attempt to hold the small footing which had been established on the opposite bank. Three times the central Bailey span had been blown into the river by the enemy, and rebuilt at the cost of many lives. So perfectly was our press camp aligned with the bridgehead that the 88s which missed the bridge fell neatly within our yard.

The air was whispering with 88s by the time we had reached these conclusions, and we hurried indoors just in time to catch sight of three shadowy GI figures about to escape through the kitchen. They were dragging out sacks and scrubbing pails filled with wine bottles; it took only an instant to realize that they were cleaning out the whole block.

"Hey, this is our house," we cried. "We've requisitioned it. We have a Mil-Gov sticker on the front door."

"We haven't done the house next door yet," the boys said. "You can have whatever's in their cellar."

"That has been taken over by the Armored for a Battalion CP," we protested. "We can't take the wine supply away from a tank battalion!"

Realizing that they had completely cleaned out the cellar of what really was our house, the boys left a few bottles on the kitchen table and took an embarrassed departure.

Sergeant Asch, quickly appraising the needs of the moment, hurried out in the jeep to explore the next block before the GI team got there. In less than a quarter of an hour he was back with enough wine to start off the press camp, and with a jeep-load of coal.

All along the line we were amazed at the lavish food stores which we found in German cellars and at the excellent wardrobes hanging in the closets of the homes we requisitioned. Always, in these well-stocked houses, there was ample evidence of the owner's membership in the Nazi Party. Ever since we had occupied Cologne and had seen the women crawling out of the rubble piles in fur coats and silk stockings, we realized that the notion of a Germany starved into submission through food and goods shortages had been wishful thinking on our part. The hoarded loot of conquered countries had kept them comfortable, even though after defeat they were to know the starvation and suffering from cold which they had brought to other countries. But the looted clothes were smart and durable, and for months our soldiers, in quick forgetfulness, were to find delight in fräuleins dressed attractively enough to remind them of the girls back home.

The cellar of Heinrich Baehr, contractor, who was unwittingly our host, was even better stocked than most. The Baehrs had fled across the river, their neighbors told us, when the city was being shelled. That Herr Baehr was an enthusiastic Party adherent we knew by the framed certificates of merit we found in the cellar; that his wife had profited by the building contracts her loyal husband had received we knew by her clothes. She had two of everything: two fur coats, two quilted bed jackets, two pairs of riding boots, two brocaded evening wraps. She had so many monogrammed bed sheets and damask tablecloths that I felt sure all this linen was just one more investment for her husband's money, as no single household could have used it all. We knew by the empty ring boxes strewn over the cellar floor that she must have invested in jewels as well.

After we had taken up residence in the Baehr home at 17 Waidman Strasse, the Germans started a thorough mortaring job on our block. It was rumored that the townspeople had wanted to surrender, and the burgomaster of Frankfurt had offered to do so, but the SS officers refused to allow it. As we had heard so frequently before, crowds of fanatical Hitler Jugend were manning the ack-ack guns—the dual purpose 88s— wicked weapons when they were fired horizontally against the invaders. By now our block was filled with tanks, and in the yard of each fine old house, enclosed by its beautiful wrought-iron fence, was a tank or halftrack. Our armored boys kept hammering at greater Frankfurt across the river, and the Hitler Jugend fired back at our tanks on Waidman Strasse. During this interchange of metal, Sergeant Asch and I spent a good deal of time down the cellar.

One day I unearthed a box of military medals, which the Sergeant applauded as a glorious find: all American soldiers were collecting German medals. In the next five minutes he discovered a coin collection, each item carefully wrapped and classified. Then I came across another box of medals, civilian ones this time, of an incredible variety: Arbeitsfront, Todt Engineering decorations, Volksopfer or National Sacrifice awards, May Day medals, Motherhood medals for child-bearing, Fatherhood medals for "Reliable Service," Hitler Jugend medals for boys, Bund Deutscher Mädel's badger for Hitler maidens. The need for such incentives must have been great for the authorities to produce them in this profusion. The civilian awards were of cheaper materials than the military decorations; studying them by dates we noticed that they became increasingly flimsy and trashy as the years progressed. We could almost read the collapse of Germany in the medals.

During let-ups in the shelling Sergeant Asch was a very busy man, getting the press camp ready for the return of Colonel Boyd with the other correspondents. We were also preparing to house a group of super-briefing officers, Air Force specialists from London who had helped select bombing targets and had apportioned the weights and types of the bomb loads to be dropped on each. These men were eager to see the results of their calculations at first hand, and were corralled by Colonel Boyd to conduct the correspondents through the Frankfurt factories as soon as the plants were captured.

In preparation for this influx Sergeant Asch requisitioned extra beds along Waidman Strasse, interviewed the few remaining civilian women on our block, picked out two who he thought would do for servants, and whisked them down to CIC headquarters. As soon as Counter Intelligence had screened them and made sure of the political purity required before they could be allowed to work for us, we engaged them at the rate of pay set by Military Government. One of the women we had hired did some scrounging in the Baehr cellar on her own, and came up the stairs dragging a bicycle. She asked the Sergeant if there was any reason why she shouldn't take the wheel home, since the Baehrs had run away. He raised no objections, although we did a good deal of amused speculating on how neighborly the atmosphere would be on Waidman Strasse after the Baehrs came home and found who had appropriated their bicycle.

The Pandora's box of a cellar seemed inexhaustible. Even when the rest of the press camp arrived, with its staff of bomb-damage experts and constant streams of newspaper people passing through the house, there was hardly a time when a war correspondent or an expert couldn't go down the cellar with an excellent chance of finding and liberating almost anything he needed. This extended from major items like army swords, spiked helmets with the Imperial eagle, and similar trophies of the last World War, which were in demand for souvenirs, to minor articles like new zippers to replace jammed ones, darning thread, clothes brushes, or eau de cologne.

Sergeant Asch was busy breaking in the two servants preparatory to the eagerly awaited coming of Major Vessels and Don. Major Jay Vessels, Minneapolis newspaperman and former AP writer, prince among press camp managers, had attained unmatched popularity earlier in the war when he ran an Air Force rest camp in Naples for fliers on leave. He was extremely ingenious at solving all the unpredictable problems of housekeeping which attended the running of a press camp under war conditions, whether it was bedding down unexpected hordes of newsmen, overcoming faulty plumbing, or cutting out the drafts when shelling had broken all the windows.

Assisting him were Staff Sergeant Harry Cowe, ex-AP photographer; Sergeant Claude Farmer, ex-Anzio-infantryman, who seemed able to do anything that needed to be done; and PFC Don Jordan, a Harvard graduate who was something of an author and playwright by choice and a superior cook by instinct. Don could turn Army rations into astonishingly delicious dishes; the routine fig bar in the breakfast K-ration furnished raw materials for a dreamy pudding, and what went into the paper-thin, crinkled pancakes with ambrosia syrup that were plopped hot onto our breakfast plates, wc grateful correspondents never knew.

In preparation for the arrival of Don, our chef, Sergeant Asch launched a program of making friends with the mess cooks and quartermasters of all nearby infantry and armored outfits. Out of their abundance they gave us cases of "ten-in-one" and other Army rations to stock our press camp. After a trip to one quartermaster, to whom he applied for a few cans of peas, the Sergeant came staggering home under a quarter of beef that must have weighed a hundred pounds.

While we were waiting for Don, Sergeant Asch directed the German servants in the preparation of meals for himself and me. One morning he told one of the women:

"We want cherries for breakfast. Bring up a jar of those big ones from the cellar."

"The German people have not had such things as cherries," objected the woman. "We've been eating plain black bread."

"For that," said Sergeant Asch, squaring his broad shoulders and gazing at her intently from his deep-set eyes, "for that, you have your Führer to thank."

In the midst of our efforts to set up housekeeping we had two terrible days when the retreating Germans threw everything they had over to our side of the river. In the course of establishing the bridgehead, our 5th Infantry and 6th Armored were fighting block by block into Greater Frankfurt, while the 90th Infantry Division was cutting off escape routes and the 4th Armored was by-passing the city and rushing forward. Tenacious SS troops, Hitler's Elite Guard, were making a desperate stand to hold fast to their shrinking portion of the city. During the last terrible night of resistance the Tank Battalion CP next door received eight direct hits, and we emerged from our cellar in the morning to find our yard littered with the tops of trees which had been cut off neatly just above our roof top, as though severed by a saw. We ran next door to see the tank boys. "How's your house?" we asked.

"It's kind of tore apart," they said. But a timely descent to the coal cellar at the beginning of the barrage had saved the personnel.

"We were just like rabbits jumping hedgerows when it started," one of the boys described it. "For my part, I'll never go rabbit hunting again. I'll know the way that rabbit feels when you start hunting him down. We thought every flak battery in town was centered on us last night."

They were able, however, to give us the happy tidings that Greater Frankfurt had surrendered at last, and we could go across the river. I learned later that the tall handsome Corporal whom kind Colonel Black, C.O. of the 11th Regiment, 5th Infantry Division, sent to lead us through the fallen city was his best rifle man and had been detailed to protect me from snipers and keep me from touching anything that might be mined. "Never let that woman out of your sight," the Corporal had been ordered.

It was hard to believe as we crossed the Main that we were really driving at last over this Bailey bridge which had been such an intimate and yet unseen part of our lives during the past few days. "Our men bloodied their noses plenty on this bridge," said the Corporal.

As we entered the mangled ruin of Greater Frankfurt we had to drive carefully to avoid the twisted figures of the newly fallen dead. But it was the living in the devastated streets that first caught my eye. Most of them were women, and they were wandering around dazedly with their arms full of flowers. Rising between the skeletons of houses were magnolias and lilacs, filling the incongruous ruins with reminders of spring; and it seemed that these women, climbing up out of the darkness where they had hidden day and night from the terrible shellings, with their first glimpse of daylight were drawn irresistibly to the flowers. It was a sense of return to life that had impelled them to fill their arms with all the pink and purple boughs they could carry.

In the center of the city, under the famous old Rumpelmayer restaurant, a food riot was taking place in the cellar where the crowd had broken into the sugar. At the municipal icehouse quantities of frozen meat had been blown into the street by concussion; after the fighting had ceased, citizens of Frankfurt descended on the meat like maggots. An advance echelon of Military Government had sent guards to food stores to try to prevent looting, and as these MPs' jeeps swung into the street a hundred Germans dropped quarters of beef before disappearing into the rubble.

We passed a moth-eaten old man who stopped us to explain that the horse he was leading was a military horse, and to inquire where he should take it. He was too dazed to understand that there was no German Army in Frankfurt any longer to lay claim to the horse.

An excited woman was posting a sign on the door of a bookstore, which stated that the premises had been inspected and passed by American Military Government. Actually this was not true, for there had not been time yet for any such procedure; but she was the proprietor, and German property owners were greatly alarmed about American soldiers' looting. Next door was a camera shop, and inside it there was already a group of infantry boys, hacking open wooden packing cases, greatly annoyed to find that they all contained either developing trays and chemicals, or large quantities of optical mirrors for installation in cameras. They had not found one camera in the shop; the proprietor had either hidden his stock somewhere else or carried it with him.

The night before, we learned, the Nazis had put into effect a sweeping evacuation order. Broadcasts told the people that although life might be hard under present conditions, when the Americans came in they would not be able to live at all. American soldiers would rape their daughters. American soldiers sucked blood like vampires. Moreover, Hitler was promising to launch a "counter-death mist," or last-minute offensive. The Gestapo promised to return and punish all who collaborated with the invader. The werewolves would come with fire and sword. Anyone who did not evacuate, it was announced officially, was a traitor.

Thousands of inhabitants risked being called traitors and remained. Some of them, finding their families divided, committed suicide rather than face the loneliness and confusion of the future. But thousands of others, with the traditional obedience of Germans, followed orders and streamed out of the town. This was one of the purposes behind the evacuation order: to choke the roads with people and slow up our tanks. It was noticeable that while the common citizens walked out on foot, the Party officials rode out in private cars, taking all the supplies they could carry with them.

Just before leaving, the Nazis had been swept by a sadistic lust for destruction. They set food stores on fire, threw hand grenades at typewriters, and burned a supply of thousands of cigarettes, rather than give them even to their own people. Even in their haste, they had found time to seek out the archives of the *Frankfurter Zeitung*, records which the editors had hidden away because of the newspaper's anti-Fascist tendencies. Their last act had been to burn these papers.

Sergeant Asch drove our jeep through the almost unrecognizable streets to the great opera house. Far below its monumental ruins, in a labyrinth of stone passages, we found some rocky chambers where Sisters of the Convent of Almighty Passion and Love were living. Throughout the bombings these Lutheran nuns had nursed the sick and wounded.

"This may be the great chance for religion," speculated the sergeant. "The religious groups, Catholic and Protestant, seem to be the only organizations left to which anyone can turn during this formless period. It is too soon for politics. Maybe there will be a later turning against religion, when the famine starts in, especially if it is followed by chaos. Perhaps then people will doubt whether the church can solve their problems. That will be interesting to watch. But the fact remains that the religious groups seem to be the only ones who were able to keep some kind of integrity and organization during the rise of Fascism, and throughout the war."

We climbed out of the underground caverns into the gargantuan snarl of twisted beams and rows of seats where the great theater had been. It was a difficult ascent, for a bomb had fallen

directly into the center, tearing up the pit; but finally we
arrived, breathless, on the remnants of the enormous stage,
Sergeant Asch stood quietly for several moments on the buckled boards, and then he said, "It seems impossible when I think
of it now. But the first play I wrote opened here in the State
Theater. My stuff was always more popular in Europe than
America, for some reason. And now here I am, a Jew. It feels
strange to be coming back after that opening of my play fifteen
years ago. There were thousands of Jews living in Frankfurt
then. If the estimates that we hear are at all correct, there are no
more than two hundred Jews left alive in this city today."

Technical Sergeant Nathan Asch, immigrant from Poland,
had served his adopted country with deep and grateful patriotism in World War I, in the U.S. Navy; and in the second war, at
the age of forty, he had volunteered and flown proudly as
machine gunner with B17 crews who were half his age. Like his
father, Sholem Asch, author of *The Nazarene*, he is a sensitive
and discerning writer. He has a benign, ugly face, with little
yellow pouches under his deep and thoughtful eyes. He was as
ingenious a jeep driver as a photographer could hope to have,
and he was passionately eager to participate in all experiences
shared by GIs.

My good fortune in having the talented Sergeant assigned to
me temporarily as jeep driver was due to our mutual connection
with USSTAF. Sergeant Asch had completed a number of
bombing missions and was attached to the public relations
division of the United States Strategic and Tactical Air Forces,
and USSTAF, the heart of an extensive bombing-survey group,
was my special accreditation: *Life* Magazine had assigned me
to make a thorough-going series of photographs of the bomb
damage inflicted by our Air Force on major German cities and
industries.

The Sergeant's and my youthful chief was shy Colonel Max
Boyd, white light among PROs. He stood out spectacularly
against the generally discouraging background of the Public
Relations Division. The Colonel, who has now returned to the
Associated Press, wangled jeeps, airplanes, and special briefing
officers, improvised courier service and even good cooking for
war correspondents, many of whom had a hard time. Among
us, the men who handled the straight news had the greatest

problems. The swift-moving front combined with the frequent lethargy of Public Relations to create a difficult situation. Each day the correspondents were forced to commute many miles forward, if they wanted to see with their own eyes what was happening, instead of being satisfied with routine releases. Then they must go all the tiresome way back to find communication centers to send out their stories. Even after the end of the war, when the Army set up in Frankfurt, from which all the news came, correspondents were housed in a rathole of a hotel in Wiesbaden, which forced them to waste two hours on the road—going and coming between Wiesbaden and Frankfurt each day—if they wanted to file stories. The mailroom, something a correspondent needs in order to receive cables from his office, closed down at six, and did not open until morning—that is, it opened if one of the enlisted men could find the key. Well, there are always some helpful and efficient individuals in all organizations, and we had a couple of hardworking Corporals (without whom we would have completely perished), one American WAC Captain, and one British woman Flight Lieutenant, whose memories shall be forever blessed.

CHAPTER 5

All the Threads Were Loose

I KNOW of no way to convey the feeling of rising violence that we witnessed as we drove deeper into Germany: the waves of suicides, the women throwing themselves after their loved dead into newly dug graves, the passionate denunciations of friends and neighbors, the general lawlessness. Each street corner had its open tragedy; every life seemed shot through with its own individual terror. And over all hung the numbing realization that this newly conquered world was facing a sterile future.

In normal life one rarely sees violent emotion openly expressed; usually such torrents of fury and desperation as we were observing are released behind closed doors. But as we advanced through Germany during the course of this incredible spring, life was like a page of melodramatic fiction. Were these hysterical people in any way like Americans, we wondered? What was a German really like? What kind of people were these, whose acquiescence, either passive or criminal, had made it possible for such evil forces to grow? How deeply had the ferment in the secret depths of Hitler's country eaten into the soul of the average man? If we could look beneath the surface of defeat, what sort of being would we uncover? Outwardly, the motives of the conquered were reduced now to three very simple ones. How shall I feed myself? Where can I get shelter? When will I find my lost family? But under these immediate problems of self-preservation all the other problems were waiting.

In the midst of chaos I was trying to take some pictures that might answer some of these questions. I was working on a series which *Life*'s editors, from the far heights of the *Time* and *Life* Building, were describing under the working title of "Faceless Fritz." It seemed as though I were pursuing Fritz all over Germany, and yet I felt that I had never quite found him.

Although my Fritz poked his varied features into a score of *Life* layouts, to me he was only partly visible.

Events were moving too fast to leave time for the considered essays which *Life* customarily featured. No one, neither we on the spot nor *Life*'s hard-pressed editors, could keep up with the furious pace of the news. Never had any of us lived through such a spring. I used to run into our other *Life* photographers, who were as rushed and tormented and baffled as I was. There were eight of us spaced along the western front, which meant we had by far the biggest coverage of any single organization—in fact it was almost as large a total of photographers as that of all the other picture- and news-agencies put together. But all of us, whether photographers or reporters, were painfully aware of the utter impossibility of keeping up with such a torrent of news. We all felt frustrated when we tried to interpret the baffling human kaleidoscope which confronted us.

Sergeant Asch summed it up when he remarked repeatedly, "I can't pick a thread out of this maze of threads. It is still too confused. The picture is blurred."

Some rough outlines in this indistinct picture were filled in for us, early after the capture of Frankfurt, by a collection of Hitler's little people whom we found behind bars in the jail at Frankfurt-Höchst. In this workers' suburb, as soon as the top Nazis fled, the smaller ones had been clapped into jail by a remarkable organization calling itself the "Anti-Fascist Defense Committee." This underground group, composed in fairly equal proportions of Social Democrats, Communists, and Catholic-Centrists, had banded together secretly two weeks before the Allied occupation. The arrival of the Americans at the borders of the city was their signal to round up and place under arrest all the Party officials they could find. They had anticipated Allied Army law to do this, although they had made the procedure as legal as they could, drawing up formal accusations which were documented and translated into the best English they could manage, in preparation for the coming of our Military Government.

In view of the trend our administration of Germany was taking, it was no surprise that this expression of cooperation with us did not have long to flourish. Military Government at first was puzzled by it, and for a time mildly pleased with it. But before long their habitual mistrust of any movement with the faintest political tinge—even one as diversely representative as the Anti-Fascist Committee endeavored to be—put an end to this group and similar committees found in several other cities. It is impossible to escape the suspicion that a strong bias against any tinge of Communism contributed to this mistrust, although the reasons customarily given were that these anti-Fascist groups were filled with political racketeers, that they were partly composed of opportunists who hoped to increase the following for their respective political parties. Probably there were some such opportunist "racketeers"; there were also, however, some courageous individuals who might have formed the nucleus of the new and more democratic era we once hoped we could encourage in post-war Germany.

The biggest catch of the Höchst Anti-Fascist Defense Committee was Prince August Wilhelm, the Kaiser's fourth son, and a high Party member—Ober-Gruppen Führer—with the function of district treasurer. Prince "Auwi" was quickly moved out of his uncomfortable cell and back to the hunting lodge on his nearby Kronberg estate, where he was kept under house arrest, surrounded by his old family servants and a cluster of attentive royal relatives. After all, who had ever heard of keeping a Hohenzollern in jail? What happened to him later I never found out, although while the Prince was in Kronberg, *Life*'s writer Percy Knauth and I paid him a visit. He cringed from the camera, hid his face behind his hands, wailed "Do I have to put up with this?" and generally was a picture of outraged royalty.

At the time that Sergeant Asch and I visited the jail at Höchst, it had lost its royal prisoner but still contained an interesting and unsavory collection of characters. These people were waiting to be dealt with by our Counter Intelligence Corps and military judiciary units, through regular Army channels. One of the inmates, a small Party functionary named Emil Rothengatten, was so brutish in appearance that he seemed a symbolic Nazi ogre come to life. With one huge fist clenched on the table, the milky light from the single-grated window streaming over his enormous shoulders, his pig eyes cast down toward his giant-sized boots, he stood as stolid as a piece of suet.

"He was the fall-guy," whispered Asch, who had been

looking over Emil's documents. "He was the one who helped the big-wigs escape, and then they didn't want him. They didn't even bother to take him along."

In the next cell was a young man with a high intellectual forehead, fine eyes, and sensitively-shaped features. This was Jugend Führer Robert Martin, head of the Hitler Youth of Höchst.

"Sometimes they have the faces of poets and the souls of murderers," said Asch.

It was partly in the character of murderer that Führer Martin had been arrested by the self-appointed jailers of Höchst. For with his mistress, who was now separated from her lover by the distance of three cells, he had done a terrible thing. The woman, Elsa Wartz, had held a position equivalent to his as head of the "Bund Deutscher Mädels," the Hitler Maidens. This fancy pair had taken four hundred children away from the town and simply lost them. Now, in the double confusion of war and of flight from war, the townspeople had no way of finding their children.

"Every day more parents come," said one of the guards, "and say 'Where is my child?' And nobody knows."

"And the children went away singing, I suppose," said Sergeant Asch.

The guard who had shown us the prisoners' documents was a member of the civilian police, recently screened and added to the staff of our Counter Intelligence Corps. CIC, with their usual sagacity, knew a good anti-Fascist when they saw one and had put this man to work for them as a security guard.

"Not only does the directress of the Hitler Maidens share the terrible responsibility of losing the Jungvolk," said the guard, "but she is guilty of other crimes against the families of all of us. And so is her father, as well."

In the next cell was the father, Wilhelm Wartz, Nazi leader of a nearby working-class village, arrested for betraying many workers on charges that had placed them in concentration camps. Wartz sat in a daze on his cot, never even looking up as we passed.

But the behavior of his daughter was very different. At the unexpected sight of a woman in uniform who, I suppose, she hoped might intercede for her, she screamed out, "Please,

please come to me. I want to talk to you. Tell them I didn't do anything wrong." As the security guard unlocked the door and took me inside the cell, she sank to her knees, and transferred her pleas to him. Beating him hysterically on the body with her clenched fists she began shrieking, "Listen, listen to me," until suddenly he started to scream back at her, as though his grief were so fresh that he could not retain his impersonality any longer.

"I won't listen to you," he shouted. "Why should I listen? You didn't listen to my people when they came."

"I didn't do anything wrong," she cried, rolling on the floor in a spasm of sobbing, "Please, oh, please listen."

"There is no reason why I should listen to you," said the guard. "Your time will come to explain things."

"I'm not responsible," she wept, throwing her arms around his knees.

"Look what happened to my wife," he shouted, carried away now by hysteria as great as hers. "You denounced my wife."

"I personally never did anything to your wife. I'm not responsible."

"You all say that. One of your kind was responsible. Look what you did to the Jews."

By now the guard was trying to step out of her grasp, and the woman, clinging even more tightly to his legs, was being dragged around the cell in a terrible way.

"You called blameless women 'Jüdische Huren,'" cried the guard. "You attacked respectable young women."

By now she had risen to her feet and was clinging to him, and the struggling couple went swaying together around the cell in complete forgetfulness of any spectators. It was all I could do to squeeze myself into corners and keep the camera from being knocked out of my hands.

She was choking her words out now, in a kind of droning rhythm, "I never did. It wasn't I. It was others."

And he was repeating over and over, in a monotonous chant of accusation, "You and others like you. You and others like you."

"Come, Peggy, come," Sergeant Asch called to me from his post just outside the bars. "Come away. I can't stand any more."

It was out on the quiet roads, driving through the cool twilight from Höchst to Frankfurt, that we finally found our voices again.

"She ought just to be killed," said Nathan Asch. "Why should she be tortured? It's all so complicated," he went on. "It's hardly her fault. Here is a girl whose father was a Nazi. It's the natural way for her to go—it's the way she was brought up. If her parents had come to America, she'd probably have been a decent enough American girl."

CHAPTER 6

On the Road to Frankfurt

A GERMAN HAUSFRAU came running down the railroad tracks toward us. Her arms were so full of silk panties and undershirts that she was scattering a pink trail behind her, and she was laughing and crying at the same time.

"Germany is *kaput*! Might as well loot!" she shouted.

Sergeant Asch and I were driving the jeep along the Darmstadt–Frankfurt highway when we caught sight of the surging mob at the edge of a rye field. A German goods train, halted by air attack the night before as our armies moved in, was stalled on the tracks. It was still early in the morning, but hundreds of German citizens had already come out with bags, bicycles, and carts, equipped for pilfering. It was a scene of mass hysteria. Hundreds of people were suddenly filled with the stunning realization that they could have everything they put their hands on, for nothing.

This was an international crowd. Sergeant Asch, who speaks many languages, was able to catch shouted phrases as groups rushed past us. Newly freed Belgians, Dutch, Russians, French, and Poles, trekking their monotonous way westward, had been attracted by the crowd, and had rushed in and started crawling between the legs and over the shoulders of the plundering Germans. There was no fighting among the looters—only a passionate clawing toward the freight cars. The crowd was even gay; they were people of all nationalities laughing, looting together.

The Poles were radiant. One Polish woman, gathering up arm loads of skirts and dress goods, looked up at me and said. "The Germans stole all this, anyway." And taking up her words some Polish men, while they hacked away at packing cases, kept chanting through their handlebar mustaches, "The Germans stole all of this; the Germans stole it all." There was a good deal of truth in this, for many of the clothes on this train bore French and Belgian labels.

By now the scene was rising to a pitch of frenzy. People were going mad with looting. A Russian, one eye black as though he had recently been beaten, forced his way forward, sobbing loudly, while great tears rolled down his battered face. The single door to each freight car no longer admitted enough of the crowd and men began hacking holes with axes in the sides of the train. Little knots of looters set up a chainbelt system to get goods out of the human whirlpool faster. Families with small daughters sent the little girls scrambling up between the ends of adjoining freight cars, where they could squirm down like monkeys toward the newly hacked holes and wriggle their way inside.

One freight car packed with women's hats stood next to another filled entirely with hats for men. By the first, groups of plump giggling German girls were trying on one hat after another, all of them wide-brimmed gray ones and exactly alike. Their countless identical selections were then tied on the handlebars of their bicycles. Near them the men were enjoying a similar picnic with headgear, and one full-faced German strolled away with a pillar of eight felt hats on top of his head, all of them with tissue paper still around the brims. During the hat rush an American MP arrived. "Are you going to break it up?" we asked, for it was only last night in Darmstadt that we had heard from the Military Governor that stored goods would be confiscated and looting would be forbidden.

"No," said the MP. "Let them have a good time."

The crowd sacked the train in two hours. Finally, only a group of serious-faced Russian girls was left. They sat in a grave little circle around a pile of blue denim, trying on neat blue uniforms, which still bore price tags, and choosing only those which fitted best. They were too intent on the clothing to talk much, but I got one of them to tell me that they had been working in a cement factory, that the Germans had whipped them often, and that they were happy to be on their way home at last.

And soon they, too, were gone, leaving a dead waste of railroad tracks littered with broken boxes and wrapping paper and dotted with wide-brimmed hats, the one item too plentiful

for even this huge crowd to absorb. It had been a brutish scene.
"Let it be a lesson to us," said Sergeant Asch, as we drove away
from the ravaged freight cars along a highway bordered with
wild flowers. " 'The Germans stole it all.' "

The Sergeant and I took time, before pressing on toward
Frankfurt, to visit the ruins of a chemical factory in Darmstadt.
This plant had been knocked out by a single bombing attack of
fifty American planes. The higher executives had fled and the
devastated plant had been left in charge of the Foreign Director. This high-sounding title seemed to indicate that he had
directed trade with foreign countries, but we soon discovered
that it meant he was in charge of forced foreign labor. Most of
the work had been carried on by the slave laborers—Dutch,
Russians, Belgians and Poles—who had lived, until our armies
freed them, in nearby prison barracks. We learned that the
owner of the factory was a Nazi Party member who lived in the
biggest house in the most fashionable suburb on the outskirts of
Darmstadt.

"Let's call on him," said Asch, turning the jeep around and
heading it out through the rubble piles.

On our way through the wooded suburbs we had some
misgivings. We had been warned against driving through
woods because of snipers. The American advance had been so
rapid that many wooded pockets like this one had been bypas-
sed, and in some there were still remnants of fanatical SS bands.
But we soon started passing civilians, which made us feel safer.
From them we inquired our way. Everyone seemed to know
where the president of the firm lived, so we pressed on until we
found the house, which was a big mansion—indeed, still big,
even though a direct bomb hit had smashed the center of the
house, leaving little standing but the servants' wing.

"Does me good to see the houses of the rich get it once in a
while," remarked the Sergeant. "It's always the working-class
quarters that seem to get the worst plastering."

We entered a gate topped with wrought-iron unicorns, and
knocked at the entrance to the servants' quarters. The statu-
esque woman who opened the door was a vision of exquisite old
age. Her hair was piled in marcelled snowy masses on top of her
stately head, and her skin had the pink moistness characteristic
of well-cared-for maturity. She stood quite still, voiceless and

trembling, waiting for us to exercise the conquerors' preroga-
tive of searching the house. When we inquired for the owner it
was some minutes before she could speak, because of her
trembling. Then she managed to tell us in low-pitched German
syllables that only the morning before he had been taken away
by the Volkssturm. She didn't know where he was by now. Yes,
she was his wife.

We knew that the Volkssturm, the People's Army, had forced
all able-bodied men to join them in the retreat, with the hope of
turning about for a desperate resistance stand against our
Army. They must have been desperate indeed to have taken
men as old as this woman's husband.

She stepped back, a picture of mixed dignity and terror,
waiting for us to start through the house. Beyond her we could
see the enormous streamlined kitchen, equipped with stainless
steel sinks and ovens and more electric fixtures than you would
find in a medium-sized American hotel. To the left was the
servants' dining room, where a group of women, probably
relatives, were seated at a meal laid on a table bright with silver
and handwoven linen. To the right were doors to pantries and
to cellars, in which it was reasonable to suppose there were
supplies of champagne.

Suddenly Sergeant Asch said, "I can't do it." For my part, I
had lost every vestige of interest in prying.

"Of course the infantry will find their way out here soon and
make away with all the liquor, at least," said the Sergeant. "But
I just can't walk in. Let's get out of here."

In silence we drove on along the highway through forests
sparkling with anti-radar tinsel which our planes had dropped
during air raids to confuse German airplane detectors. The
tin-foil slivers lighted the fir boughs with such a glitter that we
seemed to be driving between rows of silver-festooned Christmas trees. Under the dark firs were clusters of star anemones,
and above the treetops the clean March wind blew white clouds
across the brilliant sky.

From time to time we passed knots of the dispossessed,
marching toward an uncertain freedom and pulling all they
owned in child-sized trundle carts. One of these groups was a
Belgian family who had sewn colored cloth together to make a
small Belgian flag which fluttered eloquently from their baby

carriage. The oldest child carried the baby, for the carriage was needed for potatoes and rags. A few miles farther we passed a French family who had somehow acquired an enormous French flag. The man and wife, harnessed together like horses, pulled their two-wheeled wagon; behind them tagged their children; and as they trudged along, the huge tricolor floated gloriously over their heads, dwarfing and seeming to protect the little family group below.

The comparison between these people and the household we had just visited was inescapable. The Krupps, the Stinneses, the Goerings, and others like them had torn these families from their homes and forced them into a highly integrated war-shaped industrial machine. Holding the controls, these industrial families had supported the Fascist rise to power, had grown richer on slave labor, and many of them were still living in comparative comfort while those whom their system had made homeless were roaming the roads.

CHAPTER 7

April in Germany

"WE DIDN'T know! We didn't know!"

I first heard these words on a sunny afternoon in mid-April, 1945. They were repeated so often during the weeks to come, and all of us heard them with such monotonous frequency, that we came to regard them as a kind of national chant for Germany.

There was an air of unreality about that April day in Weimar, a feeling to which I found myself stubbornly clinging. I kept telling myself that I would believe the indescribably horrible sight in the courtyard before me only when I had a chance to look at my own photographs. Using the camera was almost a relief; it interposed a slight barrier between myself and the white horror in front of me.

This whiteness had the fragile translucence of snow, and I wished that under the bright April sun which shone from a clean blue sky it would all simply melt away. I longed for it to disappear, because while it was there I was reminded that men actually had done this thing—men with arms and legs and eyes and hearts not so very unlike our own. And it made me ashamed to be a member of the human race.

The several hundred other spectators who filed through the Buchenwald courtyard on that sunny April afternoon were equally unwilling to admit association with the human beings who had perpetrated these horrors. But their reluctance had a certain tinge of self-interest; for these were the citizens of Weimar, eager to plead their ignorance of the outrages.

When 3rd Army troops had occupied Buchenwald two days before, that tough old soldier, General Patton, had been so incensed at what he saw that he ordered his police to go through Weimar, of which Buchenwald is a suburb, and bring back one thousand civilians to make them see with their own eyes what their leaders had done. The MPs were so enraged that they brought back two thousand.

The newly freed inmates of the camp, dressed in their blue and white striped prison suits, scrambled to the top of the fences around the courtyard. From here these slave laborers and political prisoners waited to see German people forced to view the heap of their dead comrades. Woman fainted or wept. Men covered their faces and turned their heads away. It was when the civilians began repeating, "We didn't know! We didn't know!" that the ex-prisoners were carried away with wrath.

"You did know," they shouted. "Side by side we worked with you in the factories. At the risk of our lives we told you. But you did nothing."

Of course they knew, as did almost all Germans.

Even during the short time that the two thousand unwilling Germans were in the courtyard, the white pile grew steadily higher. American Army medics, who began feeding the inmates as soon as Buchenwald was captured, were unable to stop the ravages of long suffering and mistreatment. Twelve hundred had died the month before, and people would continue to die there for some time to come. The ironical reason why the pile of naked bodies had been allowed to grow so high, instead of being burned according to regular concentration-camp practice, was that, because of the more pressing needs of the war, Buchenwald had run short of coal.

The presence of many familiar names among the inmates —all correspondents found people in the camp they had known elsewhere, or the relatives of people they had known—served to bring the tragedy closer to reality in our minds. I talked with Eddie Cantor's cousin, a Holland–Dutch Jew, whose circuit of several concentration camps had finally brought him to Buchenwald, where he had spent one year wasting away in Barracks Number 58. But he was one of the lucky ones; he had sufficient physical stamina to react favorably to food and care, and he would live.

Buchenwald was an example of the key part the concentration-camp system played in Germany's industrial scheme. I believe that during the war we vastly underestimated the importance of slave labor in Germany's military resistance. Near Buchenwald was a V-bomb factory where many operations were carried on by forced labor from the concentration camp. Allied Air Force Intelligence knew the location of the prison barracks, which were so close to the factory that our pilots were briefed with especial care to avoid them. During repeated raids on the V-bomb plant, although some bombs inevitably fell close, the camp escaped actual hits for the most part. But although aerial photographs could show the location of Buchenwald, air reconnaissance could furnish no hint of the horrors which ground invasion revealed.

Years before the war the camps existed as what the Germans so appropriately called educational institutions. Their aim in the beginning, so they said, was political: to strangle independent thinking and handle the "race problem." Probably it was with the growing need for armaments under Germany's economy of aggression that their full industrial value was realized, although the German General Staff had included slave labor in its calculations before the Nazis came to power.

We know now that the camps were managed by personnel who had been given systematic training in cruelty in special schools for their specialized jobs, and that they were run according to a horrible law of diminishing returns. The slave laborers were fed as little as possible and worked until their strength fell below a certain level. Then by various devices —such as the prolonged daily roll call in which the weak ones were made to stand naked in rainy or snowy weather, or by other inexpensive means—the slaves were encouraged to die as fast as possible, in order to save upkeep.

If we had encountered just one camp run by a maniac, we would have considered it merely the work of madness. But at a certain stage in the advance of our armies we began meeting these camps everywhere; along the western front all *Life*'s photographers simultaneously began running into them: Dave Scherman tried to photograph Auschwitz until it made him sick; Florea struck Nordhausen; Vandivert took some unforgettable pictures at Gardelegen near Berlin, and George Rodger made a heart-rending record of Belsen. It was the wide prevalence of the system that testified to its vicious purpose.

A much smaller and less publicized place than those mentioned above brought home to me the full tragedy of the concentration camps. On the afternoon of the same day that

Bill Walton and I had canvassed the City Hall, we had driven to the outskirts of Leipzig to hunt up an aircraft small-parts factory which had been an 8th Air Force bombing target. The Leipzig-Mochau plant, in a suburb called Erla, had been one of the units in the Leipzig aircraft complex.

We never found the aircraft factory that afternoon. For a time we became involved in a small pocket where the Germans had surrounded groups of American soldiers who were fighting their way out along the borders—although things were so confused that we did not comprehend the exact status of this area at the time. We did wonder, however, at the shells that were falling uncomfortably close, and were never quite sure whose they were. But soon our preoccupation with even the shelling was lost in a concern about something else. As we searched for the factory along a narrow country road bisecting plowed fields, we began to smell a peculiar odor, quite different from anything in our experience. We followed the smell until we saw, across a small meadow, a ten-foot barbed-wire fence which, curiously, seemed to surround nothing at all. Parking the jeep, we ran through a small gate into the enclosure, and found ourselves standing at the edge of an acre of bones.

There was no one there; that is, there was no living person. But flying grotesquely over the patch of skulls and charred ribs, from a tall slender flag-pole, was a white surrender flag. There was eloquent testimony that the men who had been there so recently had not willingly surrendered to death. Plunged into the four-foot wide barrier of closely meshed barbed wire were blackened human figures whose desperate attitudes showed their passionate attempts to break to freedom. Caught in the spiked coils, they had perished, flaming torches, as they tried to escape.

Nothing was left standing among the ashes, except the incongruous flag-pole at the far edge. Dotting the ghastly mottled carpet which covered the area were dozens of identical little graniteware basins and among them a scattering of spoons.

"Look at all the nails on the ground," said Bill. "The building must have gone up so fast that all the nails popped out." Then he sat down on his musette bag on the ground, and put his head in his hands.

Neither of us knew at the time how quickly people at home, and even some returned soldiers who had not seen these things, would begin to say that perhaps accounts had been exaggerated, that maybe the Germans were not so bad after all. But even though I did not realize how soon some people would disbelieve or forget, I had a deep conviction that an atrocity like this demanded to be recorded. So I forced myself to map the place with negatives.

We had been there in silence for almost an hour, I suppose, when an unexpected and moving thing took place. Survivors began drifting back. Bill and I were witness to unbearably pitiful scenes as those few people, coming back from different directions, recognized one another and ran to greet comrades still alive, falling into each other's arms while standing up to their ankles in bones. Among the first to return were a Russian in a peasant sheepskin coat, a Czech wearing the letter T for Tschechoslovakei on his striped prison jacket, and a Pole, who, catching sight of the unburned but hand-grenaded body of a Polish comrade, sank down beside his dead friend, bowed with grief.

When finally eighteen had returned, the survivors decided that these were all who had escaped out of the three hundred whom the Germans had tried to destroy. Originally, we were told, there had been eight hundred, arrested because of political ideas considered impermissible by the Nazis, and confined to the Number Three Erla Work Camp as slave labor for the Leipzig-Mochau aircraft factory. When our armies advanced so close that the Nazi authorities knew Leipzig would soon fall, the Gestapo evacuated five hundred who were still strong enough to be herded on foot to work in another factory deeper in German-held territory. The plan had been to leave the weakest behind. But finally the Gestapo, knowing that political prisoners freed by the Americans were giving whatever useful intelligence they could to our army, decided to annihilate the remaining three hundred.

Bill got the story from the Czech. He was a barber, and to Bill and to me he was the hero of Number Three Erla Work Camp. Having a little more freedom than the others, since he was called upon to shave the SS guards, the barber got wind of the fact that a massacre was planned. The greatest barrier to the chances of escape, he knew, was the 800-volt charge in the barbed wire fence. He wrote a note which he wrapped around a stone and threw into the inner enclosure at night, warning his comrades of what was afoot, and informing them that he would short-circuit the fence. As soon as the evacuations began taking place, and the camp electrician had been evacuated with certain other staff members, the barber stole out at night, cut the wires, and short-circuited the fence. After throwing in a second note warning the inmates to escape at the first opportunity, he hid at the bottom of a deep bricked hole, coming out only to make sure the wires had not been repaired.

It is surprising how many places there were to hide even in a concentration camp. Some of the inmates managed to dig themselves into holes under the buildings. Unfortunately not enough of them, in their weakened condition, were able to understand the significance of the short-circuited wires, or more might have escaped. They had feared that fence too long.

On the morning that the Americans reached the outskirts of Leipzig, the guards had set out pails of steaming soup to lure the poor hungry wretches conveniently into the mess hall. The soup cans were still recognizable when Bill and I arrived.

After the prisoners were inside, the SS put blankets over the windows, threw in pails of flaming acetate solution, sprinkled the place with machine-gun fire, and tossed in hand grenades. The building must have gone up in a sheet of flame but, even then, many prisoners got as far as the door. We know this because the concentration of skulls was greatest where the door had been. A fair number even broke through the fence. But the Gestapo had previously brought up a couple of tanks manned by Hitler Jugend, and these ferocious youngsters shot down the survivors as they ran across the meadow. We could see their bodies where they had fallen in the plowed earth.

Some of the victims were so close to freedom that it made my heart bleed to see them. A Polish professor, who, we were told, had been an aircraft technician, had squeezed halfway through the outer fence. The shriveled lower half of his body lay in cinders within the enclosure, with his charred crutch close by, but the fine intellectual bald head thrust through to the outside was still unmarred, with even the spectacles in place. He must have been much loved; the survivors shed many tears over him.

Another half-intact figure had a silver cross hanging around his neck. The dead body was covered with blisters. The Czech knelt down, gently touched the crucifix, and said, "Blood on the cross."

The barber started hunting through each hole and dugout, hoping against hope to find someone alive. Suddenly he jumped into a trench and, raising his clenched fist, cried, "My comrade. A Czech." In the dim light at the entrance to the little underground tunnel I could just make out the face of his friend, the fine features streaked with blood. The Gestapo had evidently hunted out all who hid in holes, and machine-gunned them.

Then the barber began searching for some remembrance which he could carry back to the family of his friend. There was little to choose from, and finally he took the only thing he could find to carry away. What he did will sound strange—perhaps grotesque—when I describe it from so far away. But against this background I felt I was watching one of those rare acts prompted by deep inner sympathy. The man lifted out his comrade's false teeth, and, looking up at me, said simply: 'For the wife of my friend."

I thought that I had seldom heard more moving words.

CHAPTER 8

Munich: Where It All Began

WHEN THE celebrated Rainbow Division took over Munich on May Day, they quickly selected Hitler's private apartment on Prinzregenten Platz for a Command Post. One of the first directives issued from their new CP was an invitation to a cocktail party in Adolf's flat. I was escorted to this affair by my pilot, Eddie Lyster, and by a Captain in Military Government. It was an unprecedented experience for me to be guided through a souvenir's paradise like Adolf's apartment by an officer in Military Government. But the place had been gone over so thoroughly by the 42nd Division that only the heaviest of its movable objects remained.

I was, however, both startled and grateful when the Captain suddenly threw his arms around a tall metallic nude and started staggering downstairs under this crushing weight of symbolic German womanhood, which he placed in the jeep for me. Eddie took his cue from the Captain and, sighting an even heavier art object in the Führer's parlor, a pair of dancing girls, grasped them by their unyielding bronze skirts and struggled downstairs with them. I wrapped the statues in a blanket, and when I had them packed in my barracks bag it took two strong men to lift it—not the easiest type of souvenir to cart around with one!

Major Vessels, efficient and gracious as ever, with Private Jordan and the rest of his able staff, had a wonderful house this time for the Air Power Press Camp. Sergeant Asch had chosen it in a suburb and had requisitioned it from a firmly documented Nazi. The house had big open porches smothered in fragrant white lilacs. It was surrounded with spectacular gardens and edged by a wood carpeted with pine needles and hepaticas, sloping to the River Isar. Asch had chosen a neighborhood where all the best people had lived; in the same block was a hideaway which had been occupied by Strength-through-Joy Ley.

When the Sergeant had arrived at the front gate to inspect the house, its owner, a wealthy antique-silver merchant was already standing on the front porch wringing his hands. He had always hated the Nazis, he explained, and loved the Americans. He had only joined the Party to be able better to help his Jewish friends. Sergeant Asch followed current practice in allowing the family two hours to pack their personal effects. Bedding and mattresses they must not take; we would need them for the press. The wife and daughter packed clothes, while the man laid out on the library table a collection of letters which had been exchanged between his family and their American friends. With them he placed English translations, obviously prepared in anticipation of just such an emergency.

When the silver merchant and his wife and daughter got their suitcases as far as the front stoop, they took one last regretful look at the luxurious home they had enjoyed under Fascism for so long and, turning to Sergeant Asch, protested loudly: "We have no place to go. Where shall we go?" Nazis who had joined the Party to help the poor unfortunate Jews were the Sergeant's specialty. With dignity he replied: "You are Germans. Go to your own people. Germans must help one another." After they had disappeared down the drive, he added, "They've got a pretty daughter. They'll do all right."

While Eddie and I were in Munich, we circled above the city block by block. Eddie followed a marked chart of the city, while I referred constantly to the Baedeker tucked under the safety strap in my lap. Thus we could pick out from the plane each crumbled Nazi shrine: the Hofbrauhaus in the ruined Platzl, made famous by good beer; the Bürgerbrau, the beerhouse made famous by the sinister Nazi *Putsch*; the scarred cube of the new Braunhaus, the leveled lot where the old Braunhaus had been flattened into orange-brown dust.

The residential quarter around Hitler's flat was in fairly good condition, although one bomb had fallen just outside the Führer's window. Nearby were the homes of many of his friends. The house of Hofmann, Hitler's personal photographer, seemed somewhat too modest compared with others in the same neighborhood and especially with that of Himmler's mistress, which was almost over Hofmann's back fence. Her home, moreover, had the added distinction of a pillbox in the front yard. In the two houses just across the street—a fact evidently unknown to the lady or her powerful lover—had been concealed the headquarters of the Bavarian resistance movement.

My pilot, for all his Mad Hatter ways when he was on the ground, was an accomplished flier who could roll over a photographic subject with such beautiful balance that even when I was upside down, I was hugged firmly but lightly to my seat. In a steep spin, the least unbalance builds a pressure which is paralyzing and makes manipulating a camera impossible. With Eddie Lyster, I worked with as much ease as though I were shooting inside a studio.

Eddie, who had been flying giant troop transports, complained from time to time that our little plane was no faster than a jeep if we had the wind against us. I didn't care how long it took us between spots since, when we reached our objective, the tiny maneuverable plane was ideal for airplane photography. We lived a gypsy life in that cub, with a couple of jerry-cans of gas under the seat, so we could land on a country road or edge of a field to refuel, during our long cross-country trips. We hedge-hopped in the little plane over the length and breadth of occupied Germany, photographing practically every major city and bombed industrial center, from altitudes that varied from twenty feet to two miles.

When Eddie and I flew north and landed at Brunswick, I found we were at the home of the Rolleiflex camera. It was good to hear that the factory was being operated by our Army, because both of my Rolleiflexes had reached such a state of disintegration that I would have discarded them long ago if there had been any possibility of replacing them—I was getting only one picture out of every three or four I shot. After all, the camera had gone through the entire war and received considerable punishment on many fronts. It had long been impossible for our home office to buy much equipment for us in America, for during the war there was little to be had. Photographers were finding it equally impossible to buy from GIs in Germany, for any sums, although we often tried. When soldiers were in the field, their "liberated" cameras were cherished souvenirs, and it was only when they reached the larger cities, where unbelievably profitable black markets flourished, that photographic equipment began to filter out of their hands.

Sometimes the boys did funny but unfortunate things. One soldier who came on a cache of fifty Rolleiflexes, having the exaggerated idea which so many people have of the value of lenses, pried them all out, leaving the working parts of the cameras behind. Too late—after he had reached Paris—he found that he had rendered both the cameras and their lenses useless.

It was irritating to a professional, whose own equipment had worn down to the point of complete unreliability, to pass jeepfuls of men decorated like Christmas trees with Contaxes, Leicas, and Rollicords, and not a single one for sale for hard cash offers. However, we all preferred seeing cameras in the hands of GIs who, we felt, deserved them (if anyone can be said to deserve loot) to finding them in the possession of certain officers who made incredibly large hauls. I was never able to confirm the story of the Brigadier General who sent home five hundred Leicas when his unit occupied a large photographic plant near Weimar, but it was a persistent rumor. However, I did see many Colonels in possession of equipment so highly specialized that frequently they didn't even know how to open their fine cameras. Whenever the lucky man with cameras had a genuine interest in photography, I was glad he had something that would contribute to his hobby. But often it was someone who knew just about a camera to be able to pack it and send it home to his children. I could only hope that he had bright youngsters.

Since I had had no luck in replacing my wornout Rolleiflexes either by liberation or by purchase from liberators, I pinned great hopes on Brunswick, where the Army was starting to manufacture cameras for their own personnel; and the Signal Corps very kindly gave me one of these new ones. But the Signal Corps might as well have kept the Rolleiflex. I dispatched it to our Paris office, where I had made arrangements to have it synchronized for flash work, and sent it by the safest route I knew: in the sealed and sacred press bag on a courier plane. An Army courier has the same inviolability as the U.S. mails; but the camera never reached its destination. It may possibly have reached Paris: that I was never able to check. The probability is that it did, for any good camera at that time was bringing one thousand dollars on the Paris black market.

Later even a box of old clothes I sent back from Berlin was stolen while en route by Army courier (of course, clothes were bringing fabulous sums by then in both France and Germany), and routine press and mail sacks finally became subject to frequent and inexplicable disappearances. The Hitler statues, incidentally, never reached their destination, either. I have not missed them. They would have made me feel, I think, like those persons who take pieces of hangman's rope for souvenirs.

It was not surprising, perhaps, that we heard a great deal about the Russians' spiriting away of industrial equipment, and their alleged kidnaping of struggling, protesting scientists, while American and British behavior, whether on a national or individual scale, was always referred to in the most respectful terms. It was an undiscussed but interesting point that all over occupied Germany the hasty dipping into an area's assets was conducted like a race up to the very moment of the reshuffling of the occupational zones. The handling of the Rolleiflex factory was a pint-size example: here the objective seemed to be to get as many cameras as possible off the assembly line before this area, originally captured by the Americans, should fall into the newly delineated British zone, under the SHAEF occupation plan.

At Brunswick the Americans had some production hurdles to overcome, for when the Army occupied the factory they found that though it contained a large quantity of half-completed cameras, the inside mechanical parts were missing. After an exhaustive search the parts were turned up at the bottom of a deep salt mine, along with stacks of Party files, soap, historical records, and gas masks. Through Military Government the Army hired as many civilian technicians as they could get, and under the supervision of the Signal Corps production was rushed full tilt until the British took over.

All over Germany there were similar dashes, up to the very moment that a zone changed hands. Perhaps the most feverish scrounging was carried on in the field of scientific and industrial discoveries, extending even to flesh-and-blood scientists. It would seem that the Russians did not have the monopoly customarily claimed for them, of secretly whisking scientists away; for the shipping to America of experts—including synthetic-rubber technicians, opticians from Zeiss, and university researchers—went on, even though behind a curtain of silence. Of course, coincidentally with these proceedings there were many joint U.S.-British investigation teams hard at work, cooperating on a host of scientific projects. These were top-secret missions, but even more secret, during those early days, was this quasi-legal inter-Allied looting.

An observant American officer remarked to me: "To all outward appearances the British and American specialists were very cordial to one another. But did you get the undercurrent? The competition was very keen. The British had the jump on us. They gave their representatives high commissions. Ours had only civilian status and had to go through 'channels.' Theirs could move where they liked: they had enough rank so they could get around easily. Ours had only U.S. tabs on their shoulders. But the British were even more efficient when it was a question of getting their men out before the Russians came in."

This international race was engendered partly by the competition between nations which alliance in the war never entirely erased, and also by the necessity of getting at German scientific records before the Germans destroyed them. Many of our teams of experts, briefed for months before they entered Germany, knew exactly what they were looking for, and usually where to look for it. Scientific secrets have become one of the great prizes of war and with the development of atomic energy the scientists themselves have come into that category.

CHAPTER 9

Krupp Suckles the Wehrmacht

THE RUHR RIVER winds through a golden and gray checker-board of wheat fields and steel mills in the richest coal basin of Europe. The sun seldom shines clearly in the Ruhr. Coke ovens and steel mills spread an endless veil over waterways, workers' villages and cabbage fields. Even now, with so many factories lying in smudges on the ground, the smokestacks and collieries which rim the horizon with their fretwork are beginning once more to darken the sky. If we, the victors, turn our backs on this smoking skyline, and leave unsupervised this land which we have subdued at such an immense cost in life and work, there is a great danger that the stains in the sky above the furnaces and coke mills may thicken into the war clouds of World War III.

Just south of Essen the Ruhr widens into Lake Baldenai, an idyllic body of water bordered with woods and grain fields; and above the lake, on the top of the highest hill, is the Villa Hügel, the Krupp family mansion. The very name of Krupp echoes the crunch of a military boot on gravel. Five generations of Krupps throughout five wars have been to the German Army what the engine room is to a battleship. Without Krupp the Germany Army could not have lived or become the terrible and evil force that it was.

Friedrich Krupp, who founded the Cast Steel Works at Essen in 1810, began building the firm and family fortunes on arms manufacture. His son Alfred sold Krupp guns to both sides in the Austro–Prussian War in 1866. He equipped the Prussian Army in 1870 for the Franco–Prussian War. Under his grand-son Friedrich Alfred, Krupp steel entered ocean warfare when the Krupps began building battleships. During World War I his great-granddaughter Bertha gave her name to the Kaiser's biggest gun; and as World War II was drawing to a close it was the founder's great-great-grandson Alfried who rolled the toughest tank steels for Hitler's armies.

Krupp was more to Germany than just another steel plant. As wars grew bigger and more scientific, Krupp was the experimental laboratory for the Generals. Army officers married into the Krupp family and became business representatives of the company. Krupp executives filtered into the Army and became ballistics experts. The Government was ready to finance the Krupps when they needed it during the leaner years; and Krupp cooperated during the rise of Hitler. Krupp devised a simple universal workers' tax which helped finance the Nazi treasury. The weapons of war are now shifting to nuclear physics; but during the Krupp reign, war's backbone was steel, and for more than a century the Krupps and the German Army, hand in hand, molded military history. What they have cost the world in blood and treasure is past measuring, but the lives number in millions and the treasure in hundreds of billions.

The most noted of the Krupps was Alfred, old Friedrich's son. In 1871 he decided that the time had come to move into a mansion more fitting to the Krupp dynasty. For twenty-five years he had insisted on living within the factory gates, most of that time in the original ancestral cabin beside which his father had erected the first mill and melting furnace. There was no middle ground in the living arrangements of Alfred Krupp. He stepped from the house in the plant into the Villa Hügel, or House on the Hill, a mansion of one hundred and seventy-seven rooms. The mausoleum-type architecture and the details of interior decoration and plumbing he planned himself. In the gigantic twin cubes of masonry which make up the Villa Hügel he designed the gold fixtures of his solid-marble bathtub, styled the doorknobs, laid out four stories of music rooms and guest suites, connected the floors with elevators, and topped all with a colossal skylight arched over a ballroom sixty-five feet high.

The final effect was a cross between Versailles and Valhalla. The Villa Hügel had its own private railway station, large enough to accommodate two private railroad trains, Mr. Krupp's and the Kaiser's. A special bedroom suite was designed by the armament king for his imperial friend, with a sitting room furnished in dull red brocade and a sleeping

chamber hung with tapestries depicting the Garden of Eden.
When Kaiser Wilhelm I (and later Kaiser Wilhelm II, who was
also a frequent house guest) opened his royal eyes after a restful
night at Hügel, he could lie in bed and study, in the priceless
needlework which covered his bedroom walls, the life story of
Adam, the first recorded Jew.

Either one Emperor or the other was present at all important
Krupp family events. Kaiser Wilhelm II, at the marriage of
Alfred's eldest granddaughter, ruled that her bridegroom
should take the name of Krupp so that armament's greatest
name would be perpetuated. It is because of this edict that the
present head of the firm, now held as a war criminal, a Krupp
only on his mother's side, bears the name of Alfried Krupp von
Bohlen und Halbach.

When the Villa Hügel was requisitioned to billet men of the
American Army, it was a terrible moment for Krupp's major-
domo, Herr Dohrmann. Casting a watchful eye over the breakfast tray of the King of Roumania, choosing table wines for
visiting Prussian admirals or foreign diplomats, making sure
the Shah of Persia had enough blankets on his bed at night
—these had been happier services. However, he was the perfect
retainer. There was no household emergency his varied experiences had not fitted him to meet smoothly and efficiently, so
even when the house guests represented an occupying army, he
did his best.

As a matter of fact, with the arrival of the Americans Herr
Dohrmann found himself faring better than his master, for
Alfried Krupp was placed under house arrest and held for in-
terrogation. Dohrmann was not merely not arrested, but he continued to receive his weekly wages—a SHAEF directive states
that when an occupying unit takes over an establishment's
help, it may pay the same wage rate as the former employer.

Thus for several weeks Dohrmann continued to receive his
four hundred sixty marks a month; Wilhelmina, the chief cook
who had worked for the Krupp household since the age of
fourteen (and who performed miracles with the rations which
our Army provided), drew her three hundred marks; and the
Zimmermädchen received the one hundred twenty per month
which Mr. Krupp had paid his housemaids. Major Peter
Messer, ex-English teacher from New Haven, who adminis-

tered the Villa, simply took the Krupp payroll and turned it over to the Finance Department, and the Army paid. The pay did not mean as much to the staff as did the rations and the temporary security which the arrangement provided. But what must have meant most of all, at least to loyal Herr Dohrmann, was the excellent job that was done in running the Villa Hügel, and the conscientious care taken of the house.

When I arrived in ruined Essen to do a picture series for *Life*, I drove out to the Villa Hügel hoping to find a place to stay. On the grand staircase of the salon I found Major Willis Biggs, an Engineering officer from Chicago, supervising preparations for the expected influx of scientists and financiers—the Villa had been requisitioned to billet a task force of experts. Major Biggs looked like a plump child playing house, in his one-piece coveralls, with his chubby face and bald head an unbroken pink from his housekeeping activities. When he learned I had no home, he said, "We're looking for customers." And he installed me at once in Herr Krupp's own suite, ordering up sheets for the spacious Krupp bed, and towels for the gold-fitted bathroom; Herr Krupp by this time had been moved into the servants' quarters.

It took me less time to unpack my limited supply of clothes than it did to choose which of the twenty walnut wardrobes I should hang them in. These had sliding doors of exquisitely matched woods, and lined a dressing room two stories high. The lofty ceiling was painted with a goddess rocking dangerously on a crescent moon, her hair pinned back—as one might expect —with a star; and just under her was a balcony, carved with foxes and hounds, running completely around the dressing room.

I never was able to discover the purposes of all the gold levers for the showers, the multiple goosenecked water taps for the handbowls and toothbrush bowl, and the other extensive accessories in the Krupp bathroom. But the gold-and-marble tub I put to use at once. After the heavy bombings, running water in Germany was not easy to find, and to find water not only running but also hot was indeed a rarity. Later I learned that old Alfred Krupp was responsible for this beautiful hot water, just as he was for the faucets. When he built Hügel, he devised an installation which took water from the Ruhr and converted it to steam in a plant by the river bank. The steam-pipes ran up the hill to the big house, sunk under the driveways. He had bestowed the same attention to detail on the bathtub itself: at one end a seat had been carved out of the solid marble slab. Undoubtedly he must have enjoyed sitting on that half-submerged marble bench, reflecting that the water which gushed so hot from his golden faucets had already accomplished a chore in melting the ice from his driveways.

Down in the cavernous drawing room I found Major Biggs supervising the laying of a Spanish rug, which measured just under one hundred feet in length and weighed two thousand four hundred pounds. Alfried Krupp had worried a great deal about this rug during the bombings, the servants told Major Biggs. He was afraid the house would be burned down with the rug inside, and all through the war he planned to move it to some place of greater safety, but never succeeded in getting this done. As Major Biggs commented, "You can't just roll up a rug and carry it away when it weighs a ton and a fifth." Old Alfred hadn't planned on having wars fought at home.

Major Biggs and Lieutenant Frederick Wittig, his man Friday, were very busy for the next few days getting Hügel ready for the first contingent of scientists and financial experts. Lieutenant Wittig had been an assistant manager of the New Yorker Hotel, and he and the Major began by turning the ballroom under its vast skylight into an "Information Room" for the specialists. They moved out quantities of brocaded sofas to make room for desks and typewriters, they hung charts and maps over the family portraits, and set up a number of bulletin boards for the graphs and diagrams which the experts would use as they evaluated Ruhr industry and Reich finance.

Next they had enormous tablecloths brought out for the hundred-foot dining-room table, where the experts would have mess. They unpacked and counted the silver tableware and the gold ice-cream spoons, connected the automatic potato-masher and the yard-wide electric frying machines, and set up the electric ice-cream freezer. For the recreation of the enlisted men assigned to guard duty at Hügel, they filled the steam-heated swimming pool. For recreation for the officers and experts they unlocked the cases of music rolls, and had the self-propelled organ put back in shape.

Lieutenant Wittig, in the grateful presence of Herr Dohrmann, listed the entire contents of the Silver Room: the coffee service presented by Kaiser Wilhelm, with his profile engraved on each bowl and pitcher; the silver cup presented by Adolf Hitler, with his profile inlaid in a medallion; the Cowes regatta trophy presented by King George V in 1901, and the many other impressive racing trophies—some as big as beer barrels —won by the Krupp yacht *Germania*.

After inventory, Lieutenant Wittig locked the double doors of the Silver Room. There was to be no looting at Villa Hügel. And, later, there was only one infraction of this rule—by an individual so much higher in rank than these officers that no one could do anything about it but gasp.

Soon the scientific "Target Teams" began to arrive. Some of the men were members of the Army, many were civilians in uniform, borrowed from private industry by the War Department, and accredited to the Army. In the first wave, our best-known scientist was Victor Conquest, the originator of powdered eggs, who had come to study German synthetic foods. One of his finds was a sort of margarine made from petroleum, which he pronounced waxy but edible. William W. Farr, an ordnance expert, arrived from the War Department to investigate recoil-less weapons. Commander Pettijohn came from the Navy to explore details of new and radical submarine parts. Other specialists arrived to find out everything the Germans knew about rockets, atabrine, new fuels, and space lattices of silicates. In some fields the Hügel specialists unearthed new and secret discoveries—some practical, and some not yet developed. In other branches of science they reached the gratifying conclusion that the enemy knew no more, or even less, than we. But this investigation was important, whether it was with silica resins, where the Germans did much original research; in extrusion processes for screws and bolts, where our enemy was far behind; in the world of paint, where Germany developed a remarkable radar-resisting coating—though one no better than our own; or in infra-red detection, in which field the Germans developed but did not have time to put into production a locater so sensitive that it would detect a soldier at night in a foxhole two thousand feet away.

In addition to the various teams of scientists and the "Finance Investigation Unit for External Assets" who were billeted at Hügel, there were transient house guests. One of these was aide-de-camp to Prince Bernhard of the Netherlands. He came twice, and when he brought two wheels and a set of tires on his second visit, we realized how thoroughly he had "G-2'd" the situation on his first. He had apparently listed the make, condition, and motor-block number of every car in Herr Krupp's garage (there were seven, including two enormous Meybachs); and he returned with instructions not to step on the toes of any of the Allied Commanders, but to bring back three Mercedes-Benzes if possible. His arrangements for motorcars went through higher echelons than those at Hügel, and I heard that he left without the two big supercharged Mercedes limousines but with the medium-size Mercedes sedan, which had needed the two wheels and four tires.

Not far from the garage were the servants' quarters where Alfried Krupp was under house arrest. Quantities of his well-tailored clothes and a large collection of novels had been moved into the little yellow clapboard house where he was quartered, and at almost any hour of the day a housemaid or waiter from the Great House could be seen walking down the drive with a hot dish or a tray for young Herr Krupp. He was being held "incommunicado," but for weeks no definite directives were issued as to how the embarrassing prisoner was to be treated. Until somebody remembered to take out his private telephone he had communication, not with the outside world, exactly, but with his estate and his factory, which was really all he needed to keep an eye on his interests. When the phone was removed, a gloomy creature with a briefcase managed to slip in and spend occasional nights in the servants' quarters with his boss. This was Mr. Karl Eberhardt, the financial manager of the company, who was apparently pulling all possible strings to get the Krupp factories going again. No one knew just how Mr. Eberhardt got the gasoline or the permits for his extensive business trips, as journeying from one city to another was firmly restricted at this time. No one knew how the brunette from Düsseldorf got her gasoline or permit, either. For Alfried Krupp's girl-friend Alexis, a tall arrogant beauty reputed to be "very rich," got into the servants' quarters to see him, too.

In fact, Alfried Krupp had almost everything he needed to make his house arrest comfortable, except enough cigarettes.

But remedying the shortage was easy, even though he was a chain smoker. He had a number of copies of his official family biography printed in English, and he began passing them out to the enlisted men detailed to guard the grounds. I don't know the exact exchange rate for each copy of *The Krupps: 150 Years of Krupp History*, but I suppose if the volume was autographed it brought about a carton of American cigarettes. Some of his inscriptions were lengthy and flowery, and they all dealt with the dignity of family. In the flyleaf of the book he gave to one of his guards, he wrote: "Tradition, honestly kept by men, families, and nations, is one of the monuments of their grandfathers' pioneer work—yesterday, today, and, I hope, tomorrow."

In addition to having one hundred and fifty years of Krupp family history to read, the enlisted men also had the family boathouse to enjoy. This was set in a little park at the foot of the estate, where the Ruhr River widened into Lake Baldenai. Through the park ran a pleasant network of paths, and in former days the Krupps had allowed the general public occasional access to these wooded walks, for a small admission charge. Now, during the occupation, the surface of the lake was always lively with little racing sculls which Special Services had corralled for the men.

Beyond the little woods and lining both sides of Lake Baldenai were billowing wheat fields which the enlisted men found extremely convenient, since the fraternization rules were so slow in being modified. A recent directive from their commanding general stated in vivid detail that the soldiers were forbidden "to give gum to babies" and that they must not "initiate a smile or return a salute." I don't know whether the GIs or the fräuleins initiated the smiles, but smiles and wheat were frequently blended together.

It was the duty of the MPs to see that the General's directive was being followed, and in order to do this they patrolled the waterfront in small boats. This was a strenuous assignment, since the fraternizers often had small boats also, and more than one MP came home exhausted at night, saying he was "going to be all shoulders after that job." A solution for this situation was found, but it raised a loud cry from the enlisted men, who felt unfair advantage was being taken of them. The MPs were finally given a motorboat.

CHAPTER 10

Bomb Shelters Were Too Expensive

UNDER THE Krupp mansion was a network of shelters carved out of solid rock. Some chambers were fitted with furniture and electric lights, and one of them contained a bed for Herr Krupp, and a library. There were installations of tracks, and mine cars which could move out rubble, in case of a direct hit. And in no case could a Krupp get trapped underground, because there were several exits through the side of the hill, as well as one up into the kitchen.

This shelter interested me particularly because I had noticed a singular difference between Essen and other cities. Bremen had enormous bunkers, so well built that citizens within reach when the alarm sounded could be nearly certain of coming through the raid alive. I had seen bunkers in Cologne of such massive construction that they had withstood six direct hits. Frankfurt, Schweinfurt, Ludwigshafen—one could call the roll of industrial cities and find that all had huge bunkers of reinforced concrete where people lived, miserably no doubt, but in almost complete security from bombs. These remarkable structures all over Germany were so well planned that they included ventilating systems, lighting installations, and often even movie theaters. The type of reinforced concrete they used was so superior that "T"-Force sent over a commission of American construction men to study it.

But the City of Essen, with its enormous Krupp Armament Works, had not even one adequate shelter to protect its workers. The Krupps' much-publicized interest in workers' welfare ceased at the time their workers needed it most—and when other German war-industries were investing heavily in bomb protection.

It seems inconsistent that a steel plant making armaments should have ignored the necessity of protecting their workmen against that very warfare about which they knew so much. The people at Essen huddled into cellars and basements while the Krupp "Air Raid Protection Section," a committee which had no real power, drew up plans; but when appeals were made for bunkers, the projects were rejected as being "too expensive."

There may have been more than the motive of economy behind this. The manufacture of steel is a twenty-four-hour process; interruptions impair the "heat." Perhaps the Krupps did not want their workers running to the shelters too often. The possibility that production schedules were involved seems to be substantiated by the way the intervals of warning were shortened, as the bombings grew more furious. In 1944, Krupp workers told me, so little warning was given that frequently the people saw bombs dropping around them and only afterward heard the "acute" alarm.

The crane runners in the open-hearth plants had the hardest time. Sometimes they would be caught in a place from which they had to walk one hundred feet over open steel construction before they could get down and dash under some sort of shelter. In some Krupp mills, workmen leaped into the foundry pits; in others, they were grateful for bombs which had fallen before, as they could dive into the craters and pull loose steel sheets over their heads. When communications became so disrupted that the Krupps could no longer ship out their steel, the workers were thankful for the accumulation of extra ingots and armor plate which they could pile on top of their makeshift shelters.

In the midst of these difficulties, the Krupp executives still had time to draw up an extensive rubble-removal program which they planned to put into effect as soon as the war was over. They estimated that it would take two years to sort the wreckage and glean usable fragments like piping and tiles. An overhead railroad would be built to a valley where they would dump six square miles of waste; for six continuous years they planned to move waste scrap at the rate of two thousand tons a night.

During the final war years, when the bombings increased in fury, life for a Krupp worker must have been dreadful almost beyond imagination. One of the metallurgists told me that after each big bombing "in the center of the city, you couldn't tell where the houses were or where the streets had been. I just walked by the sun. And then the fumes. All the city is black after an attack like that. You can't see more than two blocks ahead, and your eyes get red and swollen from the smoke." The skilled workmen, he told me, became more discouraged than anyone else because so much time was stolen away from their specialized tasks by the constant need for rebuilding. "You work all the time," he said, "during the danger. Then every two or three days everything is destroyed. You lose courage."

Finally it all seemed so senseless, he said, that the men just wanted to collect the wood scrap, and build big fires that they could stay around all day. But still they kept working. The ingenuity which went into steel manufacture in these very badly damaged plants was tremendous. Metallurgical shortcuts were devised; speeds in processing were stepped up. During my photographing in the Krupp mills, after the war was over, I saw electric furnaces housed under structures that looked like chicken sheds, constructed both to handle the fumes and keep the light of the molten metal from the sky. For patching the blackout was a relentless necessity. Even near-misses meant flying fragments which caused light leaks and with a damaged blackout, each pouring of the heat could act as a direction finder for successive waves of bombers.

However, the constant need to mend the blackout, so insistent at the Krupp factory, was spared the Krupps at home. I don't know the total tonnage that fell on the homes of Herr Krupp's workers, but it was enormous. On Hügel buildings, only two bombs fell: a five-hundred-pounder which demolished the racing stables, and a small bomb which hit the greenhouses. Anyway, the Krupp family, like the other big Ruhr families, had an estate in the south where they could retreat if the bombings became intolerable.

At my request, Herr Alfried Krupp was allowed to leave the servants' quarters and spend one hour in his big house. I wanted to photograph him under the family portraits which lined the Grand Salon. He was haughty about having his picture taken for an American magazine, but under the circumstances complied with my request. (On an earlier trip to Germany, before *Life* Magazine was in existence, the editors of *Fortune* had tried very hard to get permission for me to photograph the Essen works, but had given up after six months of repeated refusals from the Krupps.)

Alfried Krupp had a look of bred-out aristocracy with no morals. He was thirty-eight years old, and handsome in a bloodless way. As I took his picture, I questioned him about slave laborers in the Ruhr, to whom he referred by the prettier term of "foreign workers." Although he did not seem to care whether or not he convinced me, he said that most of them had come voluntarily, and had been quite well off, as they had been fed more than German labor had.

This was an even taller story than most of the tales I heard. When I asked why the slaves had been so well fed, he replied, "To keep them satisfied. Of course," he added, "war is difficult. When transportation of food became disrupted, then there was less for everyone. But the only real inconvenience the foreign workers suffered was when their barracks were burned down by the bombings."

It was a pity that it was not until after this interview that I learned the details of the punishment camp in nearby Mülheim for those foreign laborers who refused to work for the enemy, or heard about the Polish girls who were snatched from Warsaw stores where they were shopping, or parks where they were walking, and sent off to the Ruhr without a chance to go home, or about the Russian slave workers who were killed wholesale while the Ruhr was being encircled because the Germans were afraid that when the war was lost the Russians might loot. And it was only later that our soldiers found the shell pits containing the remains of some of Herr Krupp's pampered foreign workers. When these Czechs, Poles, and Italians had passed their peak of usefulness, the Essen Gestapo had its own convenient method of disposing of them. People lined around a shell hole, facing inward, and then shot in the head, tend to topple forward, so that burying them is easy. The Gestapo had a gunman named Paschen, who took such pleasure in these assignments that they were usually reserved for him. One of his big jobs was disposing of seventy people at once. He shot them while their hands were tied together with telephone wire. Paschen had a twisted face that looked as if it had not been properly finished. He wept great tears when CIC arrested him.

But, of course, there was never any need for Steelman Krupp

to meet Triggerman Paschen, on either a social or a business basis. The Arbeitsfront handled everything in Essen. It parceled out the slave labor as needed, deducted the Government's percentage of their wages, collected from the slave workers for their "light, food, and lodgings," and took them off Herr Krupp's hands when their specific jobs were done. All this was the responsibility of Arbeitsfront and so, as usual, the Ruhr industrialists had an excuse when it came to unpleasant charges.

In one way Alfried Krupp was lucky to be under house arrest when the Essen shell holes were found. He was not called upon to help dig out bodies. When similar discoveries were made in other Ruhr cities, leading citizens were frequently required to attend and assist. When a particularly large cache was uncovered near Duisburg, while a watermain was being repaired, the Mayor of Duisburg was requested to help dig out the victims and give them a decent burial.

Although these developments came too late for me to ask Herr Krupp how much he knew of them, I asked him, as I asked many Germans in those days, to express an opinion on the concentration camps.

He shrugged his patrician shoulders. "There might have been a few madmen . . ." he paused, "a few psychopaths . . ." He paused and started again. "The people at the top wouldn't have liked the way their instructions were carried out." Another long pause, and he went on once more, "Yes, there might have been a few of them, maniacs or madmen, who misinterpreted the instructions."

Yes, he had heard rumors. That much he did not deny.

"In our country," I said, "we have public-spirited citizens who will protest when something happens which they think is not right. If you and others like you heard these rumors, why didn't you investigate?"

"The SS would have said it wasn't my duty."

I had seen all I wanted to see of Alfried Krupp, and he was taken back to the servants' quarters.

Our group of financial and technical experts at Hügel was growing steadily larger. It changed a great deal, as new units of investigators replaced others who moved on to different parts of

Germany. At one time we had with us two very eminent members of the Economic Division of the Control Council: one, a titled Englishman, the other, an American General who had been a Wall Street executive in civilian life. We used to do a good deal of talking around the long Krupp dinner table about what constituted a war criminal. We had just launched on one of these discussions one morning when these two important gentlemen joined us at breakfast. We had been carrying on our discussion with the tacit assumption that Herr Krupp was more guilty than the common German soldier.

"They are de-Nazifying washer-women and clerks, but most of the big-shot industrialists have not been touched," said Ernst Ophuls, one of the finance experts. "They are the greatest war criminals in the Ruhr, yet they are runnning free."

"That's a very dangerous theory," broke in the eminent English member of the Control Council, with the air of a curate instructing the young. "What's the matter with those chaps? They're no Nazis."

That was certainly a conversation-stopper. Ophuls was a mere Major and could say no more when the General gave him no support. The fact that correspondents later bestowed upon the General the non-military title of "Revolving-Door Smith" (his real name was not Smith) is perhaps illuminating.

Not far from Villa Hügel, in the Essen suburb of Werden, were the homes of a number of the Krupp executives. One of these, Dr. Houdremont, formerly technical director of the plant, was acting as its head in the enforced absence of Alfried Krupp. He is a brilliant scientist whose books on metallurgy are well known in America and other countries, a cultured and witty man, passionately fond of music, original in his manner of speaking, and hospitable. I was only sorry that he should have left his native land of Luxembourg twenty years ago to come to Germany and work for the Krupps.

But, "Why all the hate against Krupp?" asked Dr. Houdremont when I talked with him. "We are treated worse than any other plant. It is unjust!"

He leaned forward on the sofa, adjusted his heavy-rimmed spectacles, and chose his words carefully.

"We really cared only for our peacetime materials, our locomotives, and parts for textile machinery. Herr Krupp did not want to make war materials. The very thought made him sad. Besides, we thought we were doing what England wanted. We thought England wanted armament in Germany as insurance against Russia."

From this it was only one step farther for Houdremont to say, "Why didn't the English send men in against Hitler when he occupied the Rhineland in '36?" This tendency to place on England the responsibility for Hitler's rise was becoming so widespread that I heard it from German women on street corners, and I heard it even from American soldiers coming back home from Germany.

"The responsibility for everything that is bad is always put on us," Dr. Houdremont continued. "But we were very antiquated in the war-material department. We just made steel. It was impossible for us to control where our steel was used, and what it was used for. We had no way of telling where our steel went."

I could have told him where his steel went, because I had seen it from Africa to the western front. I had seen its tank tracks in the Russian plains, had encountered it from Cassino to Cologne. But by now Dr. Houdremont was explaining his idea of our functions as the occupying power. "All you have to do is control the political handful at the top. Then there won't be any wars. And then you don't have to control industry."

He spoke very strongly about the fate of his former boss. "I can't see why they imprisoned that young man." (A few months later Dr. Houdremont was also arrested.) "You couldn't make a single reproach against Mr. Krupp. And that fine man, his father! Herr Gustav Krupp was a very old man. His brain was in heaven during the last years of Hitler."

Where the brain of Herr Gustav Krupp resided during the early '30s, I am not in a position to say. But it was sufficiently earthbound for him to have announced, through his Board of Directors, in 1934: "We are once more free to pursue the manufacture of arms of which we had been deprived by the Versailles Treaty." And as early as 1933, in an annual report, he stated: "The national rebirth of our people has filled the German nation with a new faith. The mismanagement of political parties has been abolished. Class warfare and its decaying effect has been ended.

"Filled with happiness, we stand behind the Führer of a united nation."

Eminent Englishmen and Revolving-Door Generals, please note.

CHAPTER 11

Home Is Where the Heart Is

THE MAN from Missouri was very nervous. He ran to overtake me in the corridor as he saw me leaving the French Director's office in the Röchling Steel Works in Saarbrücken. His heavy German accent made his English difficult to understand, and there were permanent lines of worry between his eyes. He was in a great hurry to show me his American passport, and as he searched in his pocket for it with his left hand, he managed somehow to start shaking hands with me with his right. He kept pumping my hand until I thought I would never be able to free it from his moist grasp.

"All that is necessary is to tell them I was detained by events of war, is it not so?"

I couldn't catch the drift of this, and he rushed on to say, "The Military Government wanted to tell me my citizenship had expired. That was because you are supposed to go back every two years to America for keeping your passport good. But I said to them 'No, I was not able to get back.'"

I had managed to free my hand by now, and I took a look at his passport. He was Eugene Pracht of St. Genevieve, Missouri, a naturalized American citizen, who had come back to the homeland with his wife, also a naturalized American, and his son, who had been born in St. Louis. Mr. Pracht's specialty was lime, he told me. He had been a superintendent in the St. Genevieve Lime and Quarry Corporation, and had also worked in the drafting department of Babcock and Wilcox in Ohio, designing boilers. Then, after coming back to Germany with his family, he "got mixed up in the war situation and couldn't get home."

Like some of the greater industrial figures in Germany, Mr. Pracht was ready with his handout. He had photostated copies of a seven-year-old blurb about himself in a cement-and-lime trade magazine called *Rock Products*. This had been written on the occasion of his breaking away from St. Genevieve to go back to Saarbrücken, and it was the kind of flattering farewell that might have been expected: how much his lime-and-cement friends would miss him; what a fine fellow he had been; and so on.

Mr. Pracht had held a very nice job during the war. His post as technical expert on lime at the Röchling Steel Works had mushroomed during the German occupation of France; between 1941 and 1944 he had spent most of his time actually in France. This was because his boss, Herr Hohlshuh, at the Röchling Works, had been a German Iron and Steel Director for eastern France.

It was an interesting detail that the French industrialist who had been assistant to Herr Hohlshuh then was the same French director who had been sent back to Germany to manage Röchling now. And as new director of Röchling, he chose his old boss to serve directly under him. Thus the German steel director during the occupation of France became the assistant to the French steel director during the occupation of Saarland. The two had simply reversed their positions as their respective countries alternated between defeat and victory. After this exchange, Herr Hohlshuh and Monsieur Georges Thedrel continued to work amicably together as before, and Mr. Pracht, the naturalized American, worked quite smoothly with both of them, just as before.

I was interested in learning what I could about how well the French and Germans had cooperated when the Germans were on French soil. I had been given previous accounts of French foreign labor in Germany, and had been told that among the various nationalities the Germans could count on the best help from the French. French laborers were fed the best of all the workers, paid the most, and allowed to send home their earnings through the Reichsbank, an unthinkable privilege for any other type of slave labor. Also, the French were better organized to bargain. In Essen, for example, they dealt with Arbeitsfront through a *Betriebs Obermann*, an overseer who acted as a "man of confidence" between the French labor and the Germans. In one dramatic instance about which I was told, after a furious bombing had started fires which threatened a large quantity of machinery, the factory superintendent rushed to the "man of confidence" and secured a squad of French prisoners of war who, acccording to the German superintendent, "worked like nobody's business" and saved the machinery.

I thought Mr. Pracht with his experience in occupied France should be able to throw light on how the French in their own occupied plants cooperated with the Germans. "We got along swell," said Mr. Pracht. "There was real collaboration." During the German occupation of France, Mr. Pracht's particular area had been Lorraine, where lime has important applications in ore refining and in certain steel processes. He had found his experience with the French very pleasant indeed. "All those people in the lime plants were very nice," Mr. Pracht told me. "I improved some of their furnaces. I improved some of their products; they appreciated it. They were turning out burnt lime for making steel—that is, for the ore plants in Lorraine. The people in eastern France and western Germany have to work together."

While Mr. Pracht and I were talking, Herr Hohlshuh came down the corridor and he too started shaking my hand as though he would never let it go. I was beginning to see why British Military Government had issued a directive against shaking hands with Germans, and I resolved to obey it myself in the future. Herr Hohlshuh's hand was as dry as the skin on his face: I had seldom seen a forehead and cheeks so threaded with tiny wrinkles. Herr Hohlshuh, though without Mr. Pracht's advantage of American citizenship, spoke better English, and told me more about how the Germans got along with the French during their occupation.

"Technicians always get along," he said. "Technical people always understand one another. There was wonderful collaboration in France between the German and French engineers."

"Yes, wonderful," Mr. Pracht parroted his boss. "Good collaboration—it is the best way."

"They were no trouble at all, the French," said Herr Hohlshuh. "They produced everything we could reasonably expect." I was sure there must be a reverse side to this coin, for I knew of many French fliers—some of them were personal friends of mine—who had been rescued by the courageous French underground and shuttled away to fight against the Germans once more. There must have been some counterpart in the industrial picture. But naturally I could not expect to hear about this from Herr Hohlshuh or Mr. Pracht.

"Always we could get along with the French," affirmed Mr. Pracht, "as long as we were polite with them, and nice."

There was no doubt that Mr. Pracht had been very polite and nice to everyone on both sides of all fences, and so had his wife. This hospitable couple had been so polite and nice to the Americans who occupied the Saar with the first wave that they had achieved results at once. Whereas most good houses were immediately requisitioned for reasons of military necessity (and the necessity was very real in a place like Saarbrücken, even more grimly flattened than most German cities), still the Prachts had kept their home to themselves. They had an "off limits" sign in the yard, a tangible sign of success with the authorities. There was wine in their cellar (that was really a miracle) and packs of Chesterfields on each little coffee table in their well-furnished living room.

Mrs. Pracht, although she had been an American citizen for fewer years than her husband, spoke better English than he. She was overjoyed to see an American woman. She was longing to get back to her friends in the United States; what did I know about the possibilities?

"Do you really expect to get back to America?" I asked.

"We have to," said Mrs. Pracht. "Our house is there."

"Another house!"

"I have property in the United States in St. Genevieve, Missouri," said Mr. Pracht, with a good deal of pride. "I had it rented all through the war. The bank took care of it. My house rented for forty dollars a month. The bank took care of renting, and of repairs—everything. I have never heard from them. Mail doesn't move yet."

"But there are ways," said Mrs. Pracht.

"What ways?" I asked.

"We gave a letter to a very nice American Captain in the Heavy Field Artillery," said Mrs. Pracht, and then added hastily, "Well, you know, it is illegal, but the Captain found men going back."

There was no doubt that in the mind of Mrs. Pracht they were already rocking in their wicker chairs on their front porch in St. Genevieve, their experience in wartime Germany just an interesting memory to tell their neighbors.

"How are your friends from Missouri going to feel about all this?" I asked.

"What else could we do?" said Mrs. Pracht. "We never would have thought a war would break out. Just considering the family life, it would have been much easier over there in America. At best, we would have been together and not had all the worries."

"And not had that affair over Walter," added her husband. "Only sixteen and a half, our son is, and they tried to pick him up. What a trouble we had to keep Walter out of the Volkssturm!"

"And with the baby to think of," said Mrs. Pracht. "How could I travel with such a little baby? What would you have done?"

I knew that return to America had been made practical and convenient for people like that. After the war had broken out, there was excellent train service provided to take them from Germany to an embarkation point in Italy. And later, when Italy herself was in the war, there were American planes to fly them from Berlin to Portugal. In 1940 the American Consulate had warned naturalized Americans of German birth to go back to the United States or risk losing their citizenship.

I knew further that in 1938 Germany had made a great effort to get its German-born back to the fatherland, whether or not they were naturalized Americans. Technicians were in particular demand as were students who might be able to broadcast for the German government. When the situation became tense, in 1938, the German Consulate gave orders for Germans to return, even acrobats who were touring the United States. That was the big year for the flow back to Germany, and the "re-immigrants," as they were called, were treated particularly well and given a "special-facilities letter" which they could carry everywhere in Germany. I thought it significant that 1938 should have been the year that the Prachts abandoned Missouri for Saarland, and I found it particularly interesting that they should not have heeded the American Consulate's warnings to come home—for I felt sure they must have received them. Without my asking her, Mrs. Pracht seemed to feel the necessity of explaining.

"In January, 1940, when I took my little daughter to the Consulate to be registered, they talked to me about going back. But I didn't know why we should want to go through all the trouble and hardship, when we didn't believe war was really coming."

"You thought that Germany would win," I said.

"Just knowing that America decided the last war," said Mr. Pracht, "I thought that Hitler would keep out of a war that involved America."

"What would you have done?" said Mrs. Pracht. "It all came so unexpectedly."

"I had to do something to keep my family alive," said Mr. Pracht.

"Even working against your adopted country during a war?"

"What could I do?" Mr. Pracht repeated. "Because I was an engineer, I was always invited here and there. All I did was to help make machinery for general rolling of steel and ingots. All for general purposes."

Mrs. Pracht kept nervously passing me the cigarettes, never noticing when I still held a lighted one in my hand. She kept telling me that she so hoped I would accept their hospitality for the night. I could have the nice guest room all to myself, and it had a private bath. I had seen both the guest room and the bath, and they were indeed very nice. The bath was tiled in a dark maroon and matched the thick silk quilts on the guest bed; the bath towels were ecru, monogrammed in red. But I was more interested in keeping the conversation on the uses of the products from the steel plants where Mr. Pracht had worked.

Yes, he knew a good deal of steel went into ammunition. But sometimes metal was used for food cans. Or just for I-beams, for structural purposes only.

"We never really knew what that stuff was used for," said Mr. Pracht.

"And think of all the hardships we went through," said Mrs. Pracht. "When Saarbrücken was being bombed last October 5, the whole city was completely destroyed. And we were lying in the shelter."

"And then the way the Gestapo would listen," said Mr. Pracht. "They had a microphone on a long pole and they would lift it up to the bedroom windows to hear what people were saying."

I found this a fascinating detail, and when I questioned them about it I learned that it had been something of a comfort to have Papa in the house. Papa Kremer, Mr. Pracht's father-in-law, was first assistant in the Justice Department, a Party member, of course, working immediately under the civil court judge.

"That must have helped you," I said.

"We didn't have any advantages. We didn't have any dis-advantages," said Mrs. Pracht. "Except for the affair with Walter when they tried to pick him up, they left us alone."

Leaving the Prachts alone was exactly what I proposed to do also. There were not many roofs under which to spend the night in Saarland, but still I did not think I wished to stay in the Prachts' maroon-and-ecru guest room. Keeping my hands firmly in my pockets, to prevent any farewell handshakings, I said goodbye.

It was growing dark as I headed out of the town, but I could still make out the outlines of the Röchling's Eisen and Stahl-werke. It was a large plant, and must have produced a good deal of steel up to the time of the last great bombings. I doubted whether even a lime technician would believe all that steel went for I-beams and food cans. But then, it was Eugene Pracht, not I, who was from Missouri.

CHAPTER 12

Hildegarde Again

ALL THROUGH the time I spent in the Ruhr the recollection of my talk with Hildegarde Roselius puzzled and worried me. It seemed so strange that this educated and intelligent woman, who had been an interesting person in New York, should prove such an ardent and unrepentant Nazi. Perhaps in some way I had misunderstood her and had been unjust. It worried me, and a few weeks after the end of the war, when I was driving through Bremen on my way to Kiel, I stopped at Number Three Böttscher Strasse to call on her again.

"I have something quite special for you," said Hildegarde, ushering me into her cloakroom-apartment. "See, a surprise —a princess!"

Hildegarde's royal refugee, who had come from Bavaria on foot, with an occasional lift by truck, was Princess Marie Adelheide Heuss zu Lippe. She was related to the royal families of Great Britain and Holland through one of those typically complicated relationships of European royalty. She boasted distant kinship with an English queen and, more closely, with the present Prince Bernhard zu Lippe-Biesterfeld of the Netherlands.

During her long journey on the roads from south to north Germany, this royal hitchhiker had learned some of the ropes. When she finally arrived at the outskirts of Bremen, night was falling and, rather than try to make her way on foot through the almost unrecognizable streets, she had hunted up the nearest unit of American soldiers.

"I said to them 'Will you kindly arrest me?' " the Princess said.

" 'Why do you want to be arrested?' they asked.

"I explained that it was only a half-hour until curfew, and it would be too late to find my friend that night. I introduced myself, and said I would have no place to stay. 'Oh,' they said, 'a princess!' And they were very happy and gave me a nice room to myself and, best of all, a wonderful breakfast. They gave me eggs made with some wonderful powder, and your American flakes of corn out of a little box. They were very nice, and then they helped me find my friend Hildegarde."

Since the Princess's arrival, she and Hildegarde had been busy gathering blackberries on the moor. The two women were happy in the possession of some extra sugar which the Princess had been allotted, not because of her royal status, but because she was a refugee.

"We are four persons living here," said Hildegarde. "We get half a pound of sugar per month each. But the Princess got an extra pound because she came as a refugee, so we are able to make jam." In fact, my arrival had come during the boiling-down procedure, which was being conducted in the shelf-like kitchen, where they were stewing the berries.

"Could you find enough blackberries?" I asked.

"You couldn't make up a wholesale business with it," said Hildegarde, "but we will have about twenty bottles of juice, besides the jam."

Sitting in Hildegarde's little cloakroom, discussing the amount of jam obtainable from berries picked on the moor and from the extra sugar rationed to refugees, the Princess was just a tired middle-aged woman. Her face in its frame of bobbed gray hair had a soft charm, and her features wore a perpetual expression of piteousness, as though to say, "How can this have happened to me? I am a Princess."

She told me how she had made her way to Berlin during the bombings to see her son, who was severely wounded. "During my four weeks there I never left my helmet aside," she said. "It was the phosphorus bombs that were the worst. When a whole street is burning, the flames take the oxygen out of the air. A fire storm arises, and you can't breathe any more. You just fall down in the street and are suffocated. I have seen that myself in Berlin. One time I was trying to get to the house of a friend, and I saw many people very far down the street, crossing the street and falling down. Later on, they had to put walls all round the place because they couldn't bury all the bodies."

"You know," broke in Hildegarde, "after the bombings, it

was funny how I lost all sense of time. It is coming back. If you had asked me anything four months ago, I could have given facts but not in regard to time."

"It's the sounds you never forget," said the Princess. "In the night when you are awake, you hear the moo of a cow and you think it is a siren."

The door opened while we were talking and another of Hildegarde's house guests came in, one of two refugee artists for whom beds had been set up in an alcove of her cloakroom. The newcomer was a small mouse-colored painter named Josef Goetz, who in happier days had been a member of a Nazi-sponsored artists' circle in Berlin. The most prominent name in this Berlin circle had been that of Breker, the sculptor, whose horses and men of the bulging-muscle school were so popular with the National Socialists that Hitler had built him a studio.

Little Josef Goetz, unlike his more famous friend, had contented himself with crayon portraits or prettified landscapes, and I was astonished to find that in devastated Bremen he was already doing a rushing business. When I expressed my surprise that artists should find such quick employment, Hildegarde said, "Why, certainly! People are buying pictures. People who are fixing up their homes may want a landscape or flower piece. Many persons want their portraits painted. Josef has been here only six weeks and already four people have ordered portraits. The daughter of a North German-Lloyd captain came in only yesterday, for a portrait to give her fiancé on his birthday. And last week we had a very pretty young lady, Fräulein Rea Grieme, whose father is a coffee importer and who has an uncle in the Bronx. You see, due to restrictions on photography, people are not allowed to have cameras and take snapshots. So naturally people like to be painted."

I was amused at this new conception of the artists' pinch-hitting for the photographers.

Doing portraits brought the artist, I found, a return of two to three hundred marks for a picture in ink, and eight hundred marks for a portrait in oil.

"All the Americans want to be painted," Hildegarde told me. In nearby Wopswede, a suburb of Bremen where Herr Roselius had sponsored artists in pre-war days, the portrait painters were doing a booming business with the 175th Infantry Regiment. Men of the 29th Division, always referred to by its members as "The Dandy Fifth," considered themselves lucky to be stationed in the picturesque artists' colony. One young girl painter, according to Hildegarde, was "so busy doing portraits" that she had painted eleven soldiers in just the past fortnight, at fees ranging between thirty and forty dollars each. Wopswede also specialized in handwoven tapestries, dyed from plant colors, and Frau Heinrich Vogler, the dean of the colony, was now engaged in weaving the regimental crest of "The Dandy Fifth" into a tapestry which one of the officers had ordered for his home in the South. This art piece would set him back thirty-five dollars.

Here in Bremen, the Kaffee-Hag business was starting up, too. The factory was already operating on a small scale under our plan of operation by which food industries were given preferential licensing. Whereas pre-war Kaffee-Hag had been made of cereals like rye or bran, the factory was now using *Ersatz*, Hildegarde informed me, made of carrots when they could get them, but principally ground-up turnips. Defeat must taste bitter to Germans, I thought, when even their substitutes for coffee must be made of *Ersatz*, and even the *Ersatz* must be made of turnips.

"I think there is one great mistake the Allies can make," volunteered Hildegarde. "It would be to permit unemployment in Europe."

How readily, I reflected, the conquered were willing to hand over all responsibilities to us; especially the employment problem, with which we might have to contend in our own country.

"The soundest thing America could do would be to make a good air base in Bremen. It would be good for everybody, would be good for Germans and good for Americans. I don't mean for military purposes, but for commerce. Keeping security depends not on 'Big Three' agreements, not on political discussions, but on sound private business. As soon as American capital is interested in Germany, and as soon as Germans are indebted to America, then we will have a foundation for sound international relations."

Many Germans seemed to think we were moving into their country simply to finance it.

Hildegarde interrupted my thoughts with some remarks

about the Nazi Party: "The Party always held up good war morals," she said, as though taking it for granted that this party line would appeal to me as it did to her. "The split of last July 20 could never have taken place without underground propaganda. Many people didn't think it fair to the Führer. He had a difficult war on his hands. People should have saved their political differences until after the war was won."

Hildegarde sat silent for several moments, her serious expression heightened by the tautness of her face with its high cheekbones, her straight hair combed back. Then she leaned forward: "Now may I ask you a question?" she inquired. "Do you think we would have lost the war if you had not corrupted our morals? If we had stayed a united nation?"

"Yes," I said, "because of the bombs."

"Bombs do not break a people's spirit," she answered. "I have seen many men break down temporarily with their nerves, and I have seen them crying, but it was over after an hour and they started right on again. I believe the Germans could not have lost the war without internal moral disintegration.

"Germans are all talking about this. Some say, 'It was steel against bodies.' Others say, 'No, it was lack of morale.' And one young woman said to me, 'I would go through all this bombing again if it would make us win the war.'"

Hildegarde rose from her chair and began emptying the two pails which stood in the middle of the apartment to catch the drip from the ceiling—it had been raining heavily.

"Everything is a mess," said the Princess, getting up to help her hostess replace the pails and standing back to judge the two spots where the drip was heaviest. "A little rain is all right, but two days of rain, that the roof cannot stand. We have had a lake in here on the floor."

The two women sat down again and Hildegarde said she hoped it would not be long before we sent over some good books and magazines. "If you go into a bookstore you find some medical books, maybe, or works on psychology. You find all the stuff in which the ordinary person is not interested. You could specialize in out-of-the-way subjects, but you can't find a good detective story or novel. The only new things we get are the newspapers and bulletins which the Allies are publishing in German for us to read. Germans read all about the concentration camps. And they all say 'Why get so excited about it, after bombing innocent women and children?' "

"Have you seen the pictures?" I inquired.

"Oh yes," replied Hildegarde. "We've all seen the pictures. The newspapers you give us are full of them.

"Just yesterday I was in a shop which sold hosiery, and there was a picture of a concentration camp on the counter. Three women came in and announced, 'We have just come from a concentration camp. We ought to be served first.' They wanted all kinds of things, shirts, stockings, and drawers. A little girl pointed to the picture and said, 'I'm sorry I haven't been in a concentration camp. These women look well enough dressed. I would like to have privileges, too.' "

With memory of Buchenwald still fresh in my mind, Hildegarde's talk left me speechless. This I had not foreseen: that after it was all over, after the sufferers had finally regained their freedom, there would be resentment of them. What a refinement of punishment, that people returning from concentration camps and receiving their pathetic little extra privileges should have to endure the envious gibes of their neighbors. Of course I had no data on these particular women in the hosiery shop, but the little girl's chatter (obviously a repetition of much-heard talk among grownups) was an ugly warning of black years still to come for those who had already suffered.

"Those people from concentration camps really are behaving very badly," continued Hildegarde. "I tried to buy some flowers yesterday, and they actually wanted all the flowers. They said, 'We have a right to buy flowers first. We come from a concentration camp.' The other day I went all the way to Bremerhaven just to buy some fish. I couldn't get fish because the fisherman's house was burned out. I had to wait four hours in the station for a train, and I drank a very bad coffee. Two women sitting at the next table had been in a concentration camp. One was well dressed; the other, apparently a bit of a parvenu, said, 'Now here I have been in a concentration camp for two years just for the sake of getting a monthly allowance of two hundred marks and an extra ration card. How shall I ever live on that?'

"Other people at nearby tables resented that. We were all very much agreed that this woman was rightly put into a concentration camp. Of course, there may have been people innocently convicted," Hildegarde concluded in a tolerant tone. "But I think there were many people justly convicted. On the whole, I am suspicious. We are simply swamped with people who come from concentration camps. If things were so very bad, and if so many people were killed, I really wonder where they all come from now."

I needn't have worried about my reactions the first time I saw Hildegarde. I had not been mistaken in my judgment.

CHAPTER 13

Berlin: A River of Wanderers

"NOBODY WILL give me a place," complained the old man with the shining black fiber suitcase. He was very old, and he was a figure of dignity in his long black coat and neatly combed white beard. He was trying to make his way on to the incredibly crowded train for Halle, amid the mass of human beings who surged with their backpacks, pushcarts, briefcases and bicycles along the platform of the broken Anhalter Bahnhof in Berlin.

"Nobody will give me a place," he said. "I have been thrown off three times."

"You shouldn't let yourself be thrown off," said some luckier travelers within earshot, looking on from their precarious perches on the outside of the packed car, where they clung thick as monkeys.

"I could stand up there on the sill of that coach window," suggested the old man, "if somebody would give me a hand."

"No, that won't work," said the conductor, who was swinging authoritatively past through the crowd. "A signal post comes along, and you are knocked off."

Immediately the old man began addressing his appeals to the conductor. "You give space to others, but you don't find any place for me."

"That is typical," said the conductor. "Always the other ones. Everyone is thinking only of himself. How selfish the world is growing these days!"

The gaunt shell of the Anhalter Bahnhof, with remnants of roof clinging like scraps of lace high up on the towering arches, lent a certain somber majesty to the scene of confusion and frustration below. These wandering masses of people were displaced Germans; they wanted to go everywhere, and for every imaginable reason. There were German soldiers who, like all other soldiers, wanted to go home. There were people who had no homes planning to move in on their relatives, refugees leaving the cities because they hoped to find more food in the country, refugees coming back from the country and hoping to regain their apartments in the city. Parents were hunting for their children, wives were hunting for their in-laws, and daughters were searching for their mothers. So many people were struggling to climb up the sides of the cars and get themselves and their baggage installed that it was a surprise to see one girl equally intent on trying to get down.

"Why does this woman want to come down?" complained people near her. She was stepping on their legs and hands in her efforts to descend.

"My father hasn't shown up," said the girl. "Open the door, I must step down on the door."

Even I, an outsider in this contest, could see it would be disastrous to open the door, for the people bottled inside would come frothing out like freshly uncorked beer.

"Is it so hard to open the door?" she complained. "Here you, take my bags."

This appeal was addressed to no one in particular, and received no particular response; but by sheer force of her persistence, she managed to get a kind of conveyor belt in motion, as she passed her things, and then herself, from person to person down the side of the car.

"My God, how many small things she carries," wailed the people in her path.

"And how does this disturb the train, I ask you?" she retorted crisply, making her way from shoulder to shoulder to the platform.

An almost invisible gap on the long step of the train was filled by a one-legged German soldier who had been standing by, quietly looking for such an opportunity. With a single motion he swung himself into place, hung his crutch on the door handle, and twined his leg in some way known best to himself into the under-carriage of the car. The addition of a passenger was an unpleasant surprise to the plump man who held the next place on the step. He had previously had enough room to sit with a wooden case between his knees. His loud protests attracted a group on the platform, where people were always ready with suggestions and comments.

"Stick your legs in there," said the kibitzers, pointing out a space between the spring and the car.

"One big bump and my legs will be cut off," protested the plump gentleman.

"Listen to him," said the bystanders. "He begrudges a soldier his place."

The needs of the soldiers, most of whom were herded into cars especially reserved for them, with only the overflow having to cling to the outsides, were being ministered to by two or three German Red Cross girls. These girls made their way up and down the long platforms, collecting what they could from the German civilians to give to the soldiers.

"Has somebody got a piece of bread? Some fruit for the soldiers?" one of the Red Cross girls called out as she made her tireless way from one knot of travelers to another. "Has anybody a cigarette for a soldier?"

The girl was more successful at raising money than in getting food, and periodically she paused in the midst of soldier groups to empty her apron pockets of their accumulated mixture of black bread and Reichsmarks.

"Who has nothing at all?" she inquired of a group of bedraggled-looking soldiers. "Please don't say you have nothing if you still have something left, or you will eat the slice of bread someone else needs."

"We all want to eat," chanted the girl, as she continued soliciting along the platform. "One slice of bread less, if we can give one to a soldier."

"It's awfully sad now," commented some bystanders, who had been watching me as I used my camera now and then. "Foreigners taking pictures of us and sending them to the newspapers."

The Red Cross girl had paused by one of the cars reserved for the German prisoners of war, and was handing her supplies bit by bit through windows crowded with unshaven faces under rusty green caps.

"You've already had a piece of bread," she reproved one soldier who was pushing his companions aside.

"But I didn't get the piece of apple."

"Then we gave you something else with your bread."

"He has a whole gas mask full of food, and wants still more," said the soldiers near him.

"Comrades, this doesn't make a very good impression," she said.

I was startled to hear one of the German soldiers say, "I would like to shoot her!" and then I realized that he was not speaking of the Red Cross girl but was pointing to me, where I stood on the side-lines taking photographs. His remark made me uncomfortable, so I walked a short distance away. In the next moment something resembling a wind storm began sweeping along the platform. Like dust before a breeze all the people on the platform began running toward the front end of the train. I ran too, or rather, I was carried along in the mob, and when I finally managed to fight my way out to a clear stretch of track I watched a remarkable drama.

It was the approach of the locomotive. This was the last chance for those on the platform to get aboard. Within seconds, the steaming machine lost its appearance of a locomotive and began to resemble a wool sock covered with field-ticks. It was astonishing how agile some of the passengers were, not only in springing on, themselves, but in getting their pushcarts and bicycles tied on also.

The conductor assumed a central rôle in this episode. "There's no more space," he kept shouting. "As you see, everything is filled up. If something happens here I will be responsible."

A woman in an imitation leopard-skin coat had almost succeeded in diving into the engineer's box when the conductor caught her at it. "You can't go in there," he cried. "Come down at once. If someone burns up here, I am the one who is guilty." "Let me get up on the tender then." "The tender is reserved for our soldiers," said the conductor. "They must get home."

The lady in the fur coat was not easily discouraged. She grabbed the passenger nearest to her and started pulling herself up by his hair. At this, the conductor had endured quite enough, and he commanded the leopard woman to get off the train.

"Always the same picture," he repeated. "Everybody wants to look after himself. Nobody cares for his fellow man,"

The engine began gathering steam. White swirls licked up around the bare legs of the girls and rose, hissing, to envelop the entire human cargo on the locomotive. As the engine wheels started turning, I noticed a boy who clung in a peculiar leapfrog position to a small metal footplate at the head of the locomotive. With both feet on this plate, his hands grasping something above his head, his knees spread wide to maintain his balance, he faced a journey of an indefinite number of hours. No one ever knew how long the trip to Halle would last. In pre-war days, it would have been about three hours; now it sometimes took a full twenty-four. And even when Halle was reached, it was just one small step toward the varied destinations of the passengers. Halle is a large railroad junction, one of the few still usable in Germany's much-bombed railroad net. Therefore, whether the passengers were bound north for Hamburg, southeast for Leipzig or Dresden, or southwest in their passionate endeavor to reach the American zone—which to displaced Germans was the Promised Land—still Halle was only a waypoint where they would re-enact the same battle to get aboard some moving conveyance.

The long train was rushing past now, and the people clinging to the top and sides lost their identity as human beings and began to resemble barnacles. As the train gathered speed it might have been a chain of old boat hulls, whipping into the distance. I turned back to the station platforms and found them as thickly studded with humanity as they had been before the train had carried anyone away.

"We are going to stay here for sure," a weary-looking woman in a plaid headscarf remarked, seating herself and her three children on the edge of the platform opposite the strategic spot where the locomotive had come in today and might be hoped to come tomorrow. She removed some bundles of clothes and a cooking pot from their little wagon, so she could settle the smallest child there; the baby cart was becoming the universal carryall of Germany.

This family was among the thousands of Germans whom the Poles were expelling wholesale. They had spent weeks on the roads in Pomerania, the mother told me, and had somehow drifted as far north as Rostock, where they had spent two weeks in a camp for fugitives. From there it had taken another eighteen days to reach Berlin. They had planned to move into Berlin, but found they would not be allowed to stay; the authorities, I knew, were doing all they could to keep refugees from streaming in to this already over-crowded city.

As I talked with her, I found that the small family group had worked out a sort of system in their living. They had left Pomerania with a small supply of potatoes in the baby cart, and as these were depleted it was not impossible—although it was very difficult—to build up the stock again. In the open country people were not so selfish as they were here in the cities, and someone could always be found who would give them a handful of potatoes or vegetables, if he had anything himself from which to give. Usually the family slept in the woods, though they preferred a barn when they could find one.

The two older children were big enough to help gather firewood while the mother built a small fireplace of stones on which she could set the cooking pot. Having only one pot was hard, for she had to wash the children's clothes and every single little thing in the same pot in which she cooked the food. The children were getting skin diseases, and she was terribly afraid of their catching typhus. Now that they had learned they could not stop in Berlin, their next port of call would be Hamburg. The woman's oldest daughter had a one-room flat in Hamburg —or had had, according to a letter the mother had received long ago. Maybe she would be able to find her daughter there, and maybe her daughter would still have the flat. I did not add to her worries by describing what I had seen of gutted Hamburg; but from her hopeless tone, I think the mother knew. It was just that there was nowhere to go, and beating their way along the roads and rails was the only thing they thought of to do.

It was a surprise, when I turned from the family with their single cooking pot, to see the next couple on the platform open up a beautifully equipped luncheon case and bring out a package of sandwiches, some cold tea in a cognac bottle, and an odd-looking violet pudding, for which they carried plates and spoons. The woman wore one of those plush coats imitating fur, which are so common among middle-class Germans, and the man was in high-laced shoes and herringbone knickers. He was so eager to show me his credentials and identification papers that I was sure he had something on his conscience. The paper read: "We certify that Herr Christoph Beyer is employed by us as the head of our kitchen. The present trip to Erfurt in Thüringen has been agreed to by us." It was signed by executives of the power plant where he worked, the Elektro Werke Aktien Gesellschaft.

It was easy to tell why these people should be so well dressed, for they had access to food which they could trade for everything they needed. Herr Beyer was so secretive about the purposes of his trip that I felt sure one of those mysterious black-market negotiations was in progress in which the head of the kitchen for a power plant could hold a strong hand.

The subtle odor of the black market hung around another woman, who sat a little farther down the platform. She had planted herself sternly on a large suitcase, liberally surrounded with bags and bundles, and in her tweed suit, high halo-shaped hat, and shoes only slightly turned over at the heels, she was one of the best-dressed women on the platform. Her name was Adelheide Planner, she told me, and she had come to Berlin to "buy things." She had gone to the big Siemens Electrical Works, where she found she was unable to buy even a hot plate.

A shopping trip like this in such desperate times seemed a little odd to me, so I inquired "Was it worth coming all the way to Berlin for a hot plate?"

"I had expected to buy up five hundred of them," she said, "but nothing can be bought here, and the trunk I am sitting on is empty."

When she added that her husband had directed her to try to pick up some little machines for sharpening razor blades, I was more sure than ever that the Planner family were on the black market; for small useful articles like this possessed a high trading value. With money worth so little, a small handy item like a razor blade sharpener was a more convenient medium of exchange than a suitcase full of cash.

Seated next to Frau Planner was a gentle-faced bespectacled man who was poking the track idly with his walking stick; his striped trousers pronounced him an ex-inmate of a concentration camp, and proclaimed his unworldliness, too, for most men would have acquired something to wear in place of the hated penitentiary pants.

"Why did they put you in a concentration camp?" I asked.

"Because I predicted all that would happen because of the war," he replied. "It is all written in the Bible. All that is going to happen is written there. Mine was the voice that cried it out to the world, so the Gestapo took me away."

The Bible expert was a Prussian named Richard Blask. Vague as his predictions of doom were, they were sufficiently irritating to the authorities to bring about his imprisonment in Sachaenhausen at the beginning of the war. While I was talking with him, a bright-haired blonde, dressed vividly in a green sweater over a cobalt-blue dress, came up and followed the conversation with such attention that I wondered if she could be interested in religion.

"You are a very good-hearted man," she said, when there was a pause in the conversation. "I can see that at once."

"I am a Christian," said Richard Blask, "and live only in the Bible."

"There is a special car on the train to Halle reserved just for people from concentration camps," said the blonde. "There was one compartment in it today with only seven people. When I tried to get in, they said, 'No, there is no place,' but you, how did it happen that you did not go in it?"

"My colleague didn't show up," replied Blask. "I shall wait for him here, as he will surely find me in time for the train tomorrow."

"Is your colleague from a concentration camp, too?"

"Yes," said Richard Blask. "He is a Bible expert also."

In a practiced way the blonde clinched her arrangements to travel in this desirable company. "I am going off to get a comrade of mine," she announced, and promising to be back soon with her girl friend, she started toward the other end of the platform.

"She'll get lots of advantages now," said Frau Planner sullenly, "traveling ·with a man from a concentration camp."

The next day I returned at noon to the Anhalter Bahnhof, to watch once more the departure of the train for Halle. I found the station even more crowded than it had been the day before, and the people milling on the platform seemed even more desperate about their chances to board the train. A new rule had been passed; people no longer would be allowed to travel on the tops or outsides of the cars. Yesterday's train had met with a serious accident. One of the cars, an old-type wagon-lits, was a few inches higher than the rest of the train, and when it passed under a bridge seventeen people clinging to its curved roof were swept to death. The German authorities had been begging for some time for an Army guard at the station to keep the crowds in check, and as a consequence of this disaster some American soldiers had been sent to the station.

The GIs were having a difficult time. "We keep telling them to get off," the Sergeant told me. "When they don't get off we yank their baggage off, and then they turn right around and get on again at the back of the train.

"There's that same bird again," he said, and running to the side of the train yelling, "Back up! Get off!" he pulled a man off the window ledge by the seat of his pants. The German removed so abruptly was a neat little man with a tiny mustache. Unsolicited by us, he immediately produced his identification papers to show that he was an official of the Reichsbank and was going to Leipzig to get his winter clothes.

"That's the first time I ever grabbed a bank official by the seat of his pants," said the Sergeant.

The crowd was growing more desperate. It was becoming increasingly difficult for the GIs to keep the cars cleared. From time to time they fired a warning shot into the air. Suddenly there was a quick succession of shots, then an uproar on the platform.

"Oh, *mein Gott*. That was bad."

"Just dummy ammunition."

"No, it was real. I saw them loading their guns."

I asked a GI Corporal what had happened. "Stray bullet got one of the guys," he said.

A group of German prisoners in their rusty green uniforms stood quietly on the edge of the track, watching the GIs clear a space around the casualty. In wondered if they would show resentment at this expression of American Army authority, but they were discussing the incident with the professional attitude of one soldier to another.

"The American soldier has done what he had to do," I overheard.

"Twice the man was urged to get down, and twice he got back up again."

When the American ambulance squad arrived and hurried across the tracks to take care of the wounded man, their comments became admiring.

"That's a good litter," said one of the German soldiers.

"He will get into an American hospital and he will be well fed," the group agreed.

One of the German soldiers, his cheekbones protruding sharply from his tight-drawn face and his thin arms showing through his tattered sleeves, said longingly: "I was hurt once. I stayed in a hospital for a whole year, and it was wonderful. Just see what I look like now. Things were different then."

This young German, looking back and remembering his life as a soldier, found that the happiest year he could remember under Hitler was the year he had spent in a hospital.

Epilogue

THIS, THEN, was Germany after the whirlwind had been reaped, a bottomless pit of malevolence and malignance. Cities and people were broken ruins together, but the venom the Nazis had distilled was virulent yet and held the power to hurt and to poison all men it touched. It touched Americans as well as Germans and it was frightening to see.

It was no accident that the few good people I found were those who stood against tyranny over any other human being, people who had the democratic idea in their hearts. They were so few, so pitiably few. They were not the teachers, as one might hope, not the scientists, not those who had studied in America, not the great industrialists who might be expected to have a world view. No, the men who shared responsibility for the whirlwind, who sat unprotesting as the wind was sown, these men denied responsibility. And we, the victors, were treating them in a way that almost made it seem we didn't believe too deeply in democracy ourselves.

Women not so different from Hildegarde, will be bringing up the children of Germany, the next generation. And we have given them nothing to replace their Hitler-worship. To be sure, we have given them a few "de-Nazified" textbooks, but that is nothing more than the merest promise of something greater. We turned our backs on our greatest opportunity to do something constructive with the youth of Germany. We had no plan, no desire, no willingness, it seemed, to teach a democratic way of life. We poured out lives and boundless treasure to win a mechanical victory and now we had no patience for the things of the spirit which alone can save us from another far greater catastrophe. It was time to go home.

The driver of a staff car told me, with bitterness, of two congressmen whom he had driven when they visited Berlin.

They asked to be taken at once to the black market, even before going to their billets. As soon as they saw the crowd they whipped open their suitcases. One sold a blue pinstripe suit for $500. The other had an extra pair of trousers with his gray herringbone tweed. He got $600.

I could not blame the boys who wanted to go home with their pitiful pocketings of black market money. They had the best examples. I could only blame Americans for understanding too little, for taking part too little in the affairs of a world now shrunken to our doorstep. We had let our boys go off to war with so little comprehension of what the fight was for. Men who are ordered to put their lives in hazard should be asked to take this risk only for the highest purposes. They deserve to know what these purposes are, and to know they will be fulfilled after the victory.

We did not bring democracy to Germany, although we talked a lot about it. Even now it is not too late, because democracy isn't something a nation tools up for: it lives in its citizens, in the way they live with their fellow men. We can make up for time lost and wasted and we can give to the Germans, and to others as well, something more than techniques. Unless we do, this war will be without meaning for us, and some of the hope for a good world will die down in the hearts of men everywhere.